IMAGES
of America

TRUTH OR CONSEQUENCES

On the Cover: The picture shows the procession of a fair and rodeo parade in downtown Hot Springs, New Mexico, before the town's name changed to Truth or Consequences. (Courtesy of Geronimo Springs Museum Archives.)

IMAGES
of America

TRUTH OR CONSEQUENCES

Sherry Fletcher and Cindy Carpenter

ARCADIA
PUBLISHING

ISBN 978-0-7385-7917-7

Published by Arcadia Publishing
Charleston, South Carolina

Printed in the United States of America

Library of Congress Control Number: 2010921702

For all general information, please contact Arcadia Publishing:
Telephone 843-853-2070
Fax 843-853-0044
E-mail sales@arcadiapublishing.com
For customer service and orders:
Toll-Free 1-888-313-2665

Visit us on the Internet at www.arcadiapublishing.com

To our Jimmys, Maxine, Imogene, Louise, John, Beau, Jake, Jess, Racheal, Jessica, Colten, Grace, Dutch, and soul mates Baxter and Jay.

Contents

ACKNOWLEDGMENTS

This book exists because of the many generous people who shared photographs and their history with us. All photographs are copyrighted by Sherry Fletcher with the exception of those noted in courtesy lines—for those, the original owners may retain copyright. We could have never done this book without the support of Vicki Cecil-Sears; Ann Welborn; the Mims family; the Geronimo Springs Museum; Juanita (Nita) Nelson-Mims; Romelia Garcia; Daisy Wilson; Pat Rocco; Sylvia Gillespie; Ernestine McWhorter; Pam and John Ashbaugh; Neal, Alan, and Seth Brown (http://thedamsite.com); Dam Site Marina; Annette Smith; Judd Bradley; Jacque and Kenneth Johnston; Chuck and Karen Martin; Linda Seger; and Monty and April Brown. For feeding Jay Carpenter, we would like to thank the Arrey Café, La Cocina, Pacific Grill, Sunset Grill, Bar-B-Que on Broadway, K-Bob's, Big A Burger, and Hodgees. For feeding Rosie, the chickens, and the dogs, we would like to thank Baxter Brown. Thanks also to the farmers for the many conservation efforts they promote to help preserve our lake.

A special thanks to Hannah Carney and the staff of Arcadia Publishing for giving us this opportunity to showcase Truth or Consequences. Most importantly, thanks to the residents of Truth or Consequences for being a part of our fascinating history.

INTRODUCTION

Truth or Consequences, New Mexico, acquired its rather quirky name as part of a publicity stunt proposed by Ralph Edwards, a radio quiz show host. In 1950, to celebrate the 10th anniversary of his popular show *Truth or Consequences*, Edwards offered free publicity to any town willing to change its name to the name of his show. In addition to promoting the town to his audience of 20 million listeners, Edwards promised to provide money to help with various civic affairs. Residents of the small town of Hot Springs voted to change its name to Truth or Consequences. As promised, Edwards promoted the town, its hot springs mineral baths, and the surrounding resources.

Based on early military records from nearby Fort McRae, U.S. soldiers had begun coming to the area to bathe in the hot springs located in the center of present-day Truth or Consequences as early as 1863, despite the risk of encountering the hostile Apaches who frequented the area. Oral history suggests that the cowboys from the John Cross Cattle Company built the first adobe bathhouse over the hot springs for their own use around 1882.

Early territorial newspapers began documenting the residents of Sierra County who visited the hot springs for medicinal purposes, whether to bathe in or drink the water or lay in the mud. Many of the travelers to the hot springs stayed in the nearby settlement of Las Palomas, about 7 miles south of present-day Truth or Consequences.

In 1910, Fount Sullivan filed the first homestead in the heart of what is now Truth or Consequences and built a bathhouse at the bottom of the hill from which the spring flowed. It is not known if he charged for the use of his facilities or not.

After numerous court battles with Mexico over water rights, the U.S. Congress authorized the construction of Engle (also spelled as "Engel") Dam in 1905. Early documents referred interchangeably to the dam as the Engel Dam, Engle Dam, or Elephant Butte Dam. At one point, it was even suggested the dam be christened as the "Woodrow Wilson Dam." The name Elephant Butte came from the volcanic formation that looked like an elephant's head and back. That formation would eventually be an island in the dam's reservoir. The Victorio Land and Cattle Company battled the U.S. Reclamation Service to get more for their land than the government was willing to pay. The construction of Engle Dam and Reservoir sparked the major settlement of the town then known as Palomas Hot Springs. Even before the construction of the actual dam began, workers began arriving to construct facilities at the dam site to house the future workers. Railroads had to be built, roads graded, bridges constructed, and cables and machinery installed. This anticipation of employment and development brought people to the dam site and to Palomas Hot Springs. Stores and other dam-related businesses began to open in the town. As no liquor was allowed at the dam site, bars began cropping up as well.

By March 1911, the post office established at the dam site was named Elephant Butte. It did not take long for dam workers and their families to discover the hot springs. The town at the dam site was called Elephant Butte or Butte City and had 3,000 residents in 1914, all connected in some way to the construction of the dam. Around 1914, newspapers began using the names

Engle Dam and Elephant Butte Dam interchangeably. That was also the year that a letter was sent to the Board of County Commissioners of Sierra County from the Commercial Club of Palomas Springs. The Commercial Club's official letterhead took notice of the hot mineral springs as being "famous for the cure of blood, stomach, and rheumatic diseases." The baths were free at that time, but the Commercial Club was in the business of promoting the baths to people from outside the area, with an eye towards the revenue those visitors could bring in. The letter noted that contagious diseases were prevalent at Elephant Butte, whose residents visited the springs daily, and that already there were two cases of scarlet fever. The club recommended the appointment of their own Dr. Fries as a health officer who could make decisions immediately rather than the town having to wait for the county's health officer. The complaint was that by the time the mail ran to summon a health officer, the diseases could be spread to other parts of the state by visitors coming and going to the hot springs.

The total cost for the reservoir and dam was $8,194,025, and the dam's dedication took place October 19, 1916. The town of Hot Springs was incorporated that same year. As the buildings were dismantled at the dam site, many were bought by entrepreneurs and reassembled in the town of Hot Springs, which continued to grow.

In 1919, the State of New Mexico built the State Bathhouse, and by 1923, the first permanent school building was erected on Date Street. U.S. Highway 85, which ran through town, was completely paved in 1932, with the exception of the stretch between Hot Springs and Caballo. Bathhouses and car courts were a big commodity in town. By 1937, the basin was closed to any additional appropriation of thermal waters; the area has seen a decline in public bathhouses over the years. In October 2004, the New Mexico State and National Historical Preservation Division placed the Hot Springs Bathhouse and Commercial Historic District in Truth or Consequences on the National Register of Historic Places.

In the 1930s, the Carrie Tingley Hospital for Crippled Children was built by then New Mexico governor Clyde Tingley to promote the use of the hot mineral water in the treatment of children with infantile paralysis (polio). In 1981, the Carrie Tingley Hospital for Crippled Children was closed, and the hospital moved the services to Albuquerque to be closer to the state's other major medical services. The building is now the New Mexico Veterans' Home. In 1935, an area 38 miles in diameter (situated in present downtown Truth or Consequences) was declared the Hot Springs Underground Water Basin by New Mexico's state engineer.

The Truth or Consequences Fiesta Board voted to take over the financial responsibility for financing and producing the city's 26th annual Ralph Edwards' Fiesta and Rodeo in 1975, which up until then had been sponsored by Ralph Edwards. Today many of the residents refer to Truth or Consequences as simply "T or C." The major attraction of the area, besides the hot baths, is the recreational use of Elephant Butte Lake. As the explorer Juan de Oñate once blazed new trails on the Camino Real in Sierra County, the future Spaceport of America, located some 28 miles southeast of the town, has promised to again blaze new trails in commercial space travel.

One

Early Traffic and Hot Water

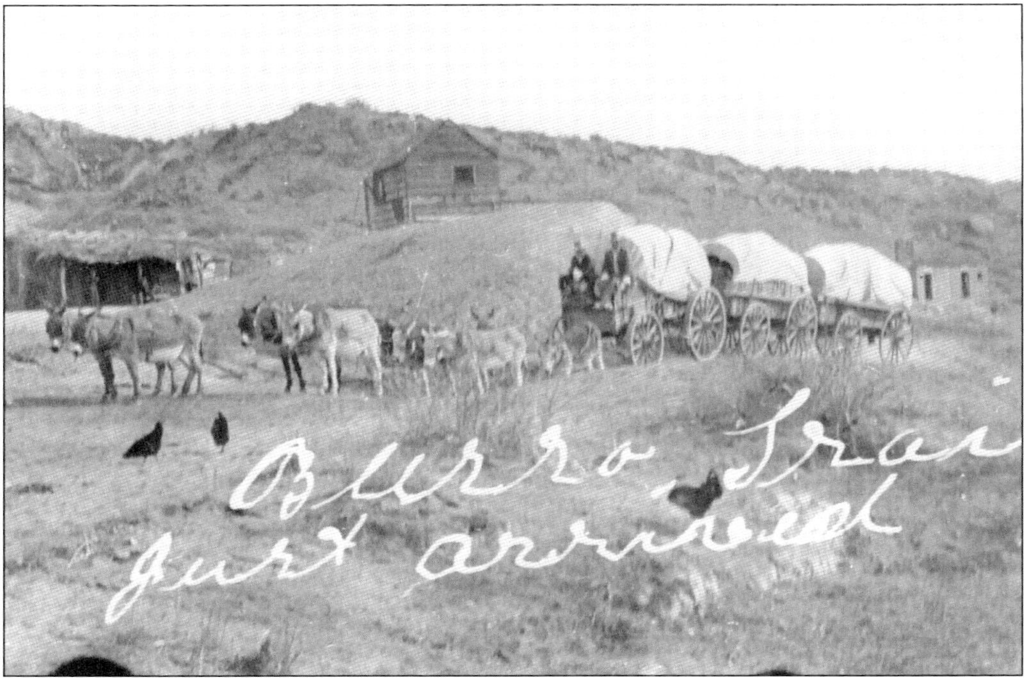

Early visitors to the area now called Truth or Consequences were primarily health seekers and commercial developers. Word had spread that bathing, soaking, and even drinking from the area's hot spring mineral waters could cure just about any ailment. The earliest name was Palomas Hot Springs, not to be confused with the settlement of Las Palomas, 7 miles to the south. (Courtesy of Geronimo Springs Museum Archives.)

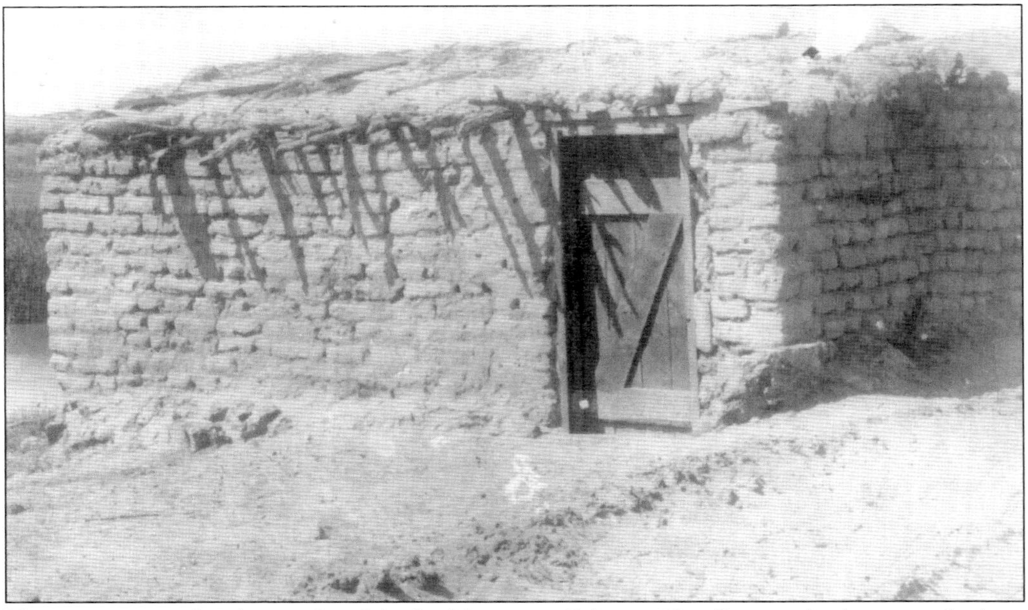

This is an example of an early adobe bathhouse in Palomas Hot Springs, built to give bathers more privacy. It did not take long for entrepreneurs to realize the commercial value of the baths; establishments offering food and lodging soon began springing up in the area. (Courtesy of Geronimo Springs Museum Archives.)

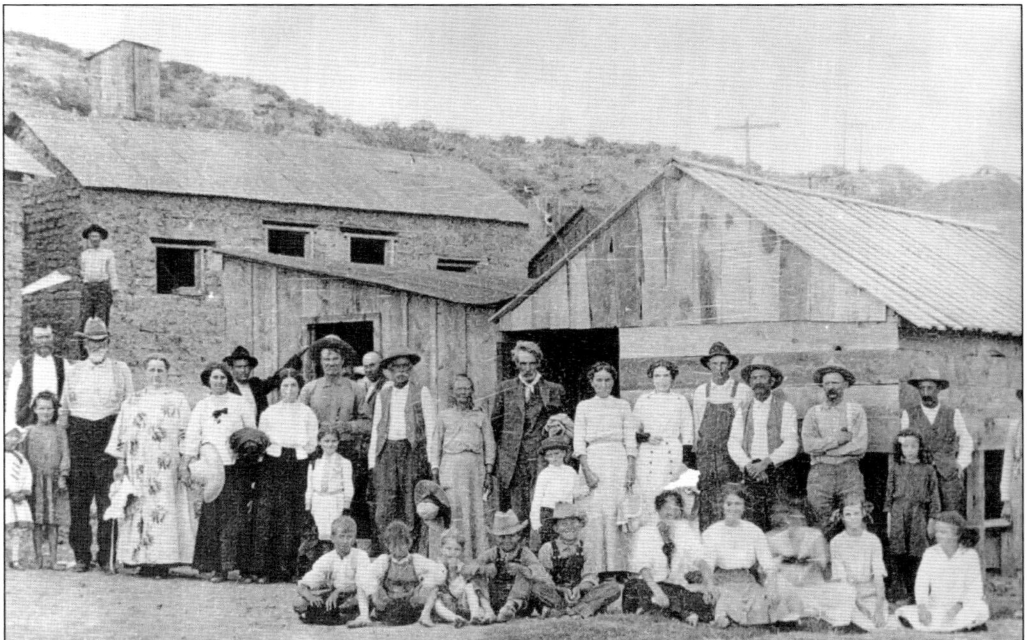

There is no information on the back of this picture, but on the front is written "Palomas Springs." Otto Goetz, the first mayor of Palomas Hot Springs, was instrumental in dropping the "Palomas" from the town's name. Nobody knows what the group seen here was celebrating. Perhaps it was the first name change? (Courtesy of Geronimo Springs Museum Archives.)

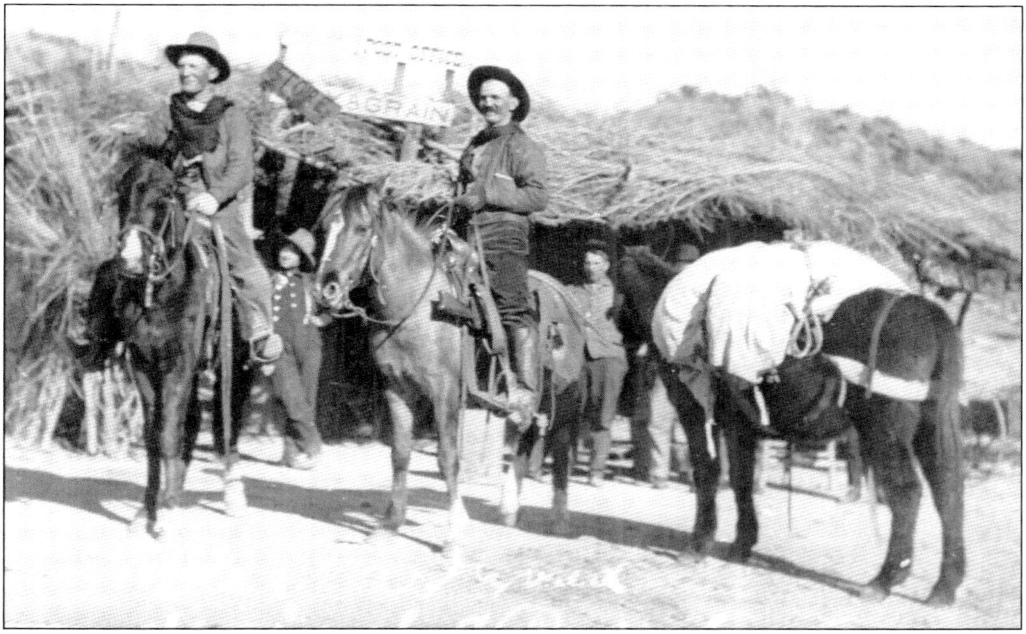

This picture shows the early post office and store where hay and grain could also be purchased. The way the two men on horseback are grinning, they must have already had their baths and feel full of spit and vinegar, ready to conquer whatever the day brings. (Courtesy of Geronimo Springs Museum Archives.)

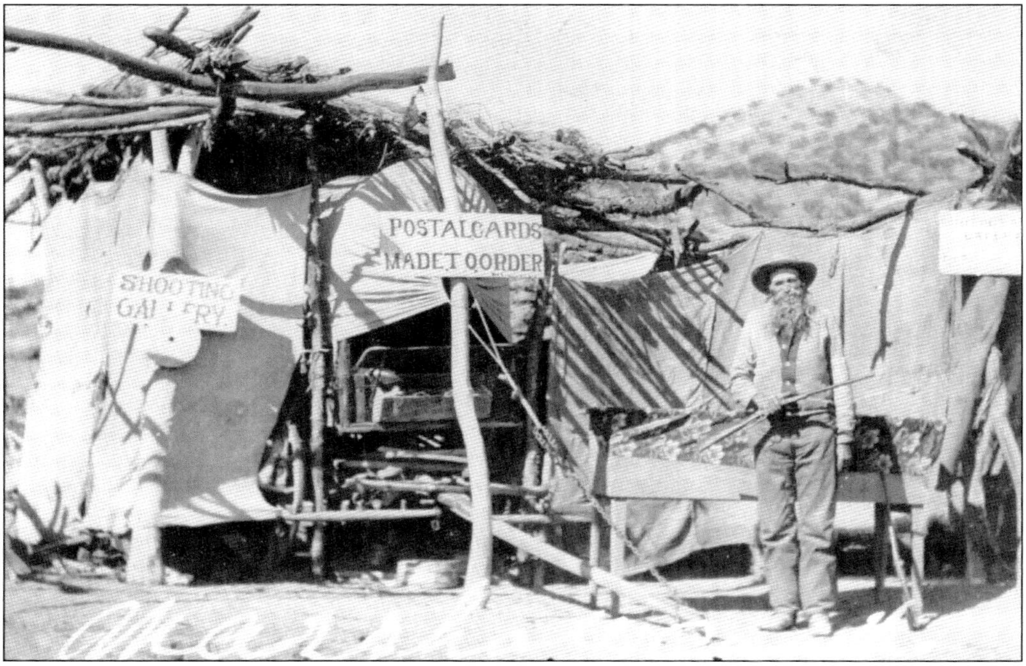

The bottom of this picture identifies the area as "Marshall Camp." To the right, a sign identifies the tent as a photography gallery. It was not unusual for people to have their picture put on a "postal card" and sent to a friend or relative. (Courtesy of Geronimo Springs Museum Archives.)

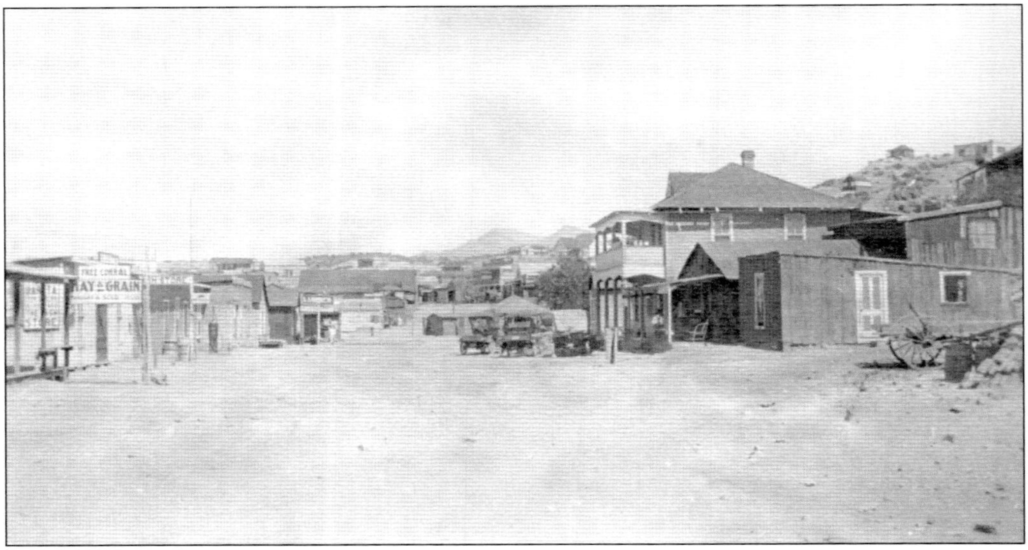

A 1919 plat of the town indicates that its name was now simply Hot Springs. The two-story building with the veranda was Pickle Johnson's hotel. Sam "Pickle" Johnson built the first hotel, which Laura, his wife, managed. Many guests slept outside on the veranda because it was felt that the air helped those suffering from tuberculosis. (Courtesy of Geronimo Springs Museum Archives.)

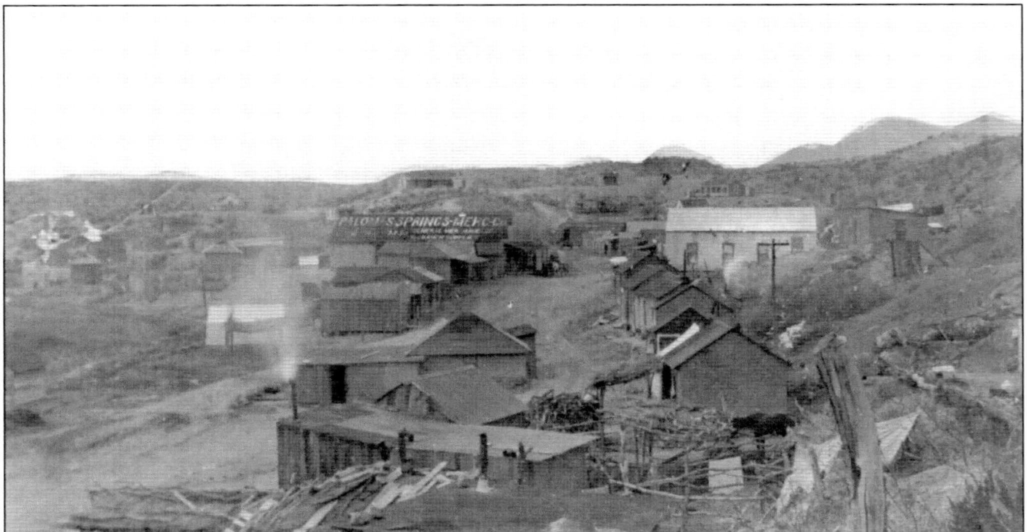

This is an early picture of Palomas Hot Springs. The original plat of the town site consisted of 59.49 acres. On September 7, 1914, the *Santa Fe New Mexican* reported that the Palomas Hot Springs Town Site Company filed incorporation papers and planned to do a general real estate business in the area that included laying out the village, buying land, issuing loans, and erecting electric lights.

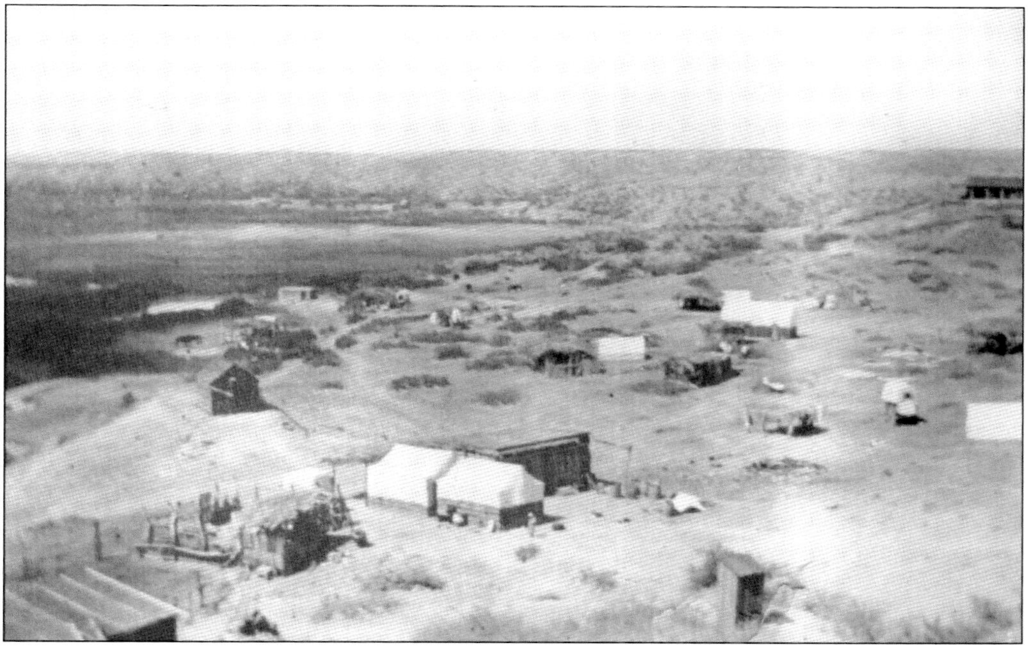

This photograph was taken by Harry S. Stanton, an engineer who worked on the construction of Engle Dam. As a newlywed, Stanton brought his wife to live on the construction site between 1911 and 1916. They returned to the area on their 50th wedding anniversary and gave this photograph to Mrs. C. L. Hedrick. (Courtesy of Geronimo Springs Museum Archives.)

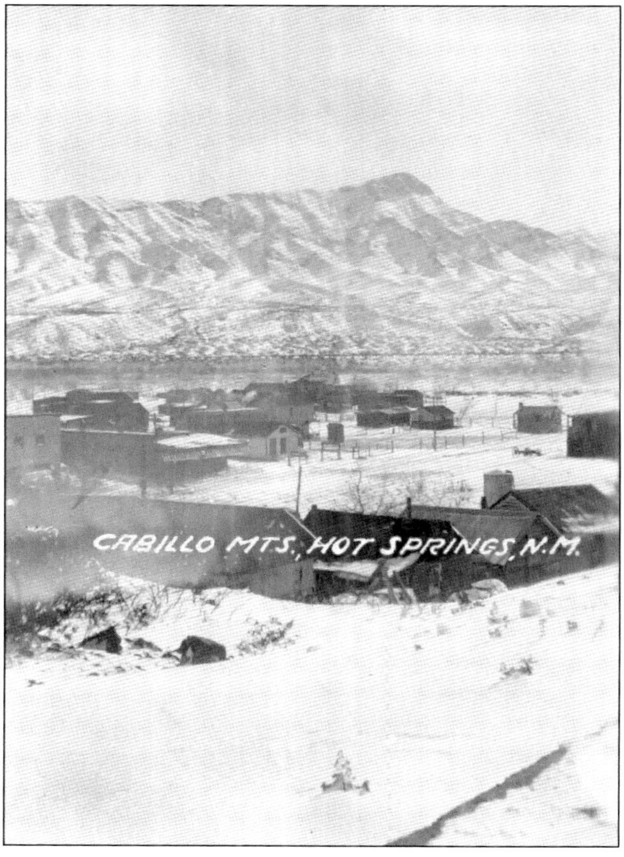

The mountains in the distance are the Sierra de Los Caballos. The mountains were mined for vanadium, lead, and copper. The Sierra de Los Caballos, or just Caballos, along with the Sierra Fra Cristobal Mountains to the north, formed the western boundary of the Jornada del Muerto. The picture has the name of "Caballos" misspelled, which was a common occurrence when early residents tried to spell Spanish words.

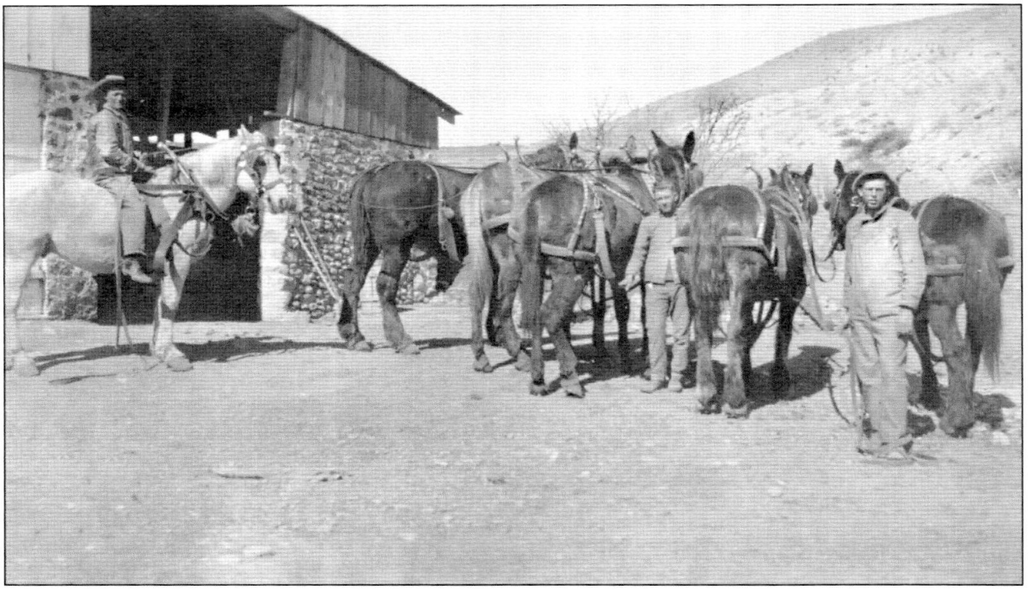

According to the *Santa Fe New Mexican*, on October 20, 1914, the residents from Palomas Hot Springs were said to be up in arms over a posting that they felt discriminated against their town. The posting by the chief engineer at the construction site said that any workers visiting Palomas Hot Springs on a "habitual basis" would be considered "undesirable employees."

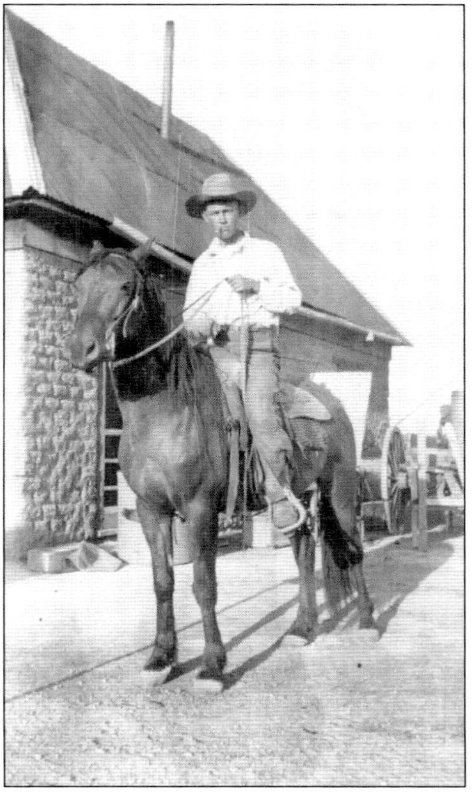

Sierra County had 3,536 residents on the 1910 Census. That year there were reportedly 4,040 horses, 26,200 head of cattle, 21,600 sheep, and 2,000 goats in Sierra County. A horse was worth about $11, a cow around $10, a sheep would run about $1.37, and a goat would set a person back about $1.

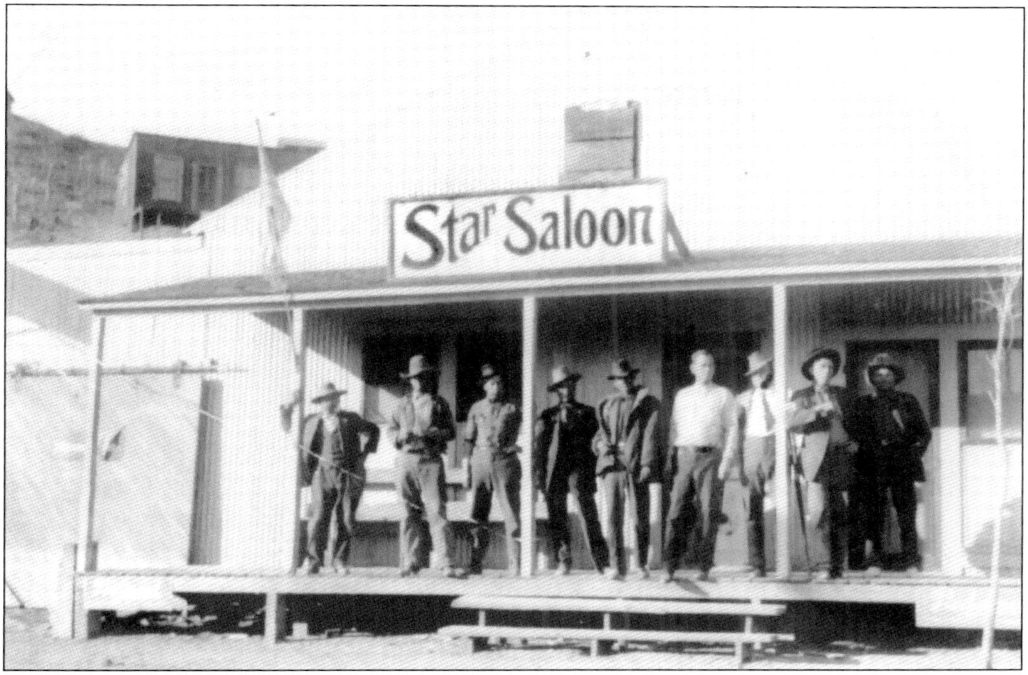

The Star Saloon opened in 1913 on Main Street. Standing from left to right in this c. 1917 photograph are Jim Adams, Navajo Red, Joe Tafoya, Joe Sena, Sam Hidalgo, Claude Hefferman, Bill Graham, and two unidentified individuals. Liquor was not allowed at the Engle Dam site, so bars became a hot commodity in the town of Palomas Hot Springs.

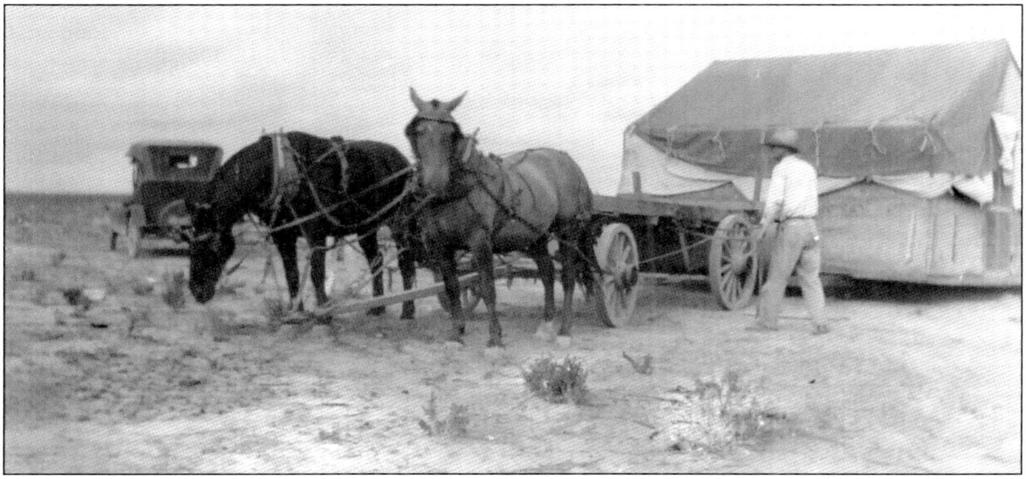

When Engle Dam was completed in 1916, the government sold off the buildings at the site. Some were taken apart and removed by horse and wagon. This picture shows how some of the building materials were then transported down to Palomas Hot Springs and reassembled.

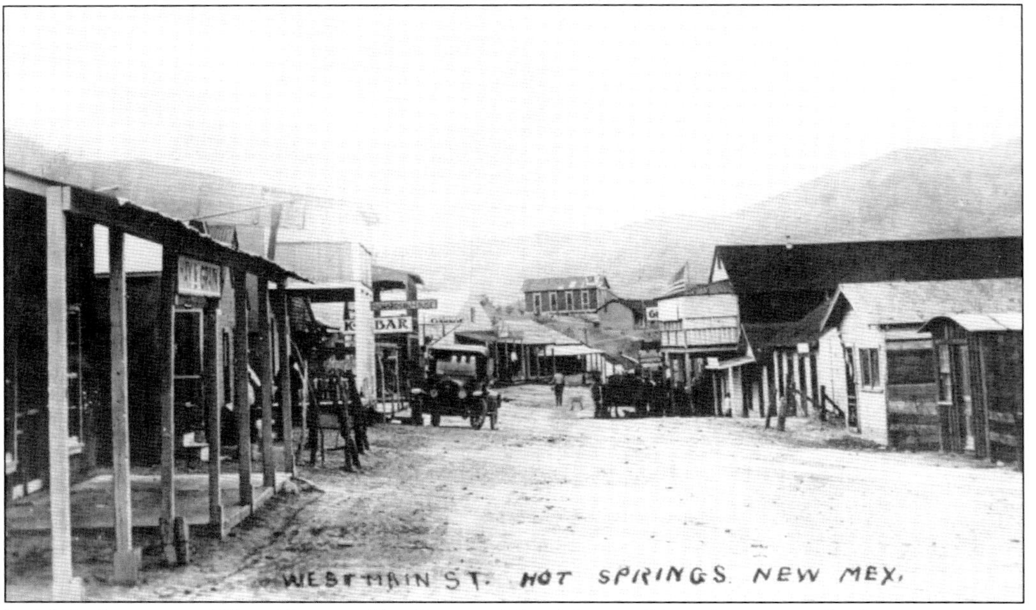

In 1920, there were 455 residents in Hot Springs, New Mexico. Main Street was the first commercial street in town. Some of its buildings had been moved from the construction site at Engle Dam. It would become a through street in 1934.

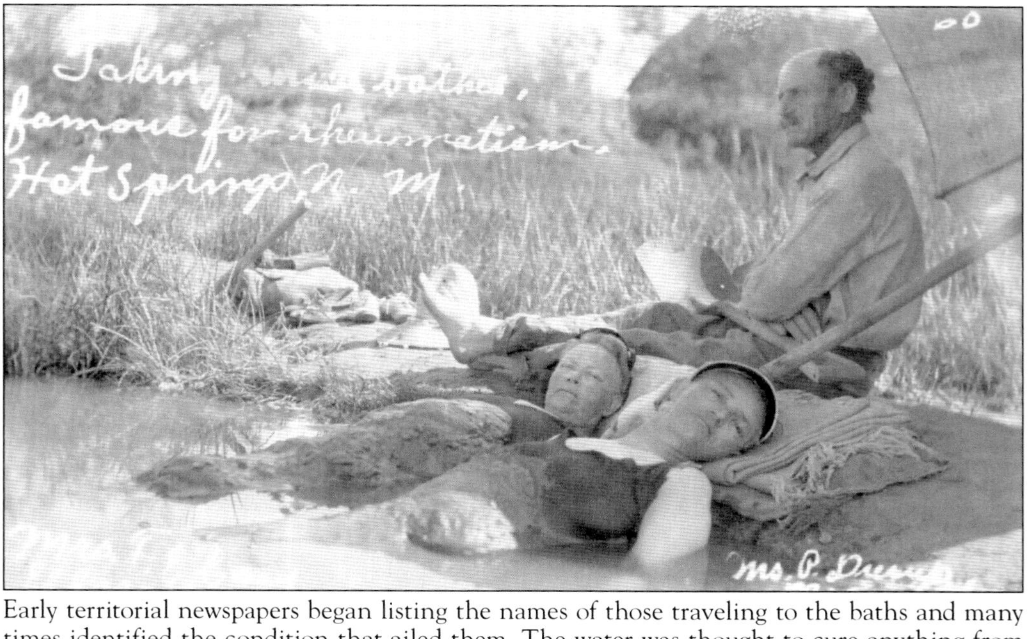

Early territorial newspapers began listing the names of those traveling to the baths and many times identified the condition that ailed them. The water was thought to cure anything from rheumatism to blood and stomach disorders. It was also rumored that the mud could improve a person's looks.

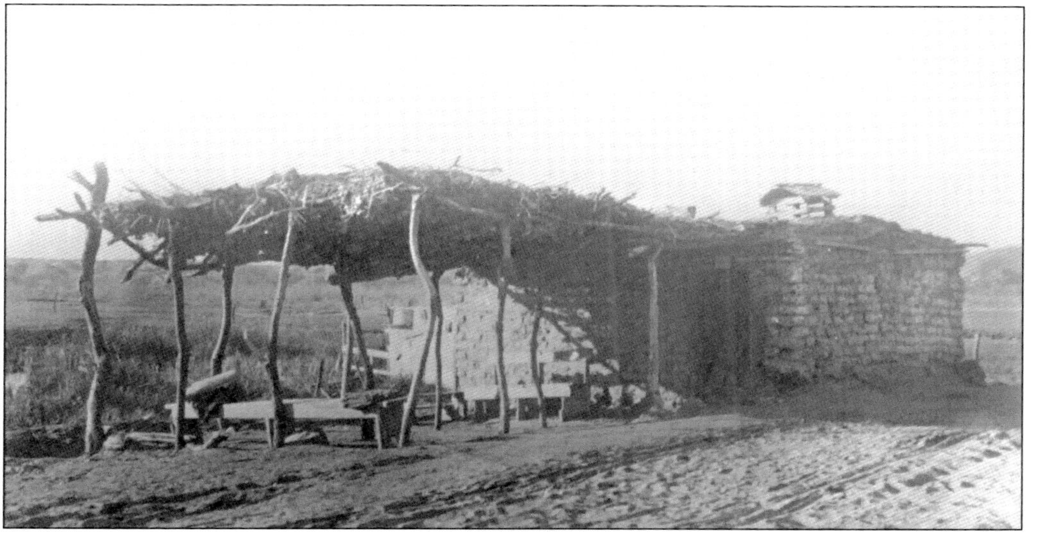

This adobe bathhouse was known as the lower bathhouse, and it was thought to be the original bathhouse built by the John Cross Ranch cowboys. After a long day of riding the trail, a cowboy likely needed a soak to get rid of the aches and pains of a hard day's work.

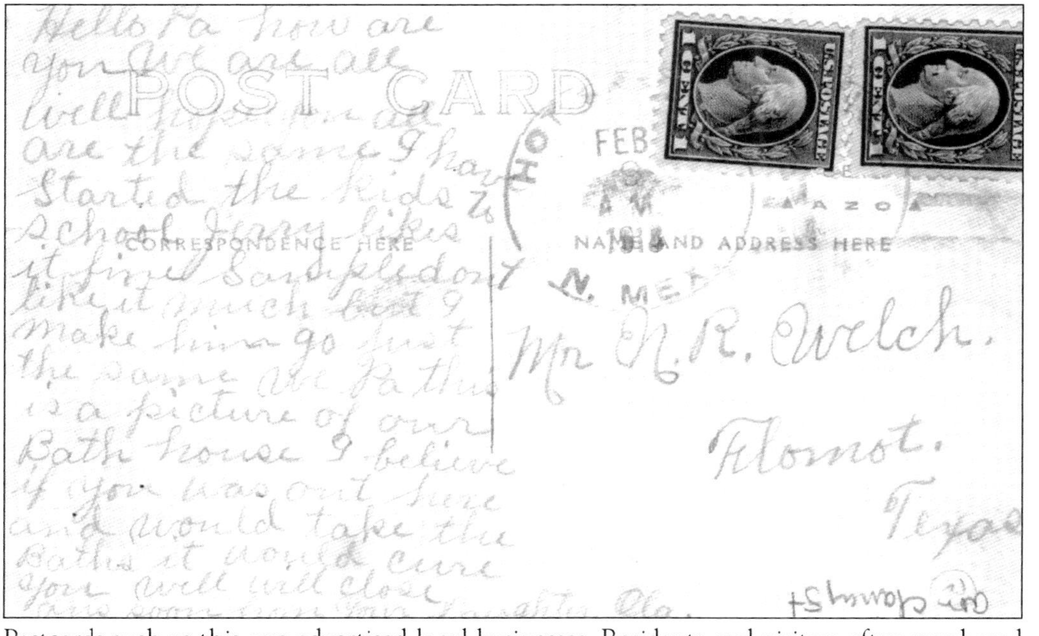

Postcards such as this one advertised local businesses. Residents and visitors often purchased these cards to send a short note home to family and friends. On this card, Ola suggests that her father come take the baths in Hot Springs—evidently he was not in good health. This is a good example of how Hot Springs's reputation began to grow.

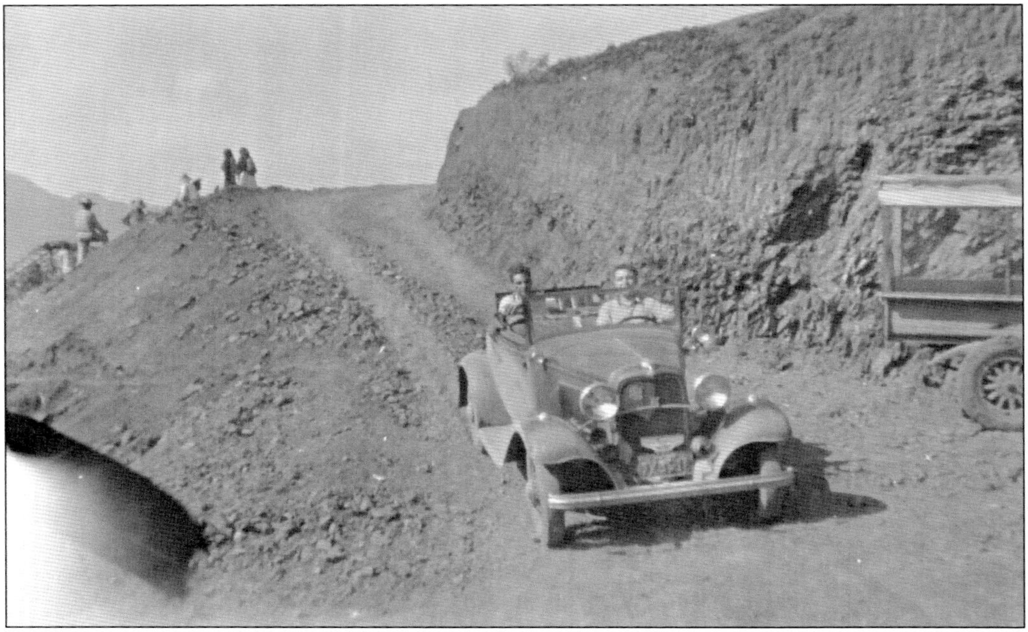

The Lonestar Auto Line advertised orange-colored Buicks that carried passengers between Engle, the dam, and Hot Springs, New Mexico. Lonestar advertised the "best dam cars, driven by the oldest dam drivers, on the dam line." The cars carried a star painted on them to identify them as belonging to Lonestar. Passengers depended on motorcars (like the one above) to take them from the train station to town through the 1930s.

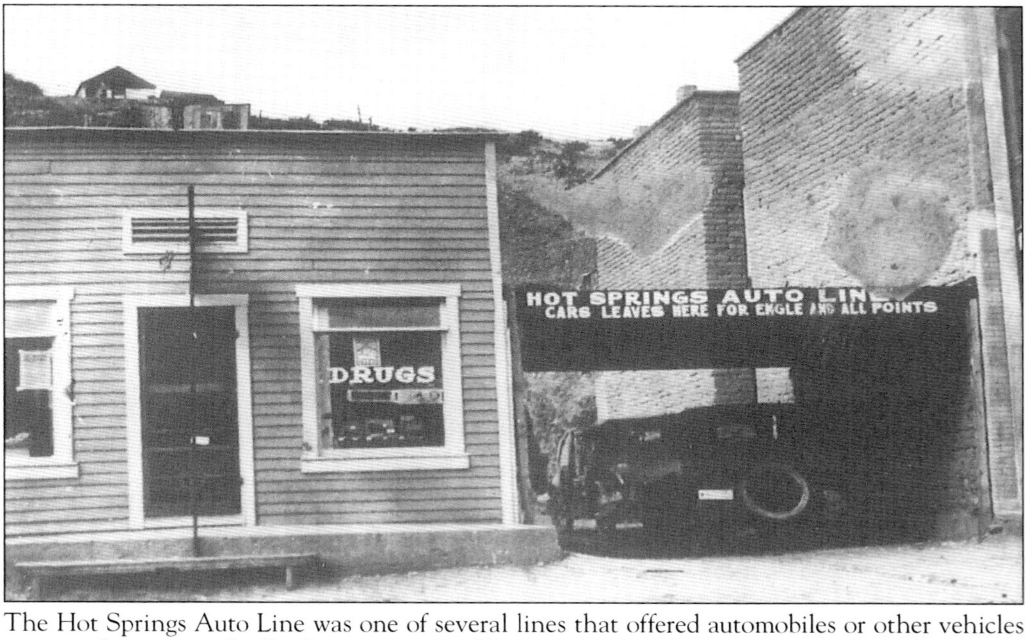

The Hot Springs Auto Line was one of several lines that offered automobiles or other vehicles to meet the train at the Engle train station. The train station depot was approximately 20 miles from Hot Springs. Visitors were usually traveling to the baths or visiting relatives in the area. Large merchandise shipped to the area was hauled by train and delivered by trucks.

Two

Soaks, Sanitariums, and Health Seekers

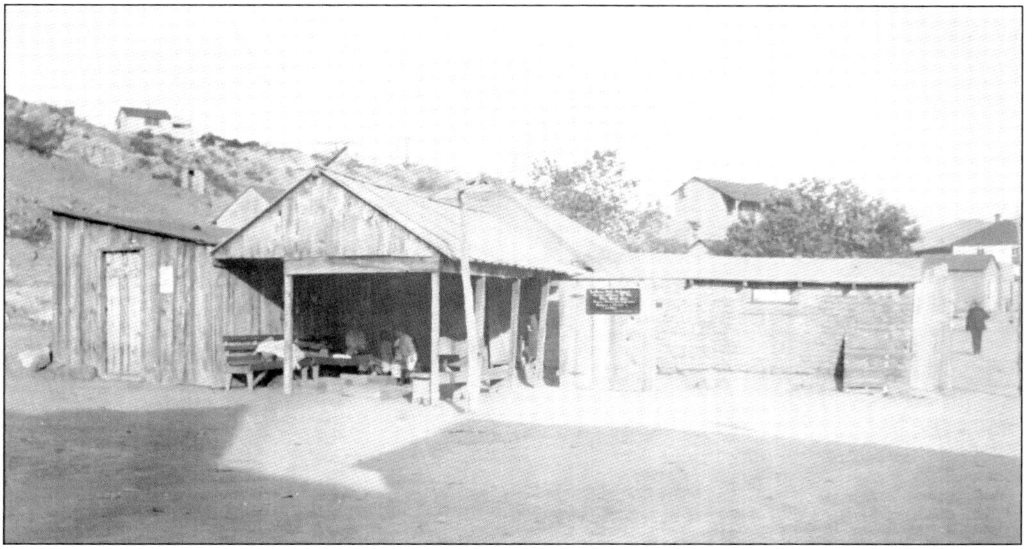

A. M. Cornell reported in the May 31, 1904, *Santa Fe New Mexican* that a boy had been partially cured from the springs' hot waters. Physicians had called his case "hopeless." His parents had taken up residence in Palomas Hot Springs hoping for a complete cure. The bath above is an example of the early bathhouses that many visitors frequented.

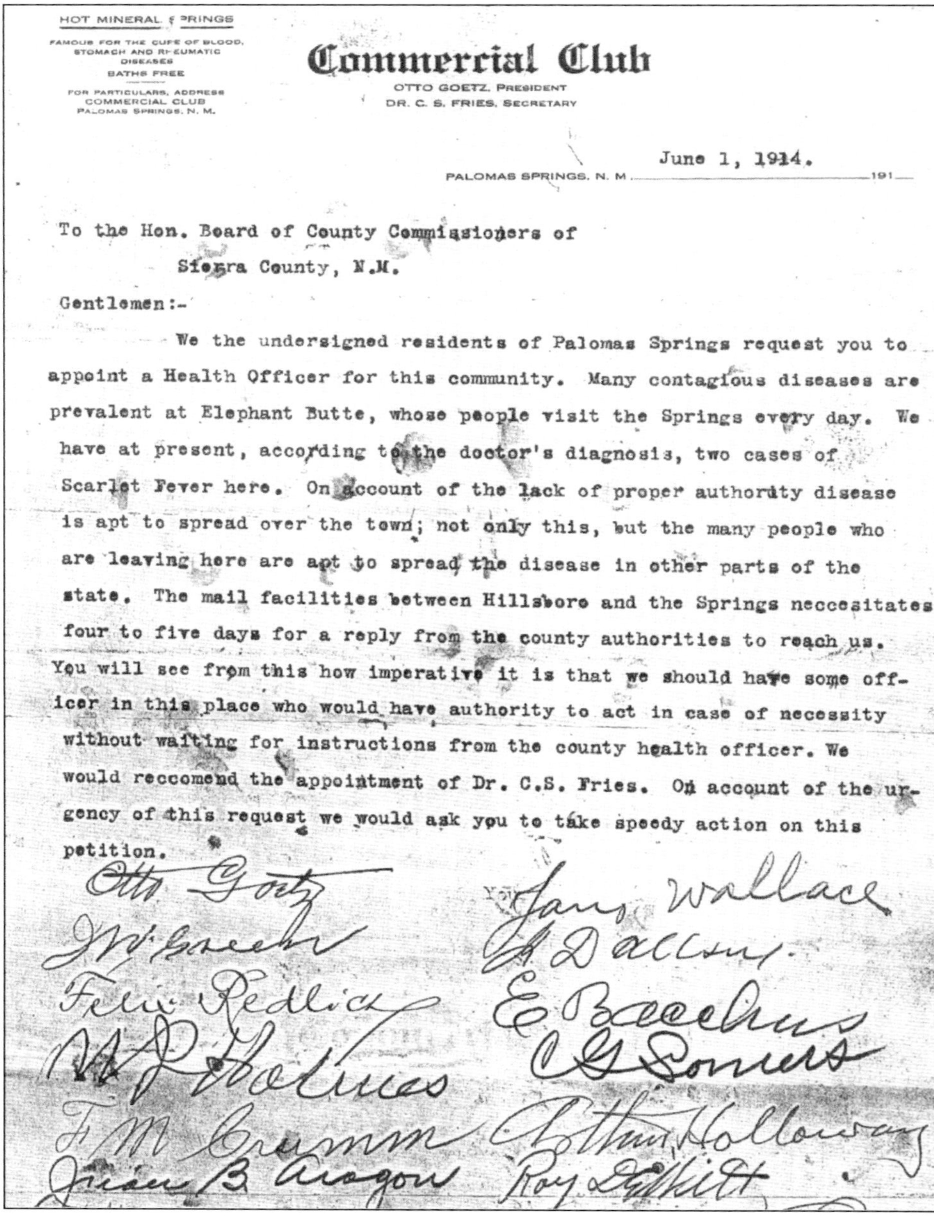

HOT MINERAL SPRINGS
FAMOUS FOR THE CURE OF BLOOD, STOMACH AND RHEUMATIC DISEASES
BATHS FREE
FOR PARTICULARS, ADDRESS COMMERCIAL CLUB PALOMAS SPRINGS, N. M.

Commercial Club

OTTO GOETZ, PRESIDENT
DR. C. S. FRIES, SECRETARY

PALOMAS SPRINGS, N. M. June 1, 1914.

To the Hon. Board of County Commissioners of
Sierra County, N.M.

Gentlemen:-

We the undersigned residents of Palomas Springs request you to appoint a Health Officer for this community. Many contagious diseases are prevalent at Elephant Butte, whose people visit the Springs every day. We have at present, according to the doctor's diagnosis, two cases of Scarlet Fever here. On account of the lack of proper authority disease is apt to spread over the town; not only this, but the many people who are leaving here are apt to spread the disease in other parts of the state. The mail facilities between Hillsboro and the Springs neccesitates four to five days for a reply from the county authorities to reach us. You will see from this how imperative it is that we should have some officer in this place who would have authority to act in case of necessity without waiting for instructions from the county health officer. We would reccomend the appointment of Dr. C.S. Fries. On account of the urgency of this request we would ask you to take speedy action on this petition.

The Commercial Club, an early chamber of commerce for the area, sent this letter to Sierra County commissioners. They wanted the state to appoint a health officer immediately so that they would not have to wait for the county health officer to be reached by mail. They proposed that their own Dr. C. S. Fries act in the capacity of the health officer in Palomas Hot Springs. Notice that at the time, the baths were free, and the Commercial Club claimed that they could cure blood, stomach, and rheumatic diseases. It leads to the speculation that Palomas Hot Springs got more than they bargained for by inviting the "sick" to their area for a cure. They had every reason to be afraid with cases of scarlet fever in their midst. Any fears of contagious diseases were not enough to close the baths, however, as the bathers brought in money to the area through lodging, food, and drink. Baths continued to crop up all over town.

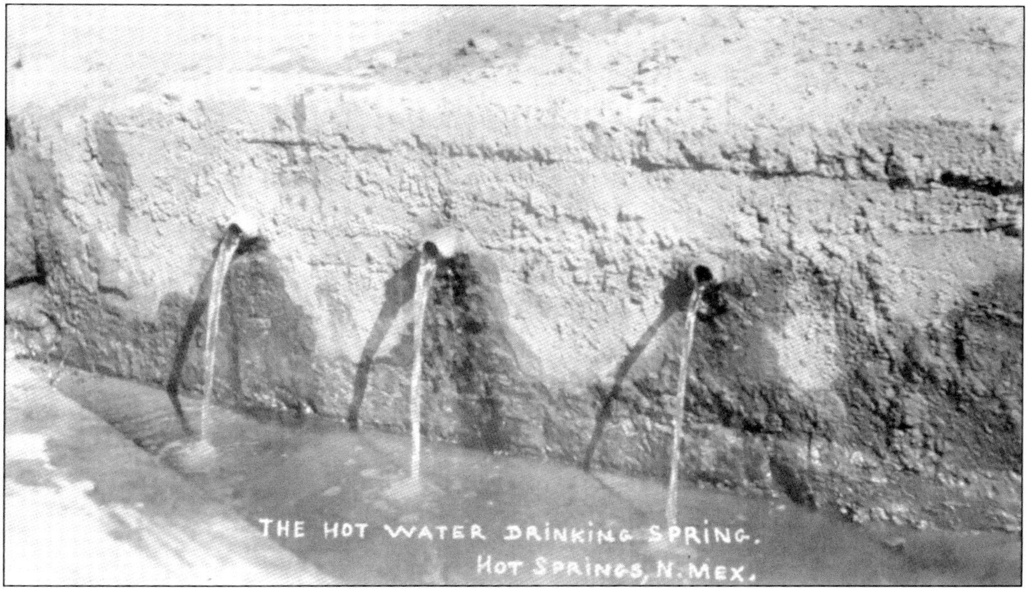

These *c.* 1900 pictures depict the "drinking springs." Not only did individuals bathe in the hot mineral springs, but they also drank the water, seeking to cure themselves of blood, stomach, and other diseases. In 1921, the Department of Agriculture did a water analysis. Using this analysis, the claim was made that the waters cured everything from chronic inflammation of the joints to asthma. The chamber of commerce claimed to have a file of affidavits, which they would willingly share, from people who had been cured at Hot Springs.

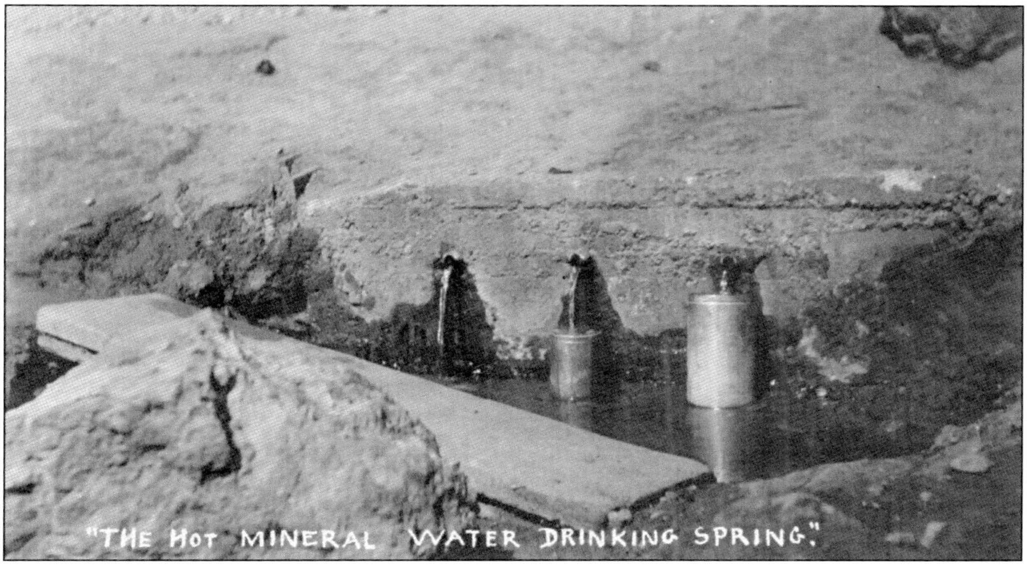

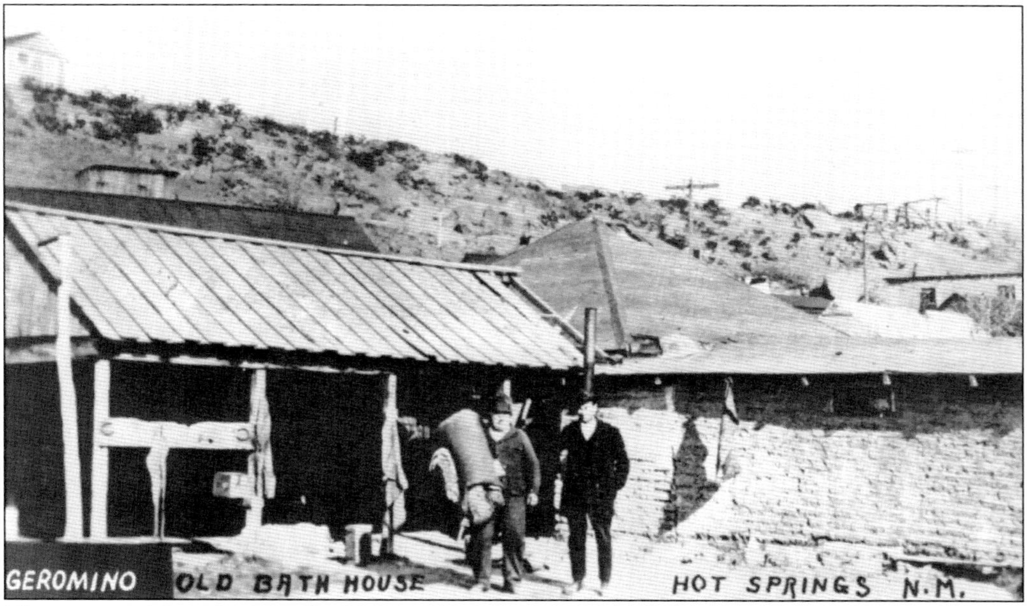

This picture shows the main bathhouse in Hot Springs. It did not take long for bathhouse owners to start realizing that as they improved the facilities, they could charge for the baths. Since oral history claimed that Geronimo had been at the springs, the entrepreneur running this bath decided to market the place as Geronimo Springs.

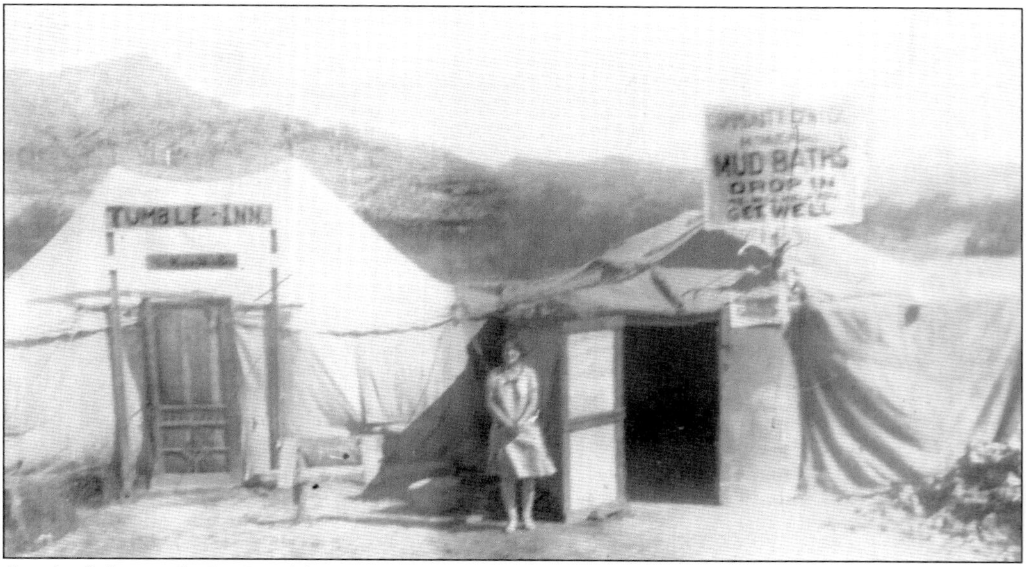

On the left stands the Tumble Inn, one of the tent hotels popular at the time in Hot Springs. On the right is the Community Center Mineral Mud baths. The woman standing in front is perhaps a patron of both facilities. (Courtesy of Geronimo Springs Museum Archives.)

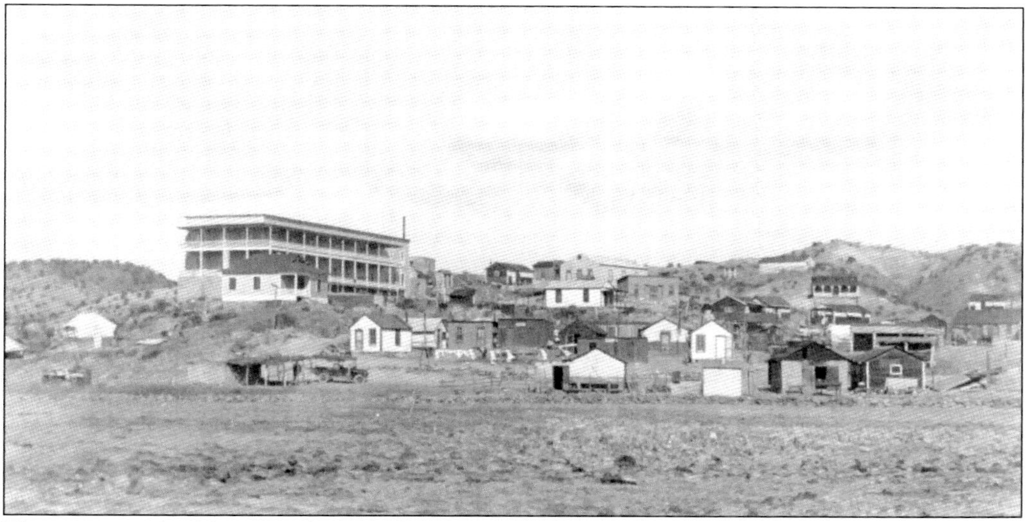

The two-story building standing on the granite hill above Hot Springs is the Vera Hotel, shown here around 1918. Owned by W. H. Harris and wife Edith, the hotel rented rooms for $1 a night and boasted of its hot and cold running water. The hotel advertised itself as "The Best Hotel in the State by a Dam Site."

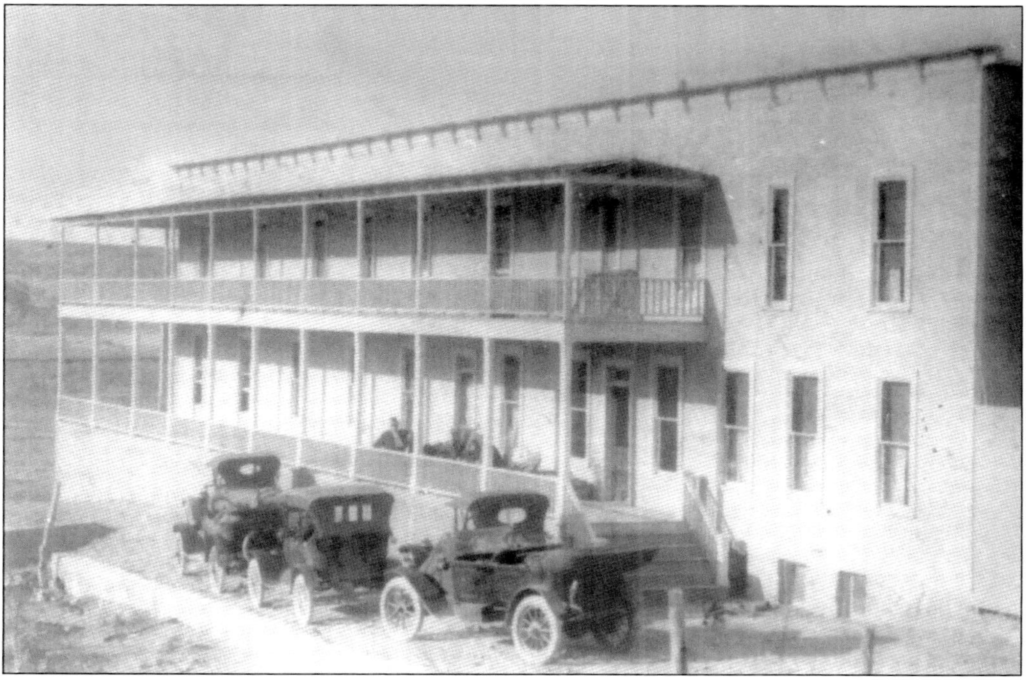

The Vera had been barracks and mess halls for Engle Dam workers before it was auctioned off by the government, dismantled, hauled to town, and reassembled as a hotel. An original 1920s grocery list shows the hotel paying 60¢ for five pounds of sweet potatoes, $1.50 for six pounds of red chili, and $15.20 for two sacks of sugar.

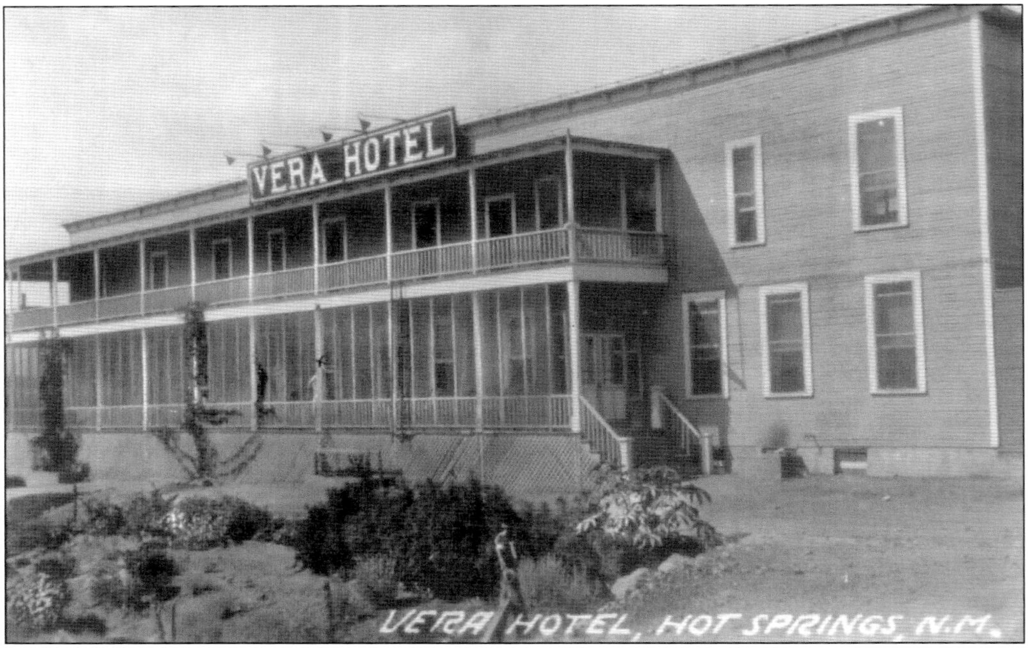

By 1923, the Vera had changed ownership twice. James W. and Florence Knox bought it in 1923 while (some say) they were on their honeymoon. In 1929, the Vera was advertising hot and cold water, steam heat, reasonable rates, and convenience for bathers. They also were said to have electric lights, amusements, and a traveling men's headquarters. Florence Knox taught dancing to the young men and women of the area and brought in local talent to play at the Friday night dances. James Knox, known as Jim, was involved in establishing the Hot Springs Fire Department and the Carrie Tingley Hospital for Crippled Children. New Mexico governor Clyde Tingley stayed at the Vera Hotel when he was in town. (Both, courtesy of Geronimo Springs Museum Archives.)

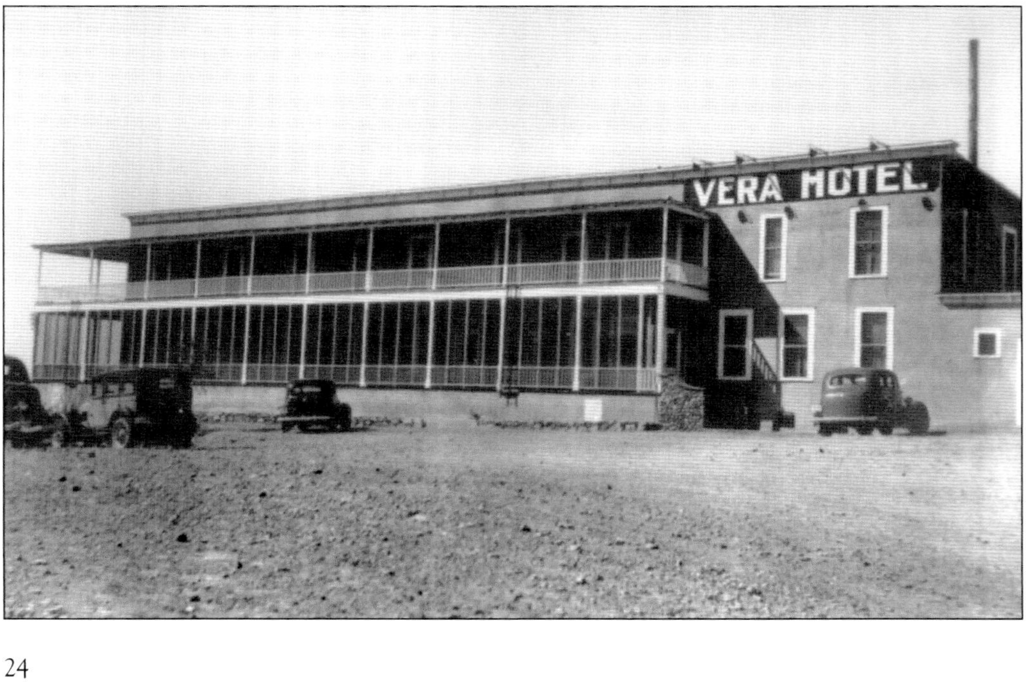

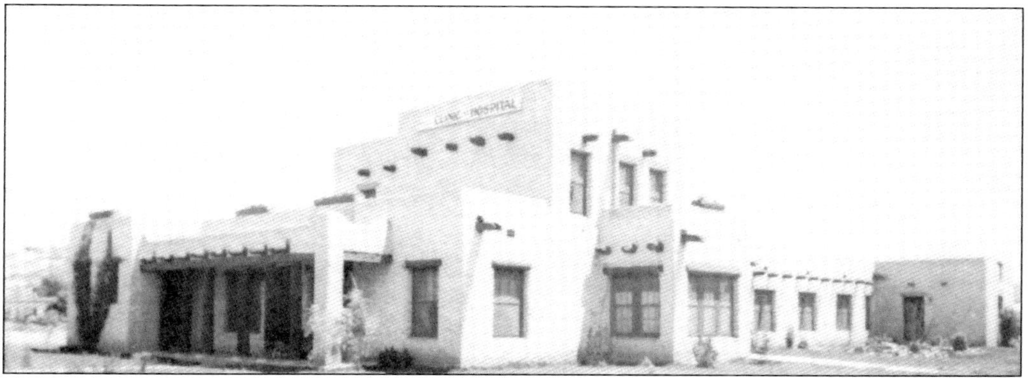

Dr. Fred Leslie built the Virginia Ann Clinic and Hospital around 1936. The Craig family operated it in 1948. The hospital was located on the corner of Austin and Clancy Streets in Hot Springs. The hospital was said to serve those patients dealing with arthritis, neuritis, rheumatism, and alcoholism. In the late 1940s, the Catholic Sisters of the Sorrowful Mother, a German order of nuns, arrived to operate the hospital, which was then called St. Ann's. A wing was added onto the hospital that employed nine physicians. The hospital was leased from a Mrs. Frost and a Mr. Collins for a 10-year period. The first sisters at Hot Springs were Sr. M. Rosalinda, Sr. M. Viola, Sr. M. Guadentia, and Sr. M. Encratia.

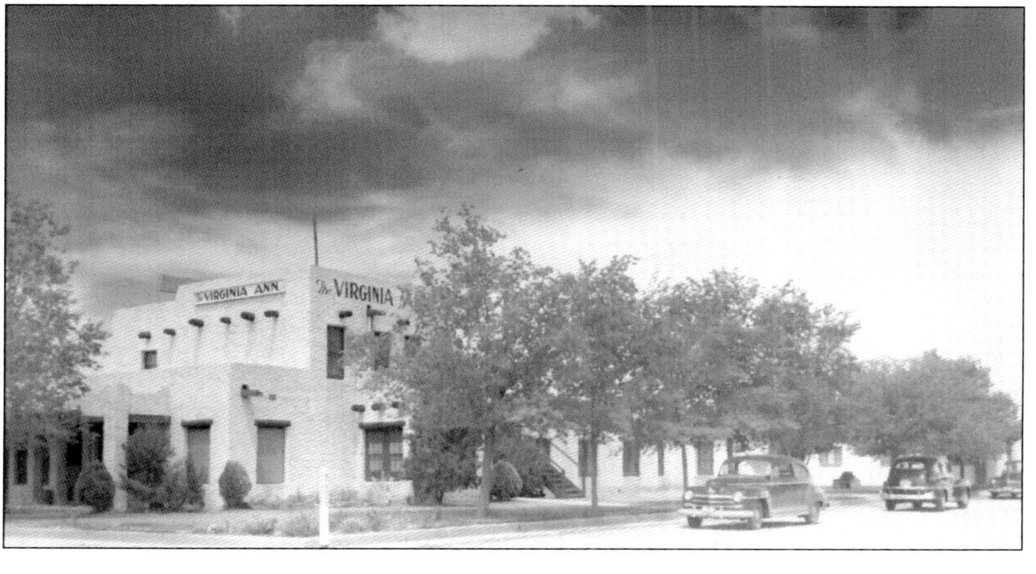

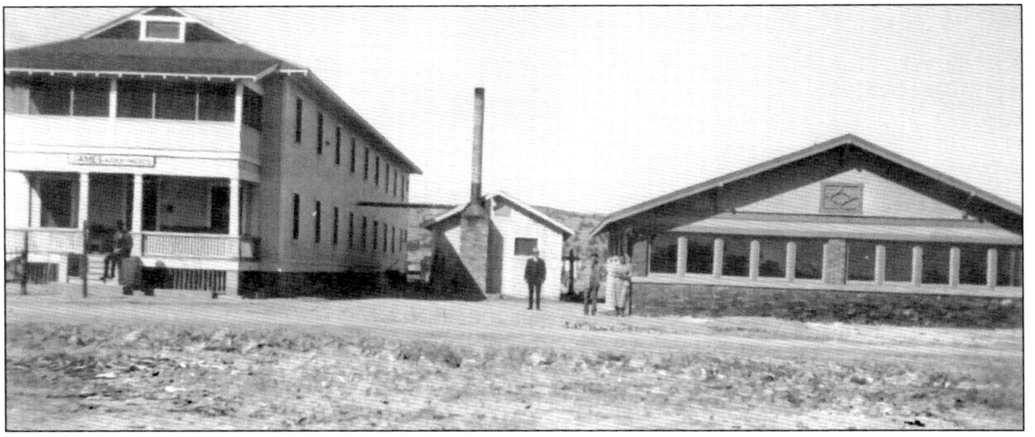

The buildings on the left are the James Apartments and their mineral bathhouse. The James was one of the buildings in use at the work site during the construction of Engle Dam. The government auctioned off the structure after the dam was complete, and Harold Scott bought it. He hired Charlie Price and the Stone brothers to bring it to Palomas Hot Springs by wagons. It was then sold to Mr. and Mrs. Charlie James, who hired Mike Knifel to reconstruct the building into apartments. The James was popular due to the location of the springs beneath the bathhouse.

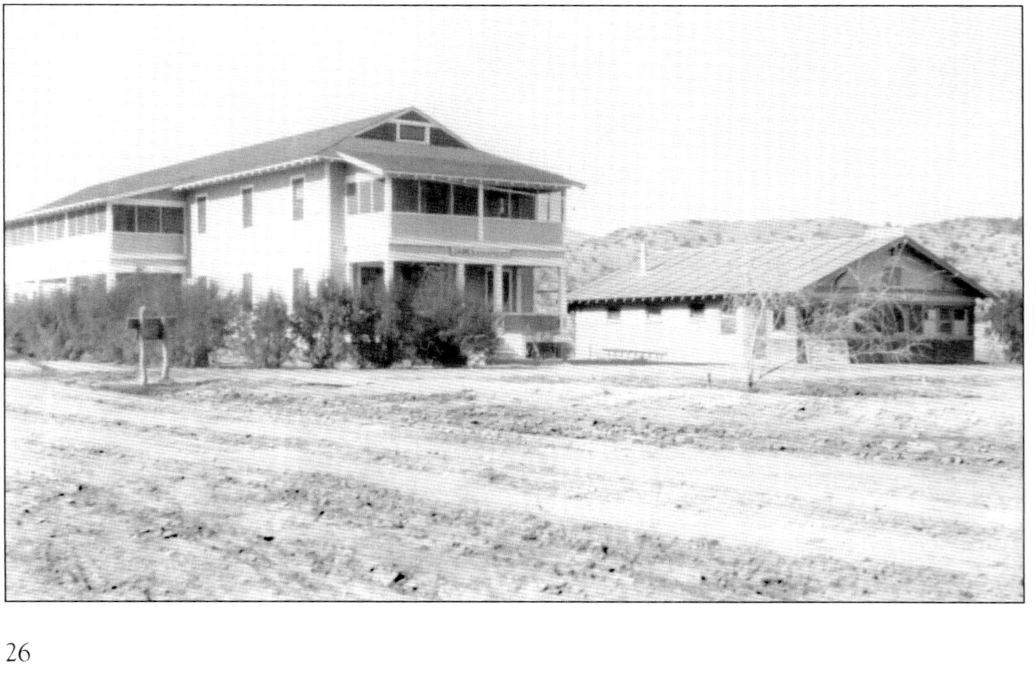

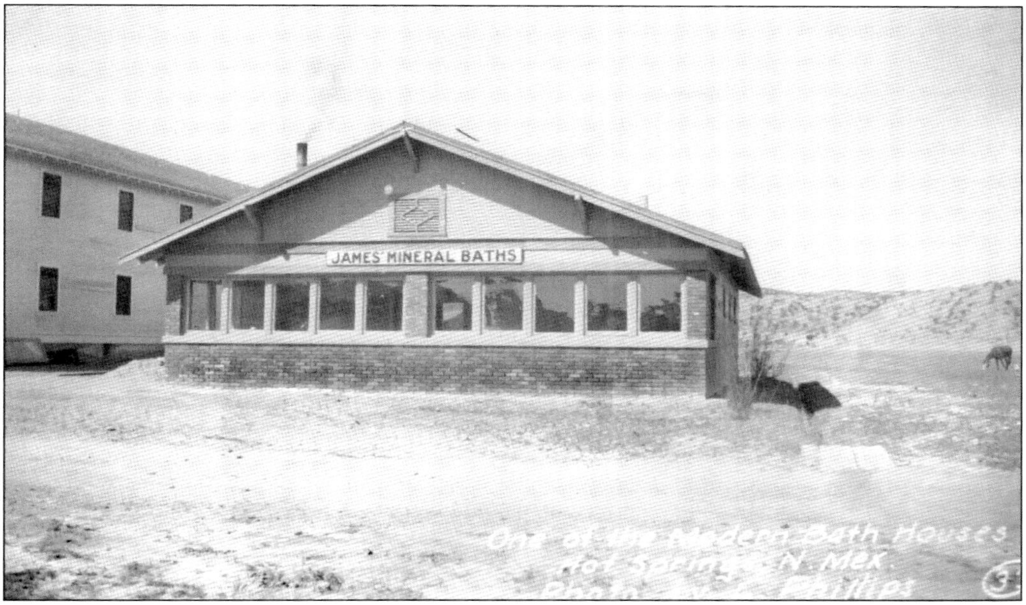

The James Apartments and Bathhouse site is now the home of the Bank of the Southwest. The builder of the present bank building did not cap the hot water, constructing a fully equipped mineral bath in the bank president's office area. This is probably the only bank in the United States to have its own mineral bath. (Courtesy of Geronimo Springs Museum Archives.)

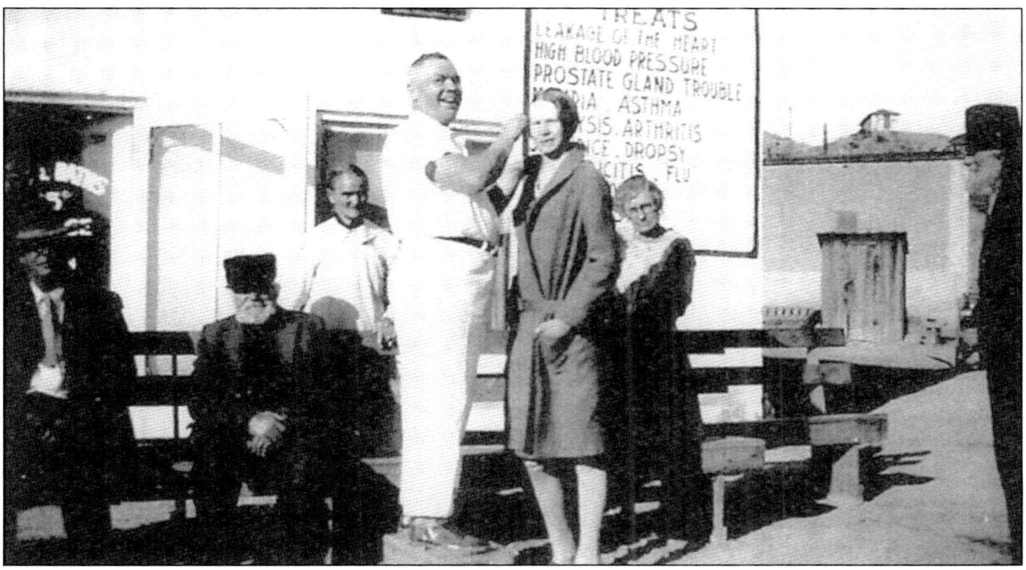

Linda Seger has three photographs of her great grandfather George L. Mills. This particular photograph had the caption that indicated Mills was now calling himself a "doctor." The "tall glass of water" standing in front of "Doctor" Mills was said to have come in on a stretcher and gone out on her own two feet. Now that would bring in the business. (Courtesy of Linda Seger.)

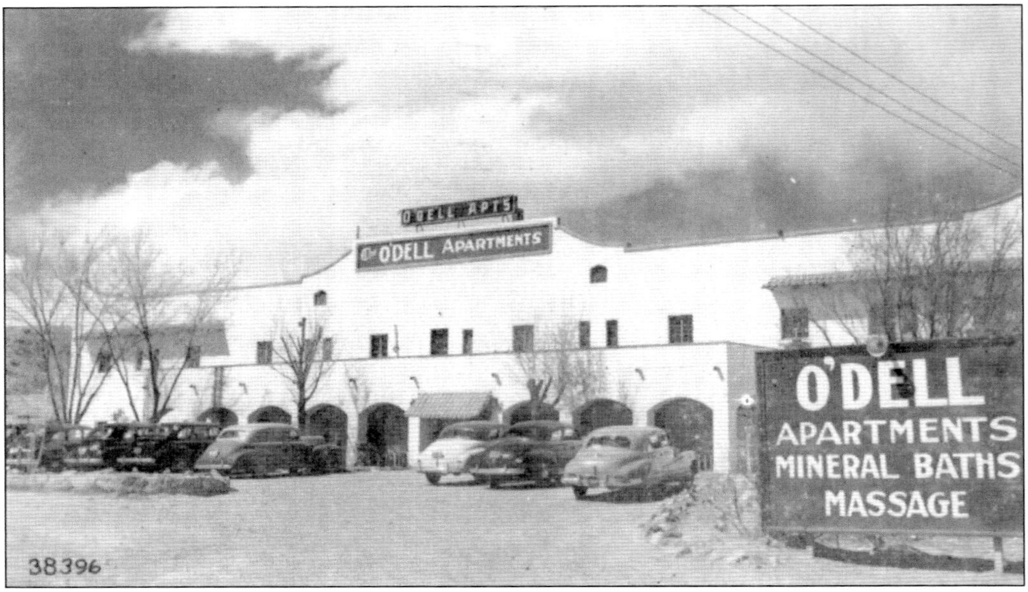

The two-story O'Dell Apartments were built in 1928 in the center of downtown Hot Springs. The rooms were the size of a typical motel room, but they were called apartments because of the added amenity of a small kitchenette. These photographs show two different spans of time in the history of the O'Dell Apartments. The well at the O'Dell was the first registered well in the Hot Springs Basin and was known as HS-1. In 1945, the hotel brought in a professional masseur to manage the mineral baths located inside the hotel. The O'Dell still stands today as the Sierra Grande Lodge. It has been fully remodeled and updated.

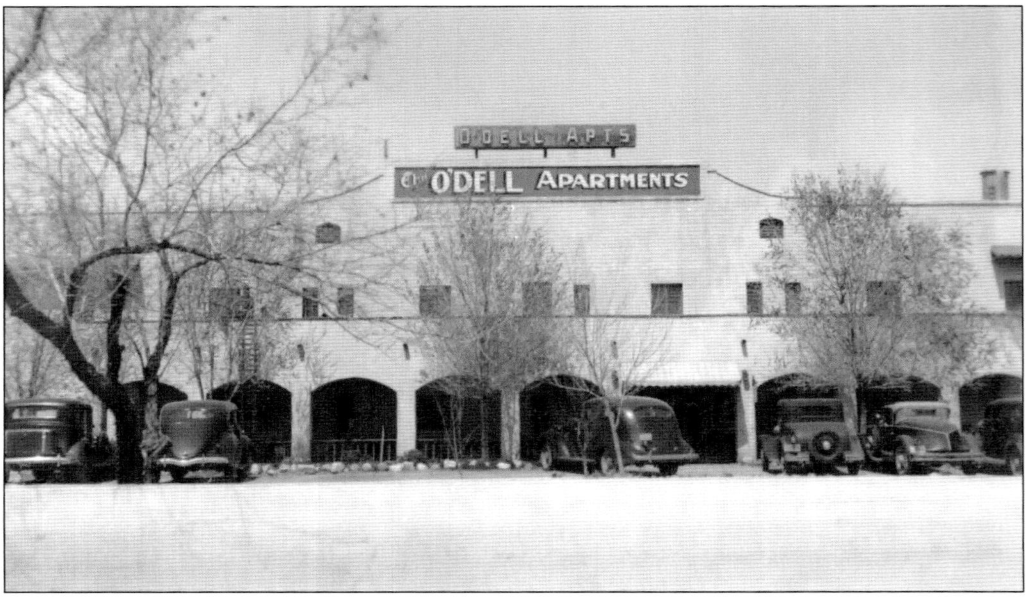

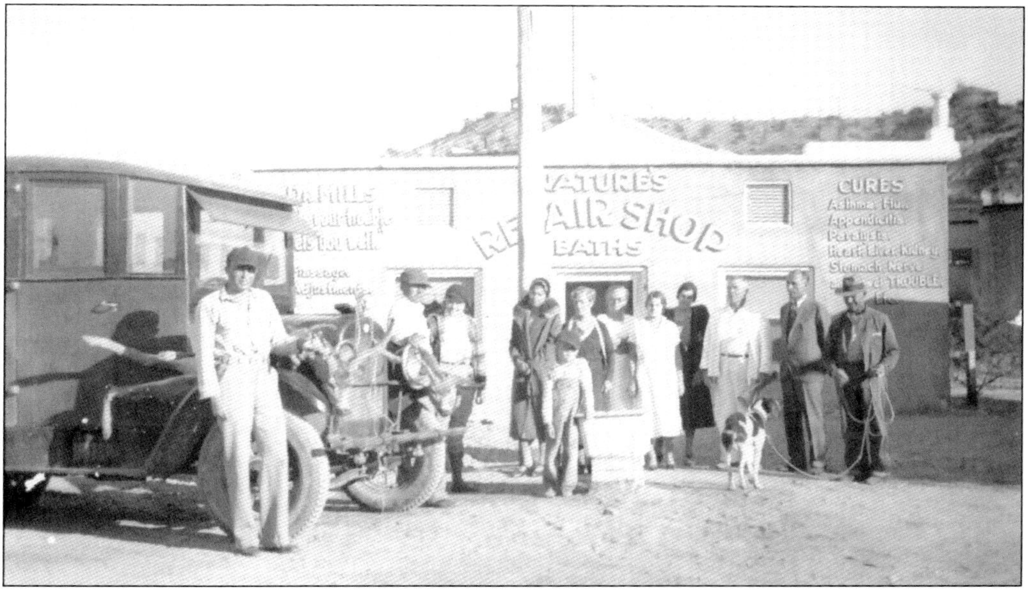

George Lewis Mills moved to Hot Springs and opened up the White House Baths, which he later renamed Nature's Repair Shop. Mills later became known as Dr. Mills, but it is unknown if he was actually a degreed doctor because he listed himself as a manager at a bathhouse on the 1930 U.S. Census. (Courtesy of Charles "Chuck" Martin.)

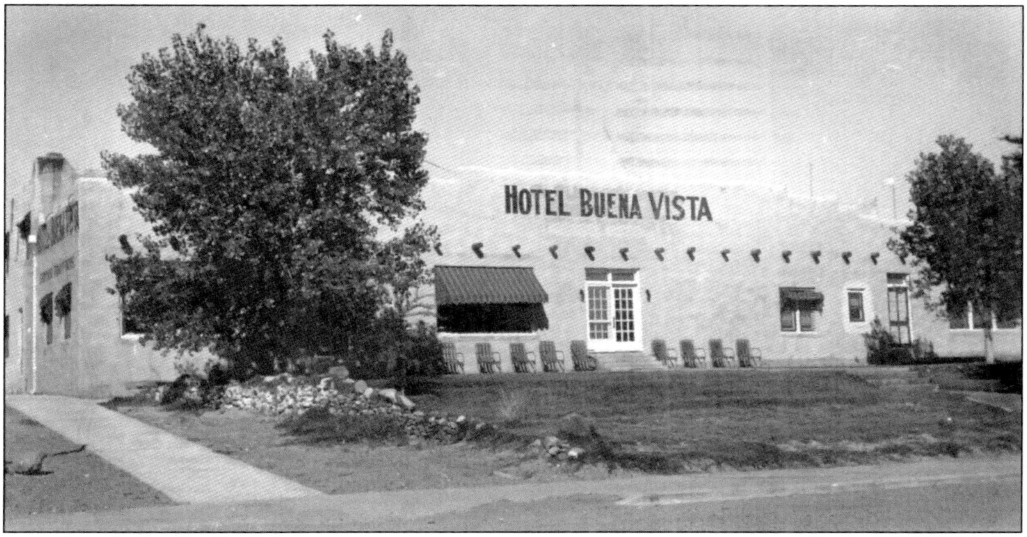

The Hotel Buena Vista was originally the Dr. Plumlee Hotel and Sanitarium. Dr. Plumlee had moved his family in 1933 to Hot Springs from Roy, New Mexico. At that time, he leased the newly constructed facilities. It later became the Sartin Sanitarium and later the Hotel Buena Vista.

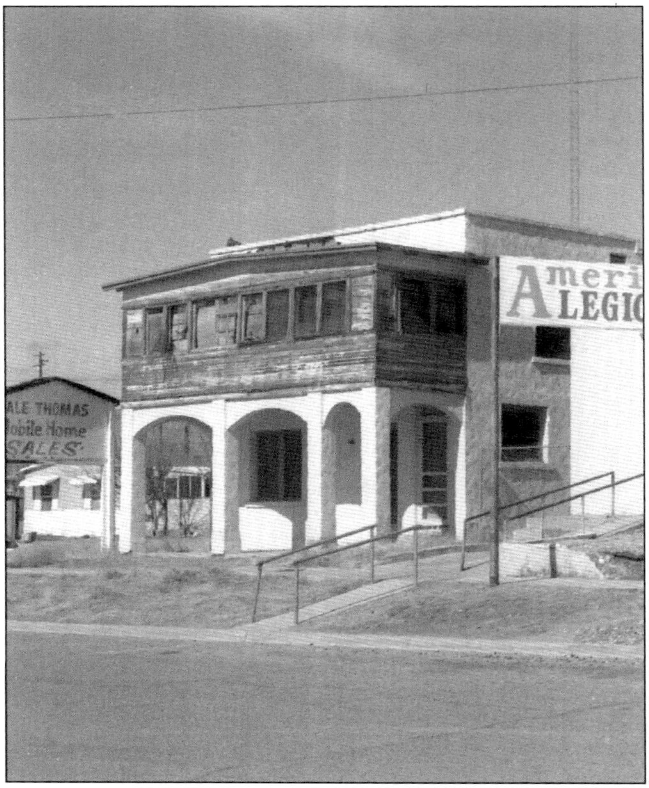

This two-story dilapidated building was considered the first hospital in Hot Springs. Starting in the early 1900s, New Mexico attracted health seekers seeking a better climate for relief of asthma, consumption (tuberculosis), and other diseases of the lungs. The terrace-style buildings accommodated individuals seeking fresh air, which was thought to help relieve symptoms. Many babies were delivered in this facility in the 1930s.

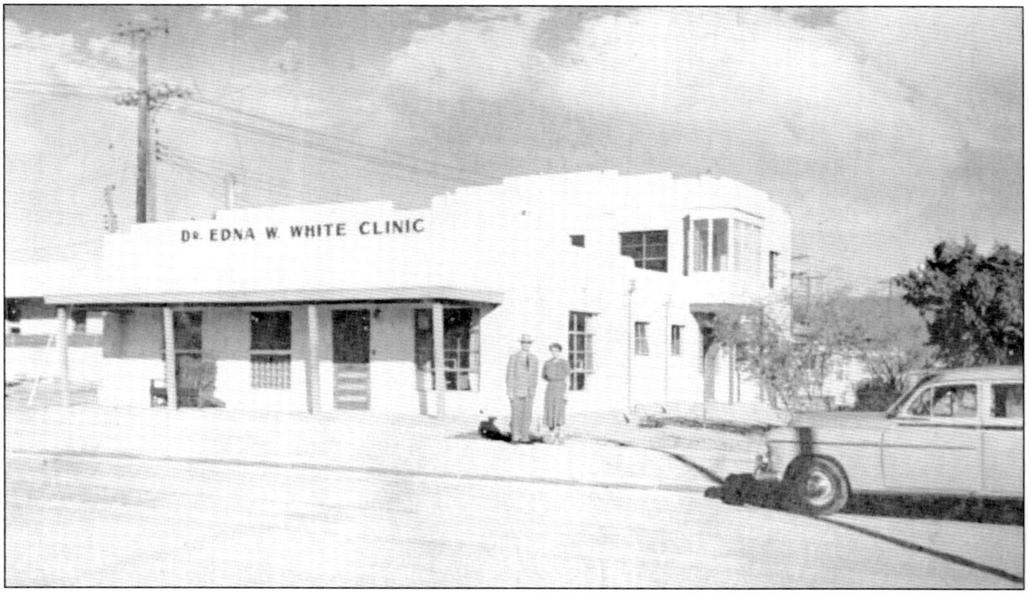

Dr. Edna White and her husband, Rev. Boyd A. White, are pictured outside of their clinic and home addition. They came to Hot Springs in 1948 to promote a Presbyterian ministry, which included healing, preaching, and teaching. Together they built the Reformed Presbyterian Chapel in 1950, the clinic in 1951, and their home addition in 1953.

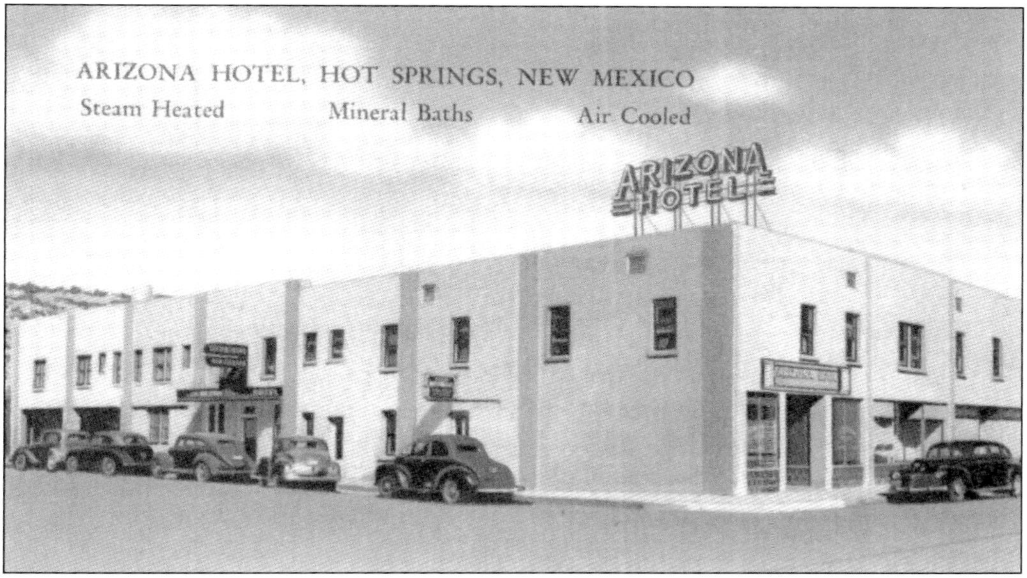

The Arizona Hotel was located at 100 Foch Street in Hot Springs. It was owned and operated by Mr. and Mrs. Barney Iorio, who had relocated here from the Gallup area. The Arizona Hotel was built in 1928. To make a phone reservation, a person called the number 17. The Arizona advertises on this postcard that it has "mineral baths in connection" to the hotel.

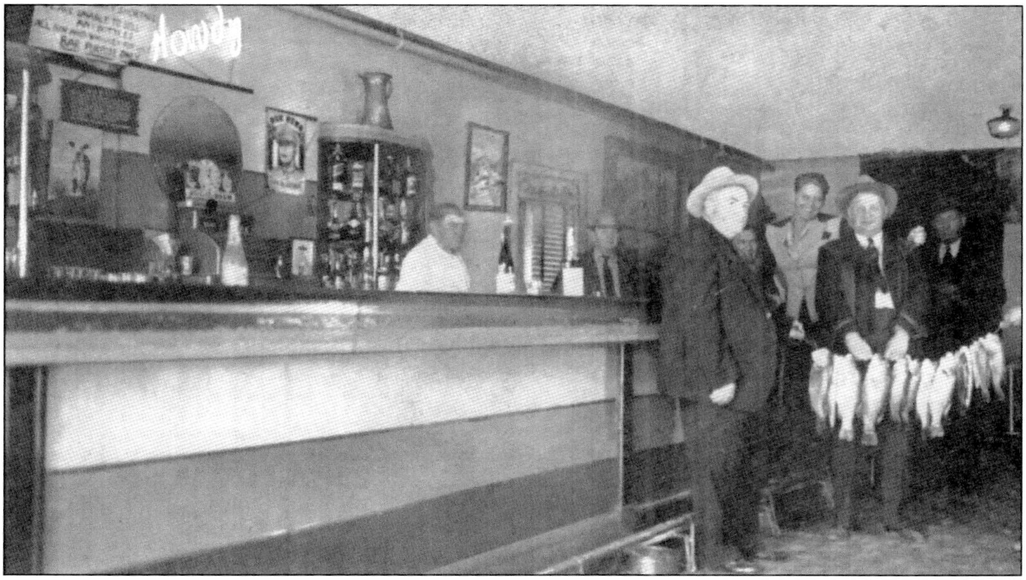

This was the Arizona Bar, and as seen by the postcard, fishing on the waters of Elephant Butte Lake or nearby Caballo Lake was a big sport. It was not all that common for the local fishermen to bring their catch in for "bragging rights" to their fellow fishermen. The Arizona also had a gambling room, another popular "sport" in early Hot Springs.

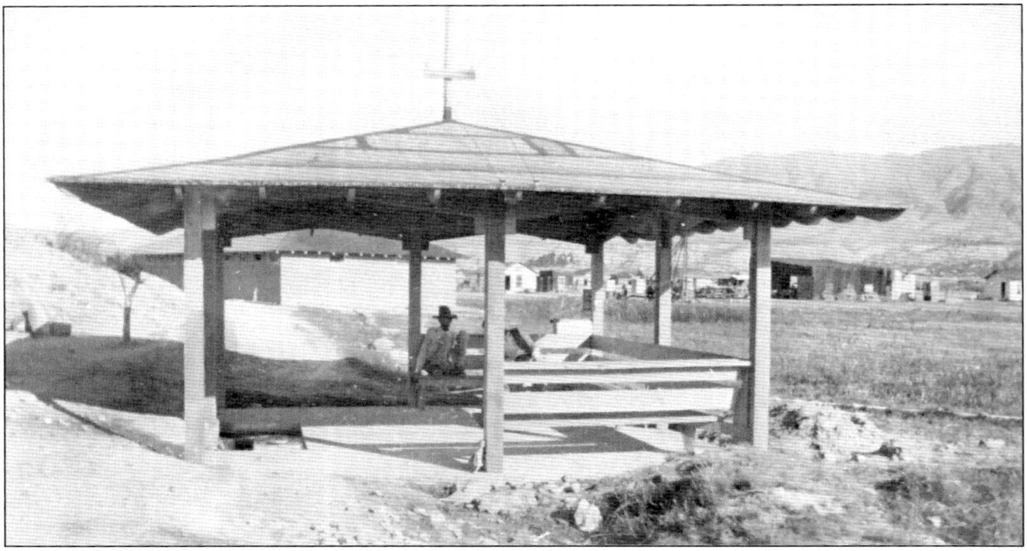

This picture depicts an early style of room used to shelter the springs. Though it was unknown at the time, downtown Hot Springs's approximately 35 artesian wells, springs, and sumps were all part of a single large artesian basin. The area was divided by the prominent limestone Magdalena Ridge upon which the water tanks for the city were eventually located.

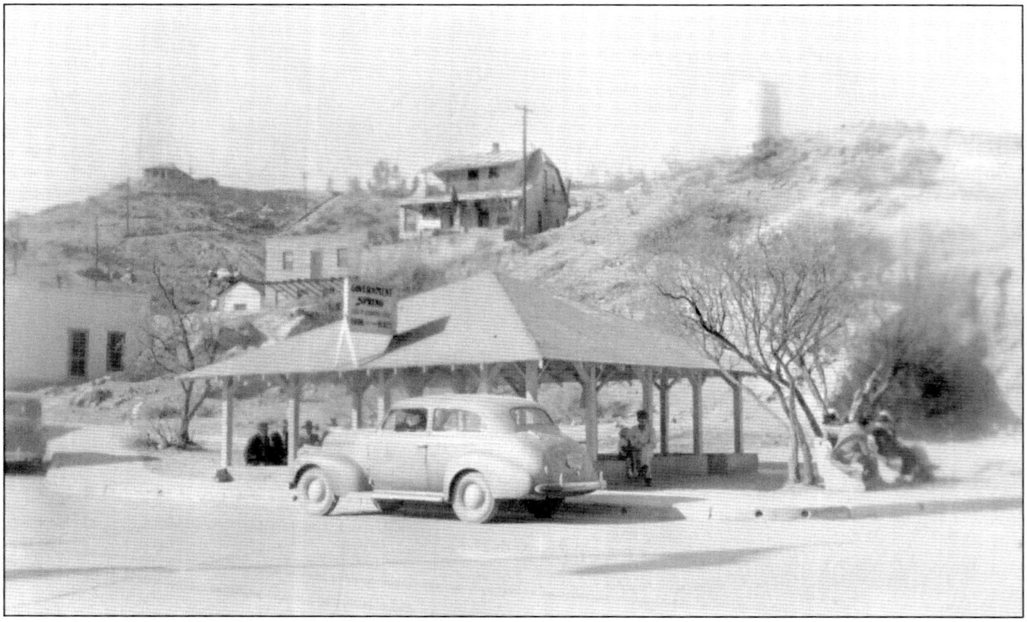

Fount (Faunt) Sullivan wanted to acquire the land around the hot springs, and so did the John Cross Cattle Company. Sullivan circulated a petition throughout the area to withdraw the land around the hot springs from settlement. Through his actions, the land around the hot springs became government land, and eventually the springs would become known as the Government Springs, shown above.

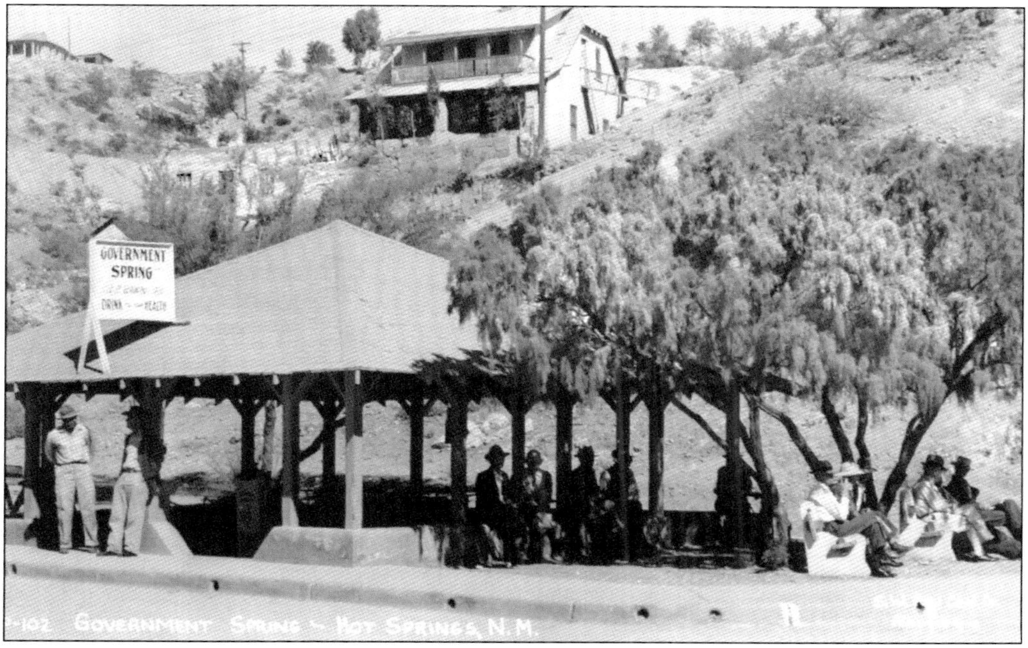

This postcard shows Government Springs, which would later become known as Geronimo Springs. Government Springs was not for bathing but for drinking. The area is now where the present-day Geronimo Springs Museum is located. In March 1947, a 20-year lease of Geronimo Springs from the federal government was executed by the city of Hot Springs. In 2003, the lease was signed over to the city.

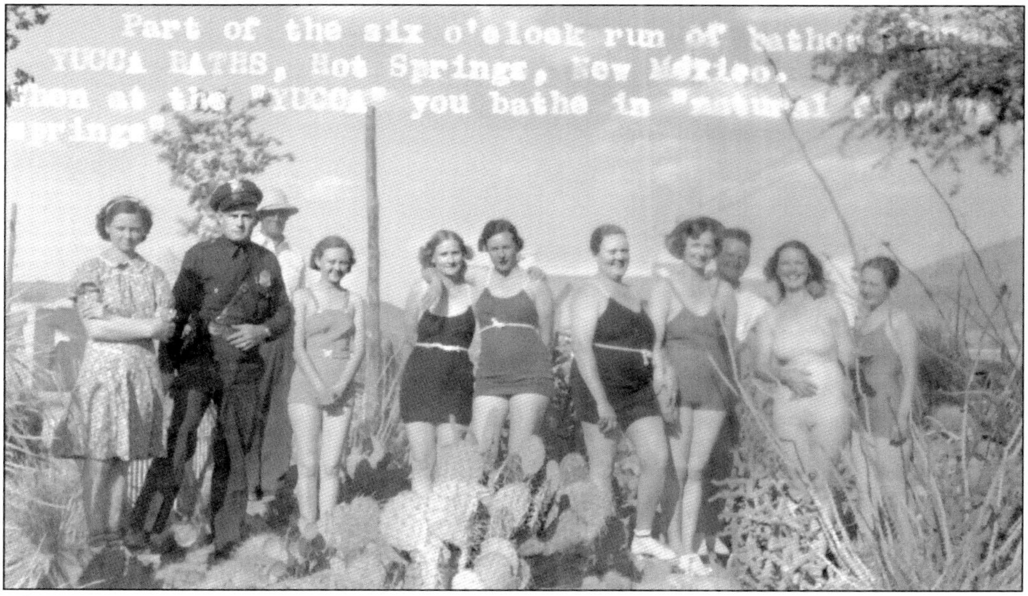

These young women are waiting to take the hot spring mineral baths at the Yucca. The Yucca Lodge and Mineral Baths were located near the business area of Hot Springs. They advertised themselves as having the area's only 20-foot pool of hot mineral water, which would either cure what ailed people, or at least make them feel better. (Courtesy of Charles "Chuck" Martin.)

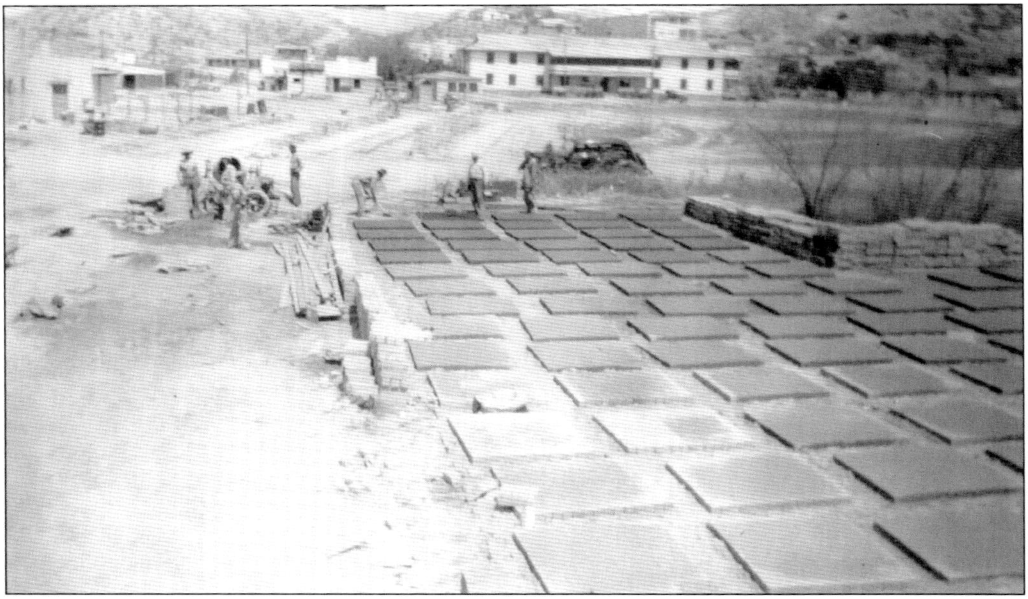

These two pictures show the early construction of the Hoosier Tourist Apartments. Harold Lotz, an architectural engineer who was originally from Madison, Indiana, built the apartments in 1938. Lotz had moved his wife, Jen, and their young son, Jimmy, to Santa Fe, New Mexico, for his wife's health and so that she could be near her sister. The family soon discovered the waters at Hot Springs and began visiting the area. In 1937, they bought property on Austin Street, Lots 5 to 10 in Block 11 of the Palomas Hot Springs town site. The blocks for the construction were built right on the part of the property that is now the parking lot of the Hoosier.

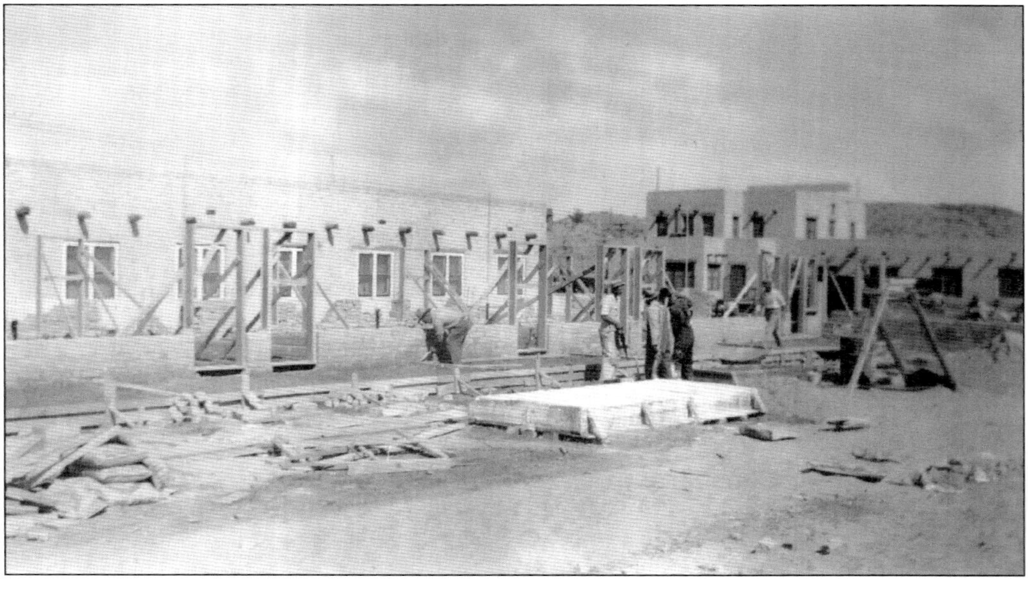

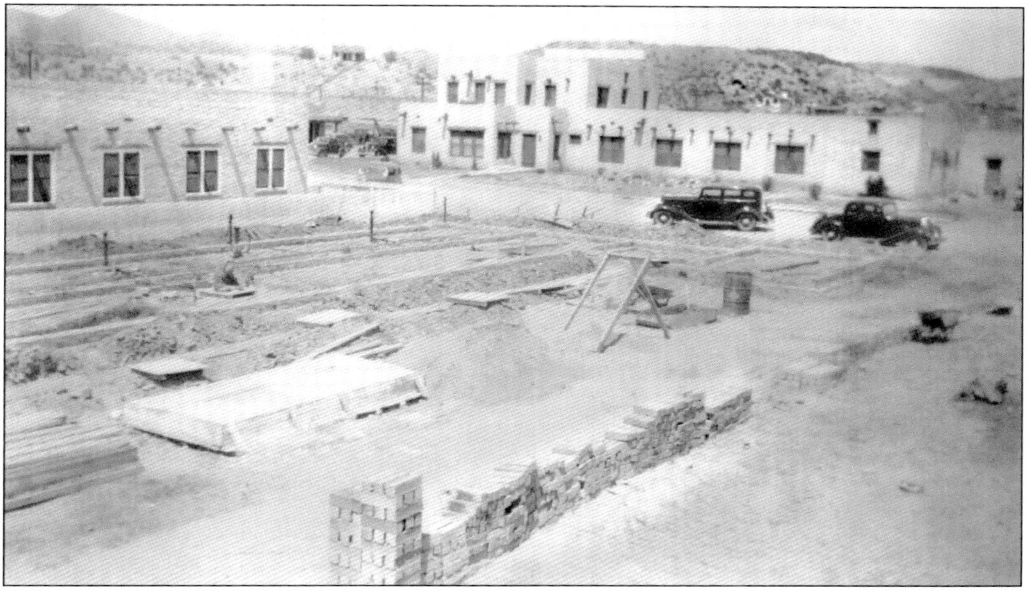

Harold Lotz designed the Hoosier but employed Earl Terry in 1937 as the contractor for the project. The only building on the east side of the block at the time was the Southern Hotel, which sat on the corner. Lotz was there to oversee all facets of the construction. The office and residence on Austin Street was the original building. The adjacent apartments were built behind this. The family moved into their new home and business in 1938. Their son, Jimmy, would attend the local school. These photographs show that the construction was completed in stages. The Hoosier Tourist Apartments would be connected to a bathhouse and a pool designed for guests staying at the Hoosier.

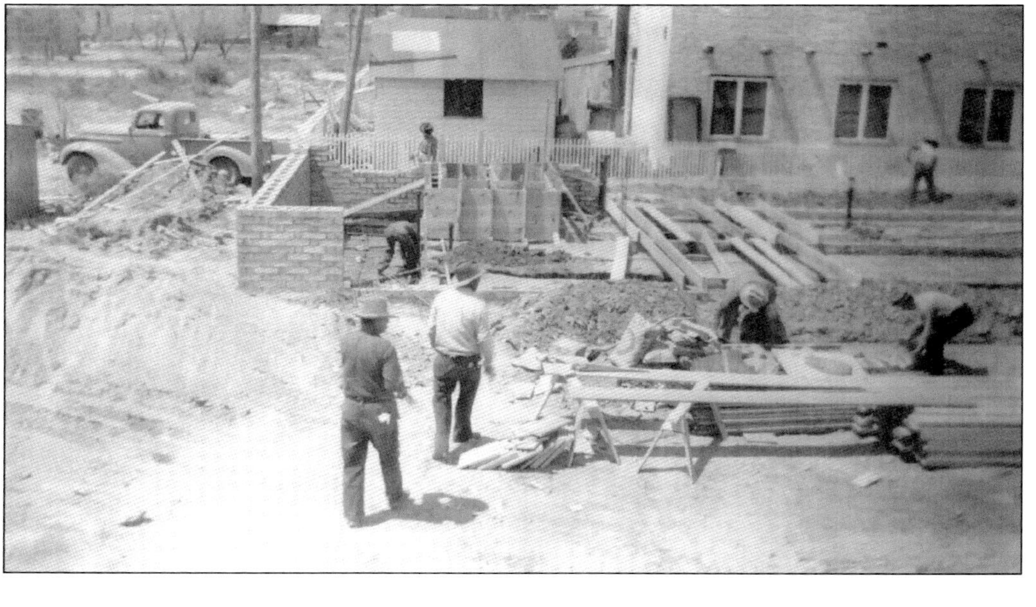

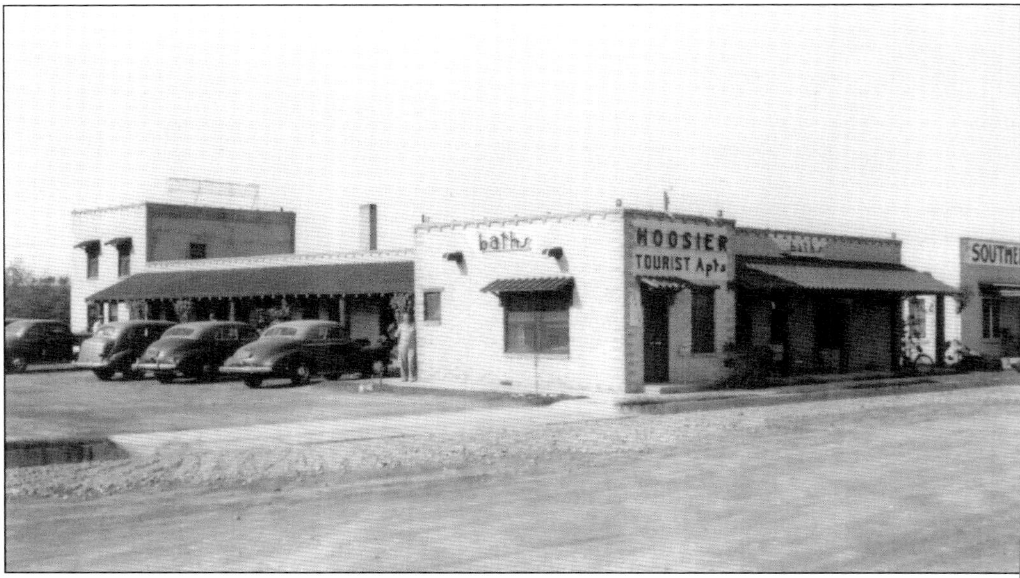

The photograph above shows the completed Hoosier Tourist Apartments and Baths. The edge of the Southern Hotel can also be seen on the right. The picture below shows the Hoosier's pool, for which an artesian well was sunk. The mineral waters would attract guests year after year to the Hoosier. The water temperature in the Hot Springs ranges from 98 degrees to 115 degrees. According to the Water and Beverage Laboratory, Bureau of Chemistry, Department of Agriculture in Washington, D.C., the minerals found in the water are sodium chloride, potassium chloride, potassium nitrate, bicarbonate, calcium chloride, calcium sulfate, silica, alumina, iron carbonate, chloride, and radium.

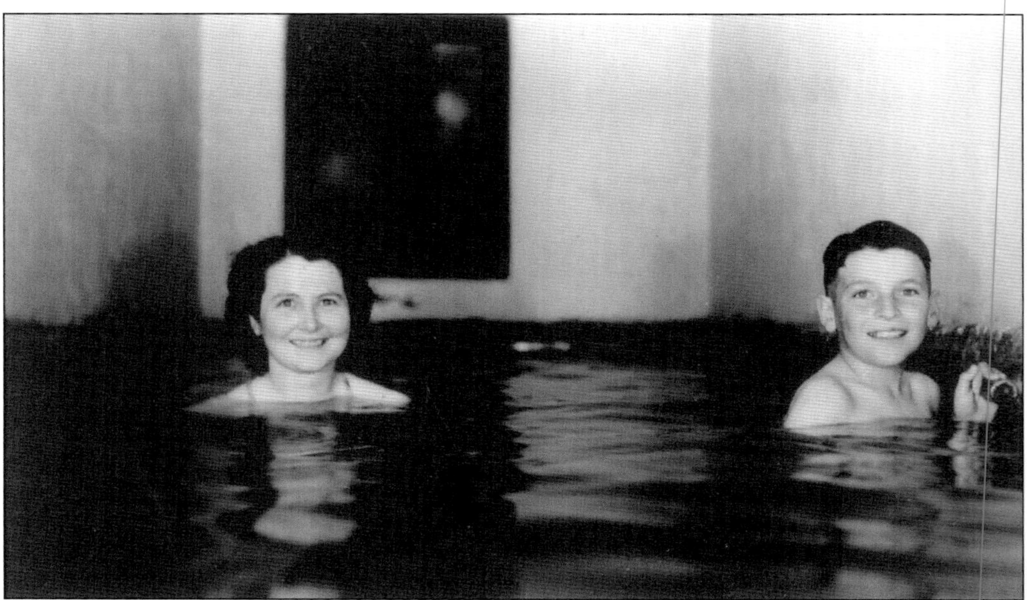

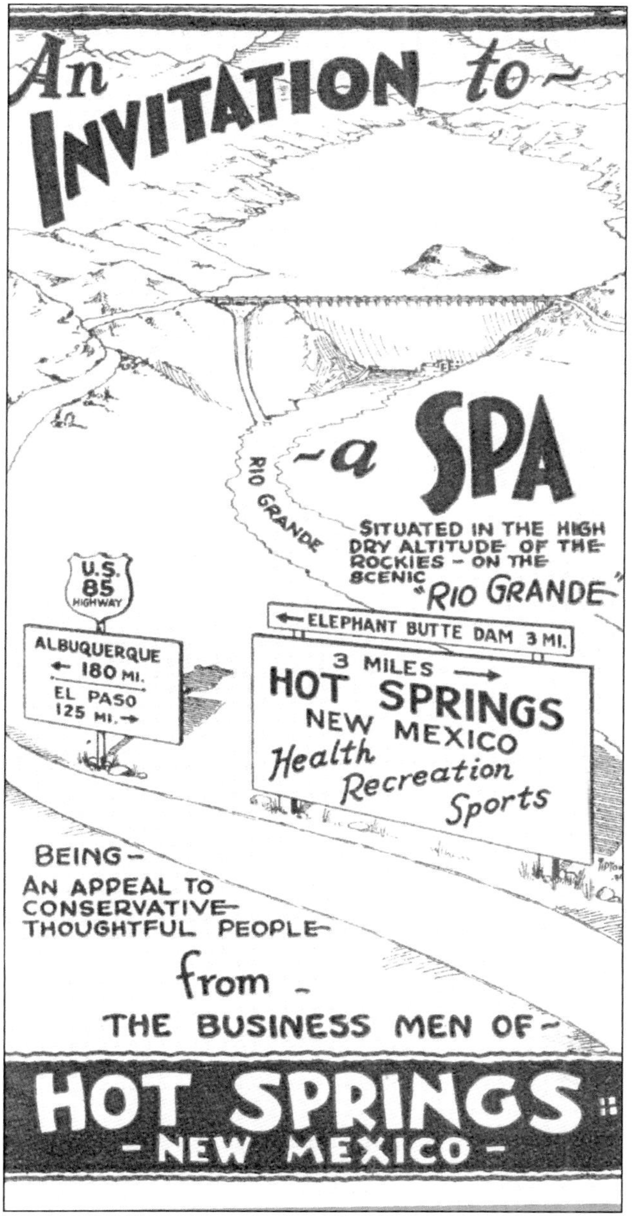

Early on, Hot Springs had begun referring to itself as "America's Karlsbad," after the springs in Karlsbad, Germany. Of course, promoters were quick to note that the waters at Hot Springs were much better than the springs in Germany or elsewhere. The claims that were put in writing as of 1921 were that the following maladies could be relieved or even cured by the waters at Hot Springs: chronic inflammation of joints, chronic joint, and muscular rheumatism, chronic bronchitis, and asthma, chronic inflammation of "empyema" (the brochure's spelling), chronic pleurisy, chronic stomach trouble, neuralgia, neuritis, insomnia, varicose veins, and generally run-down conditions. Later it became more appealing to call Hot Springs a spa town, and this brochure was put out to let the tourist know that the town not only had the baths, but also offered boating and fishing on Elephant Butte Lake. Hunters or hikers could also enjoy the mountains, a mere 20 miles away.

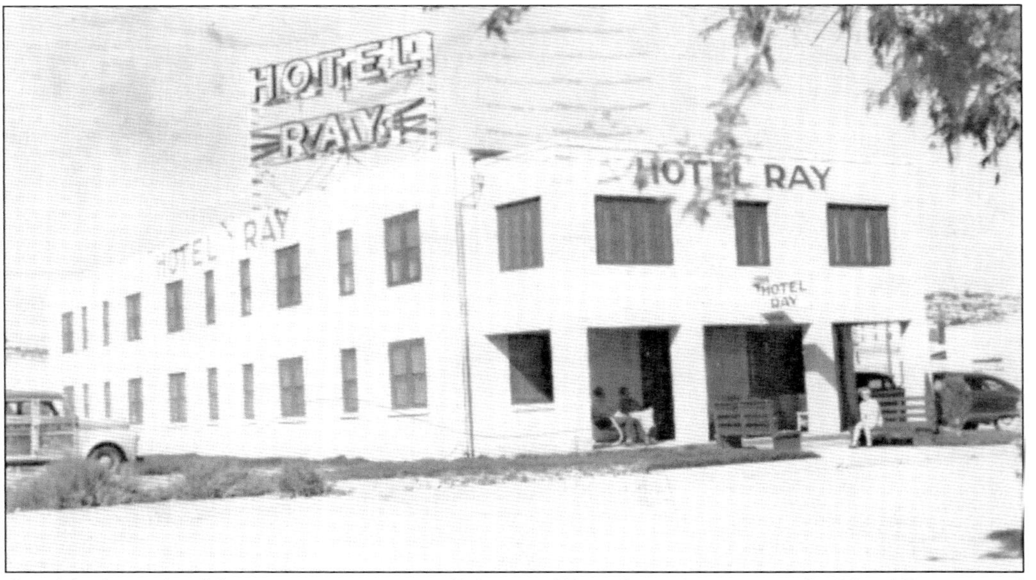

One block south of the west intersection of Main and Broadway Streets was the Hotel Ray, owned by Grace Eldridge, R.N. The new attraction offered by Eldridge's hotel was a "massage and zone therapy." This is one of the postcards printed up to advertise the hotel.

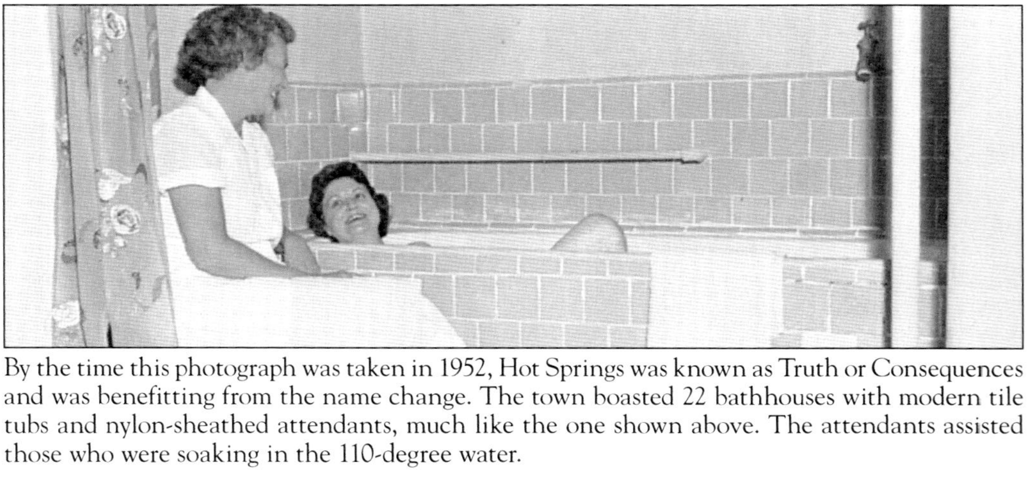

By the time this photograph was taken in 1952, Hot Springs was known as Truth or Consequences and was benefitting from the name change. The town boasted 22 bathhouses with modern tile tubs and nylon-sheathed attendants, much like the one shown above. The attendants assisted those who were soaking in the 110-degree water.

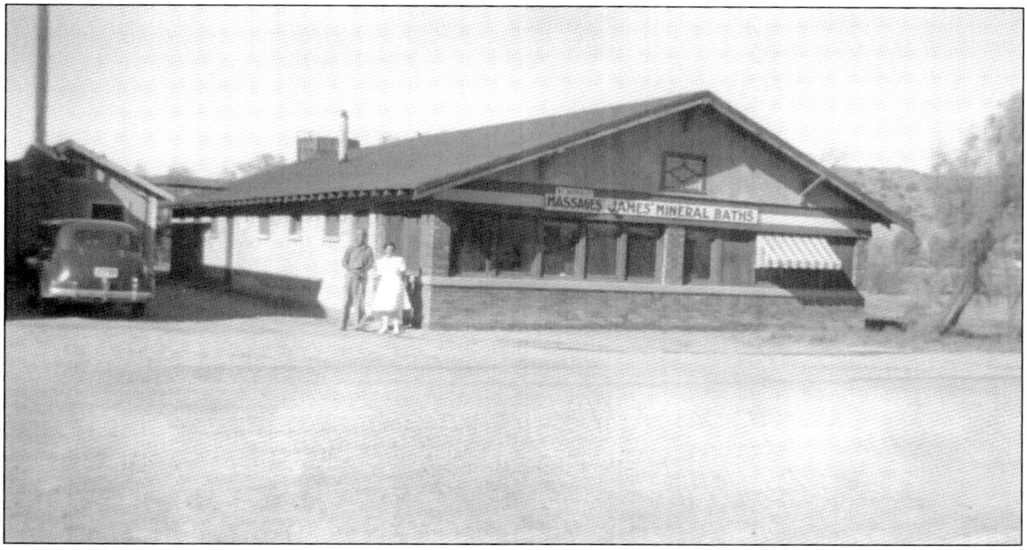

Seen here are the James Apartments in the early 1900s (above) and the James Mineral Bathhouse in later times (below). In 2004, cultural and architectural historian Dr. David Kammer wrote the nomination to place the Hot Springs bathhouse and commercial district in the National Register of Historic Places. The Cultural Properties Review Committee met in Truth or Consequences on October 8, 2004, and voted to list the historic district in the New Mexico State Register of Cultural Properties. In May 2005, the historic district, located between Main and Van Patton Streets and Date and Clancy Streets, was officially entered into the National Register of Historic Places. This included the bathhouses.

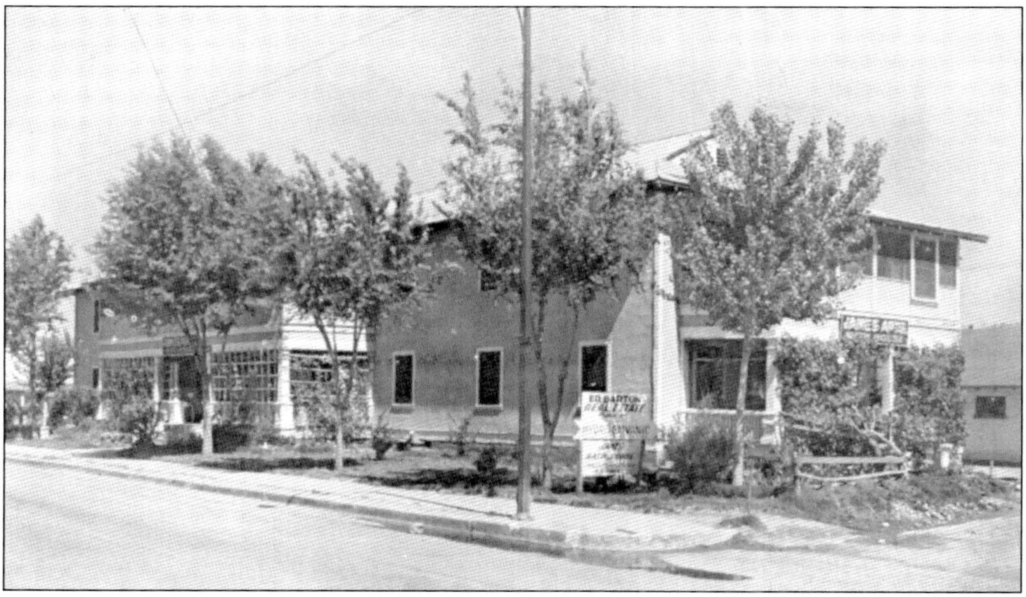

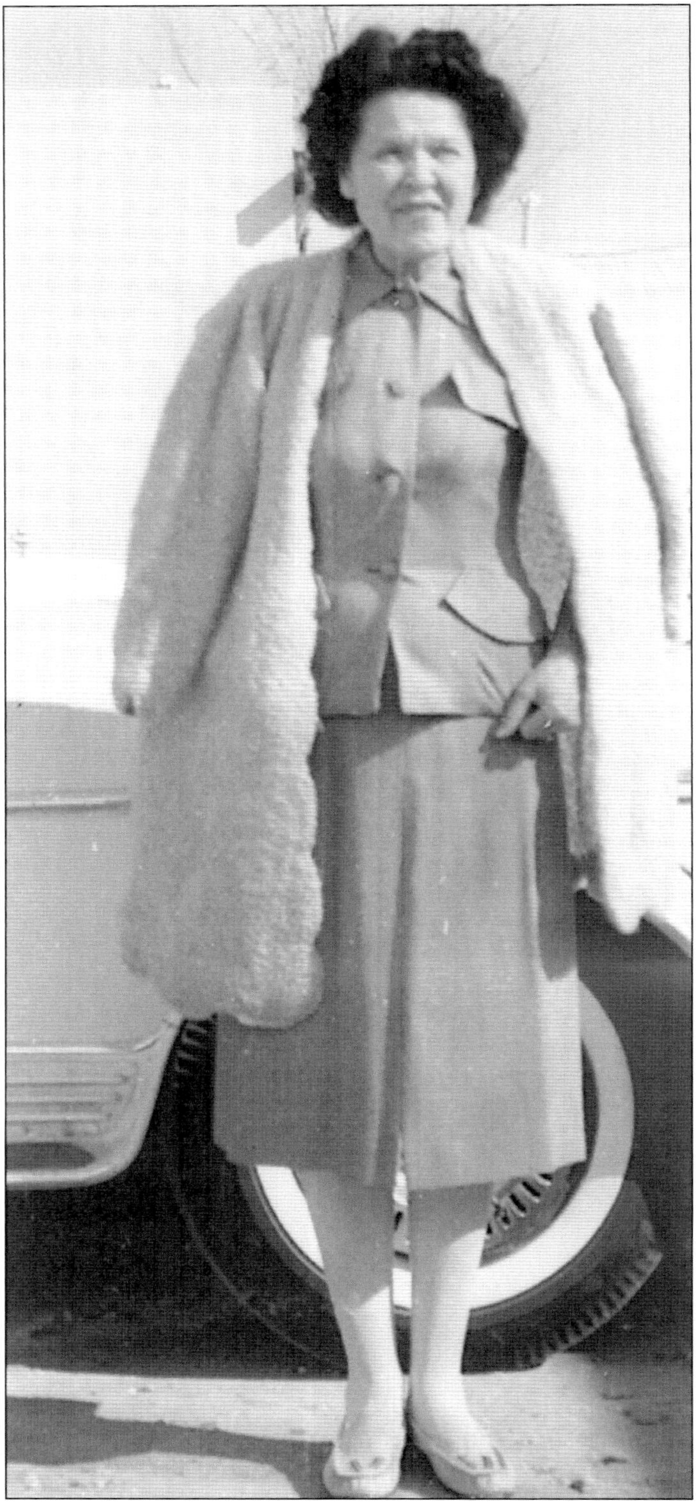

Magnolia Ellis was one of the more provocative individuals around town because she claimed to be a healer. She humbly said that her ability to heal was a gift from God. In the 1940s and 1950s, she had a very large following that included individuals from outside the United States. Her daughter's 1957 book, *A True Story about the Life of Magnolia Ellis*, claimed that Magnolia was born to a mother who was 54 years of age. She weighed only 1.25 pounds at birth, according to her daughter, and was placed in a warming oven, which served as an incubator. She was fed with an eyedropper by Ellen Pickett, the midwife from whom she received her middle name. In 1972, Magnolia Ellis retired to Wilcox, Arizona. She died in 1974 and was buried in Arizona. The sign with the name, Magnolia Ellis, still adorns the two-story building in downtown Truth or Consequences.

Three

Car Courts and Carrie Tingley

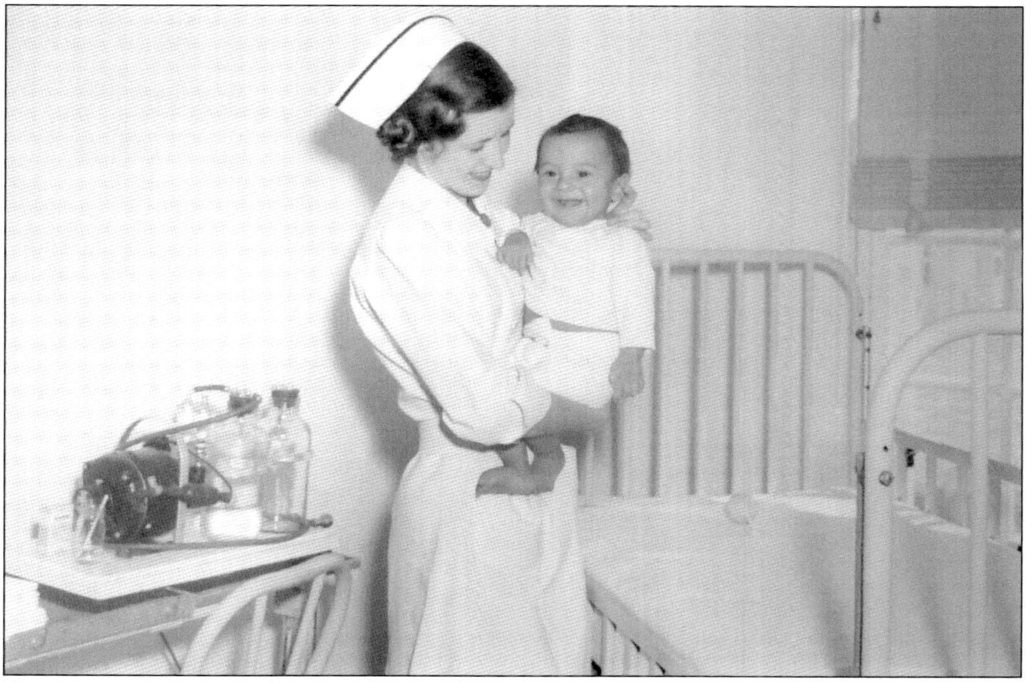

New Mexico governor Clyde Tingley and his wife, Carrie, wanted to help the children of New Mexico that were suffering from infantile paralysis (polio), talipes (club foot), and other crippling diseases. Thus was born the Carrie Tingley Hospital for Crippled Children. The 19th century had seen a rise in polio epidemics, and this prompted more attention to and care for sufferers of the disease—especially children, who were its most common victims.

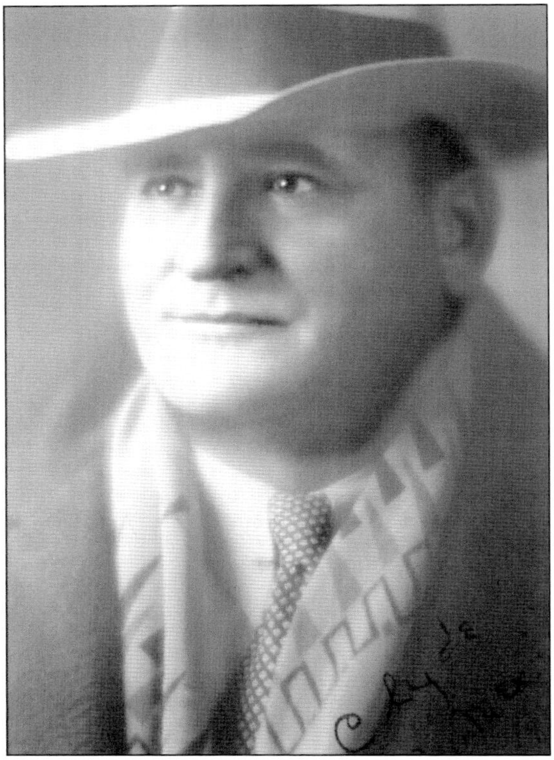

Gov. Clyde Tingley and his wife, Carrie, had no children of their own, but when the Tingleys decided to build a hospital for all of the children of New Mexico who suffered from a crippling disease, they chose Hot Springs, New Mexico, because of the hot mineral springs. The Tingleys were aware of the hospital at Warm Springs, Georgia, made famous by their friend, Pres. Franklin Roosevelt, who himself suffered from polio. The architect of the hospital at Warm Springs was made a consultant to the project. Carrie Tingley was known throughout New Mexico because of her benevolent work in her home city of Albuquerque.

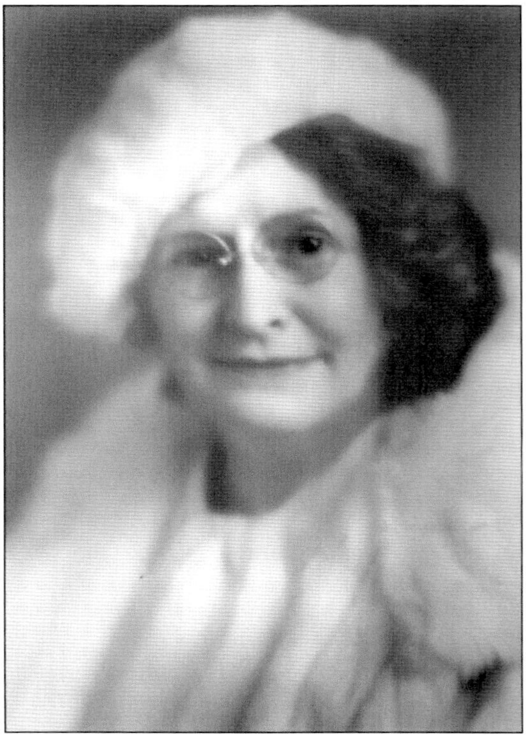

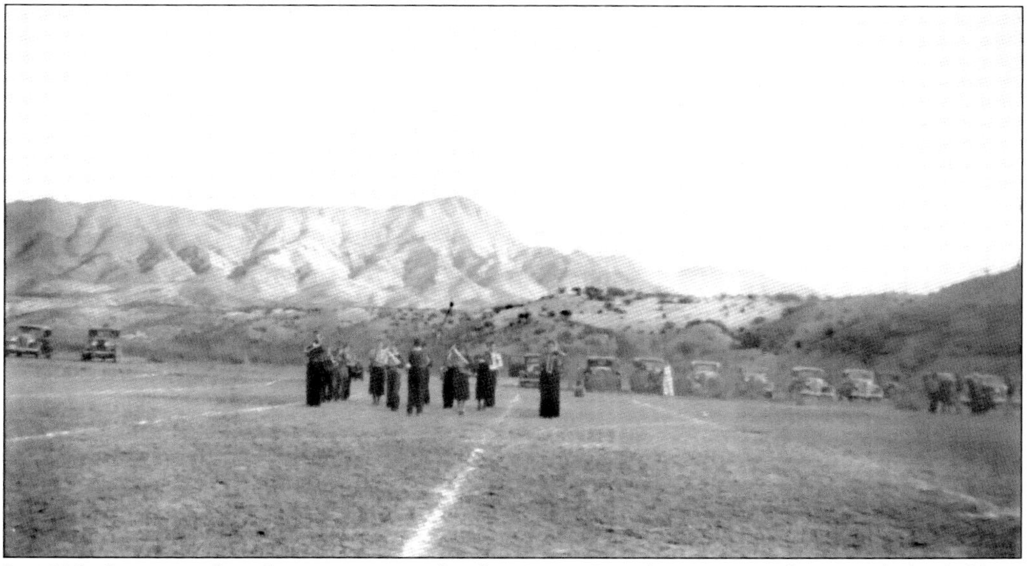

In 1935, the groundbreaking ceremony for the Carrie Tingley Hospital for Crippled Children was held. The Town of Hot Springs paid $12,000 for the original land, and the site would be enlarged to include a 66-acre plot donated by residents C. E. Henson and T. M. Hobbs. (Courtesy of Geronimo Springs Museum Archives.)

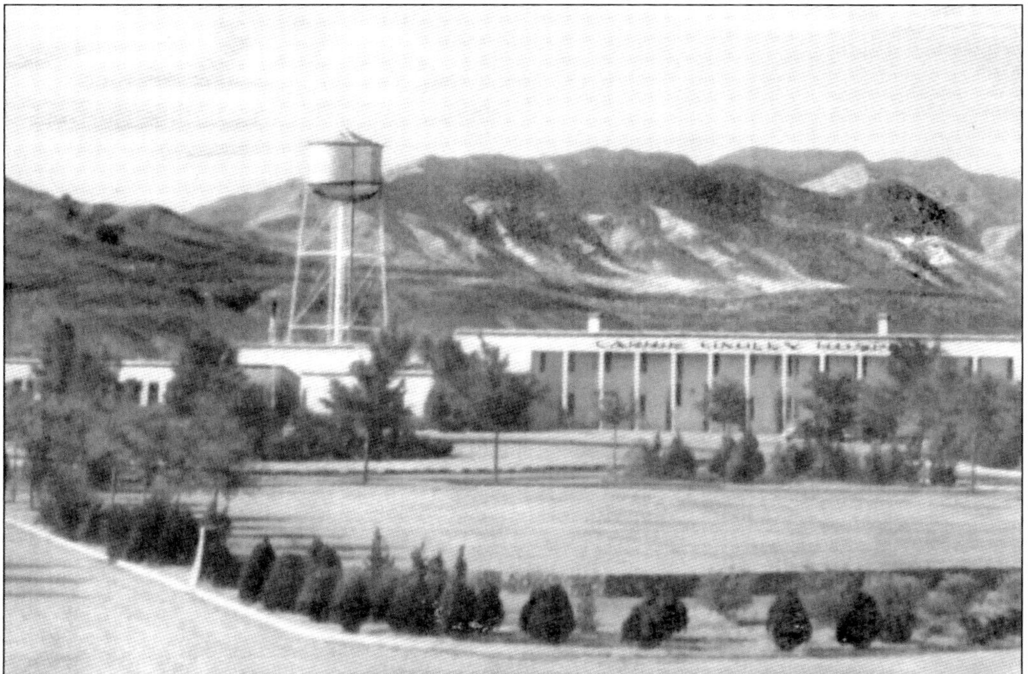

The first concrete was poured on March 13, 1936. The property had been deeded to the state by the town, and construction was begun with 1.6 million bricks made by the inmates at New Mexico State Penitentiary. Hot Springs supplied a tested hot mineral well, along with the electricity and the water needed for the construction.

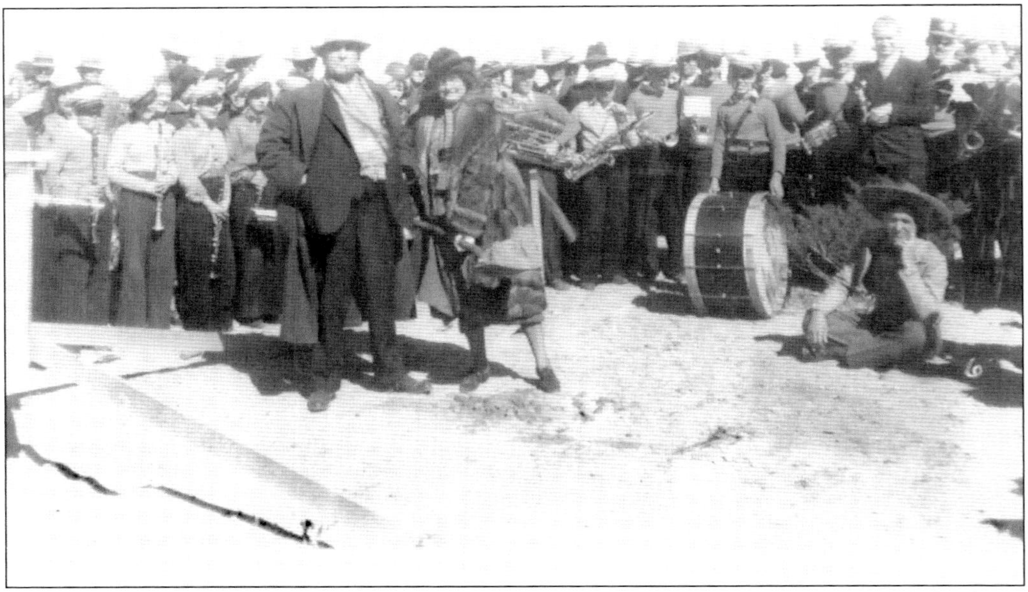

On September 19, 1937, the hospital was dedicated in Hot Springs. Town mayor A. J. Burleson issued a decree asking that all the businesses close between noon and 3:00 p.m. so that all citizens could participate in the ceremonies. Governor Tingley led a parade through Hot Springs.

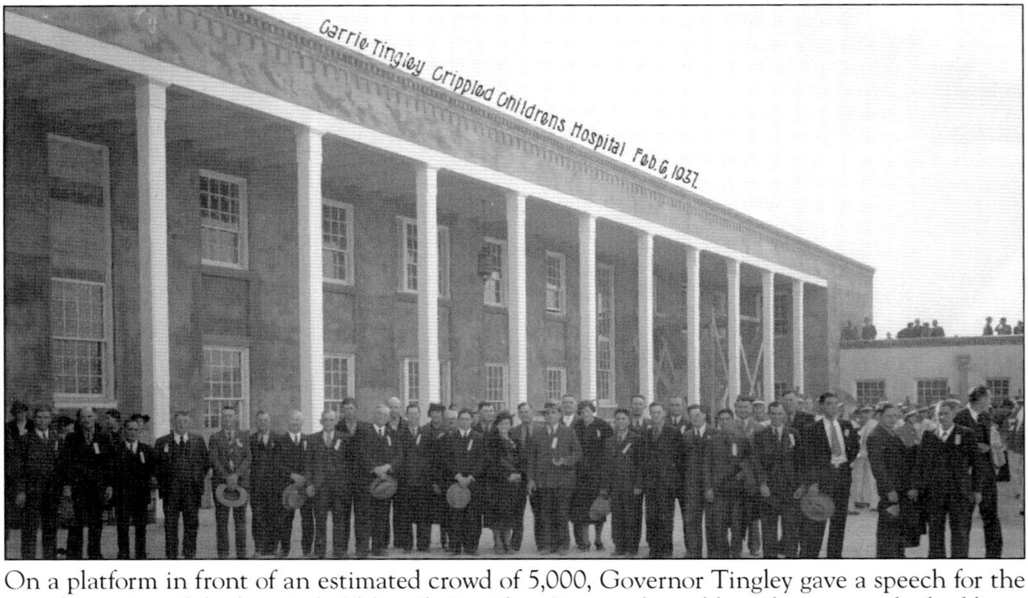

On a platform in front of an estimated crowd of 5,000, Governor Tingley gave a speech for the grand opening of the hospital. Although President Roosevelt could not be present, he had been following the progress of the hospital. He sent Charles T. West, the undersecretary of the interior, to represent him at the hospital's opening ceremonies.

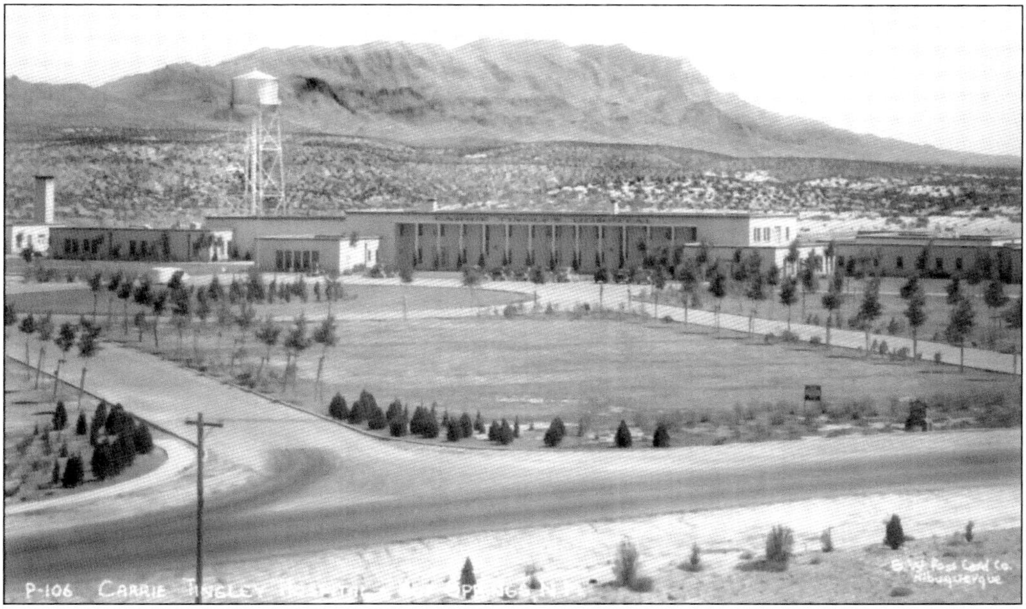

The Carrie Tingley Hospital's architecture featured a Spanish Colonial design with trees, shrubs, and flowers decorating the grounds. Wide drives lined with trees and shrubs were designed to make the entrance to the hospital welcoming as well as beautiful. It stands as the single Works Progress Administration (WPA) project in New Mexico for which President Roosevelt was closely connected due to his condition of polio and friendship with New Mexico governor Tingley.

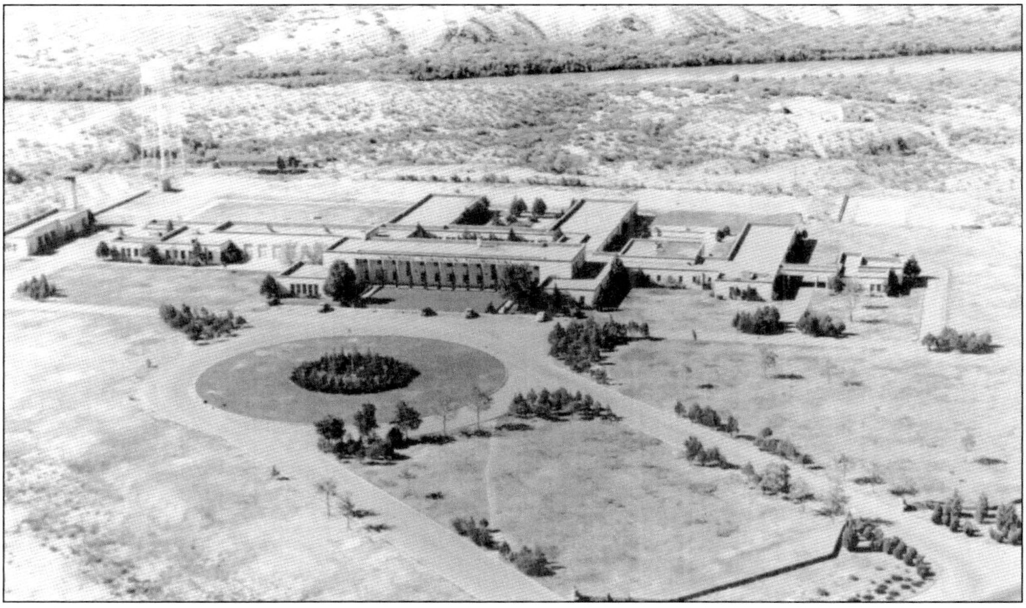

This view shows the landscape of the Carrie Tingley Hospital for Crippled Children from the air. Romelia Chavez-Garcia, a third-generation Carrie Tingley employee, noted that her father, Ambrosio "Amby" Chavez, was the truck driver who brought the trees in from Socorro on the newly paved U.S. Highway 85. The U.S. first assistant postmaster traveled from Washington, D.C., to help Governor Tingley plant the first 200 trees.

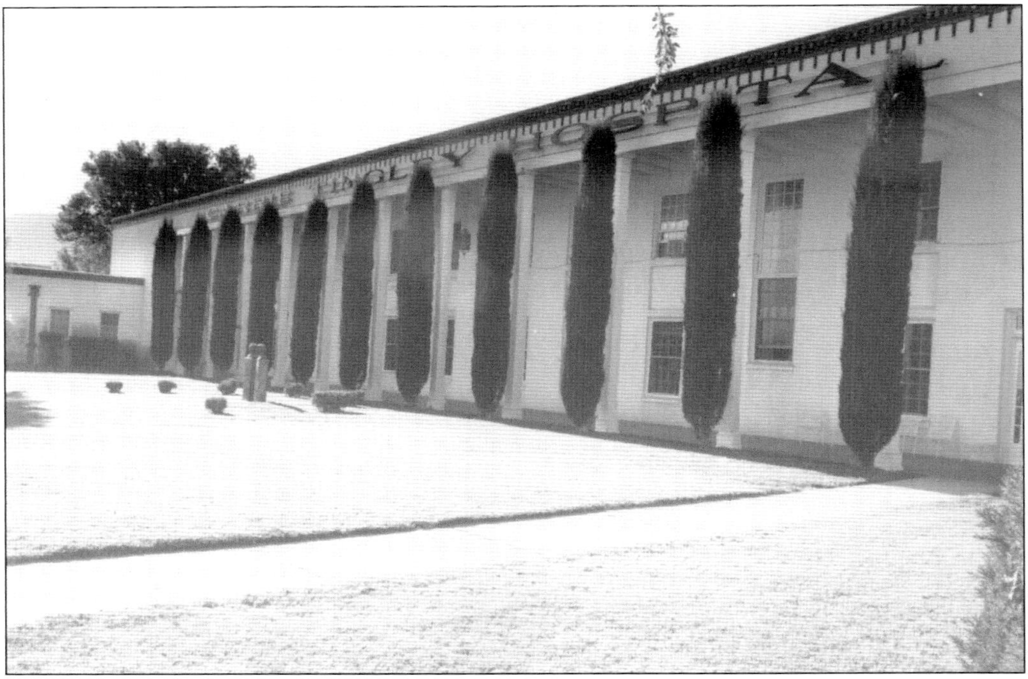

In 1935, it was announced that the WPA had approved $274,954 for the construction of the Carrie Tingley Hospital for Crippled Children. Over the next three years, two additional grants would help pay for the staff quarters and the power plant. Though young WPA architect Willard C. Kruger had previously designed only schools, not hospitals, he was clearly up to the challenge.

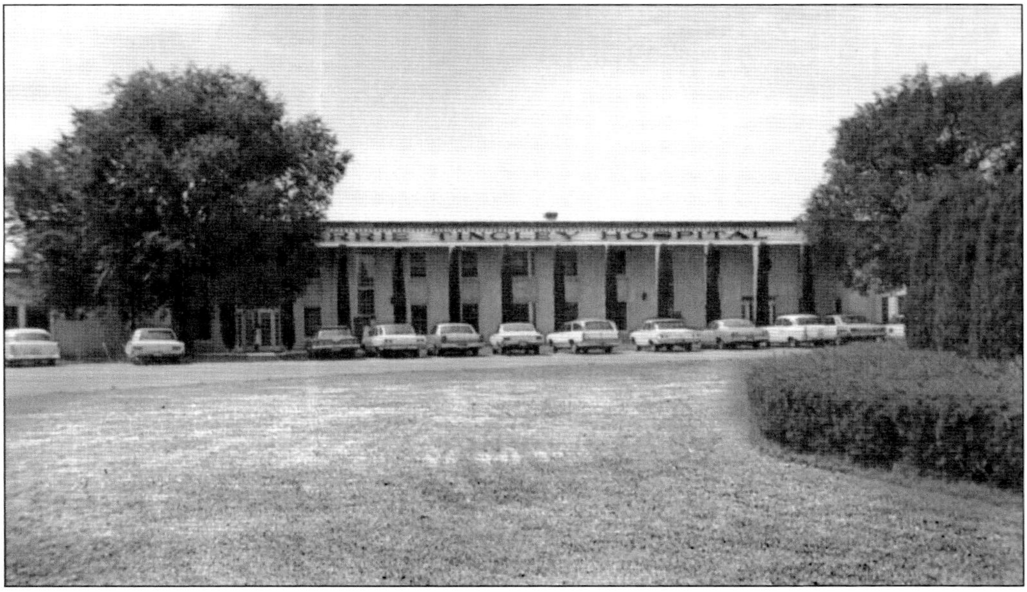

As the winter of 1937 waned, Governor Tingley became so enthusiastic over the progress at the hospital that he used a fleet of state vehicles to drive the entire New Mexico State Legislature to the site for a visit. Steel was used for the beams, and concrete was used for the roof in case hospital administrators determined to add a second story later.

This picture gives a glimpse of the Turtle Fountain, created by WPA sculptor Eugenie Shonnard. Sitting in the inner courtyard, four carved turtles faced all four directions. Governor Tingley used the New Deal programs of that time to secure artwork through the Works Progress Administration's Federal Arts Project. This allowed the showcasing of New Mexico artists and their works. (Courtesy of Geronimo Springs Museum Archives.)

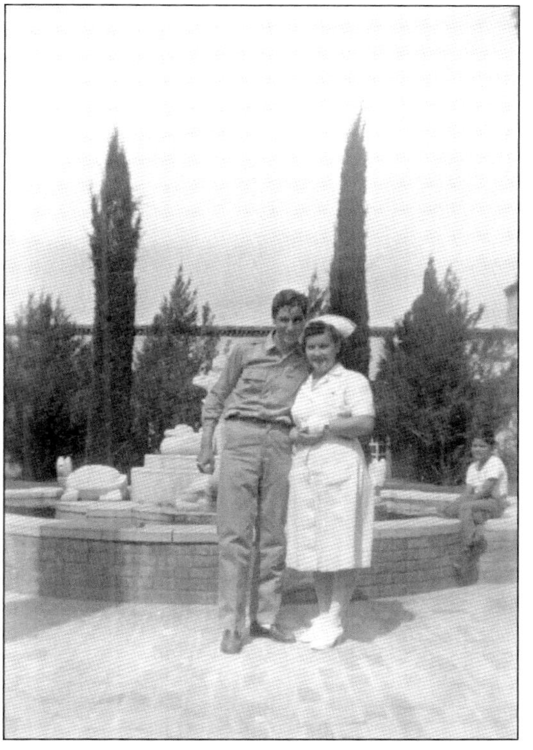

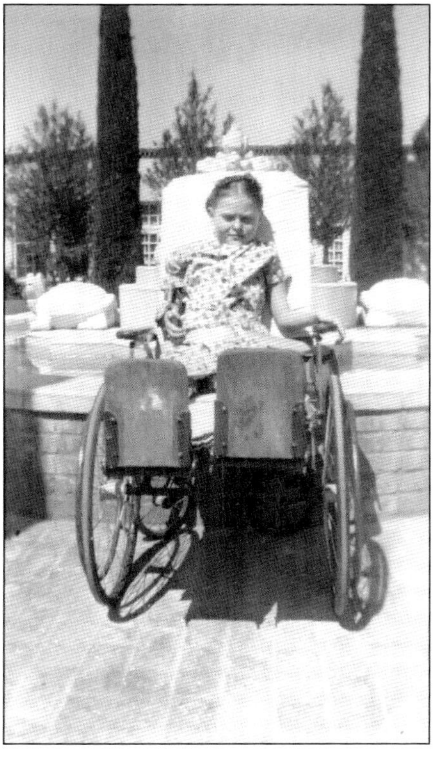

Sunshine was paramount to the treatment of children at Carrie Tingley. This young lady is soaking in the sun in her custom wheelchair. An outdoor playground was available to all who could use it. The hospital had a capacity of 100 beds with the main building comprising an area equal to more than 1.6 acres. (Courtesy of Geronimo Springs Museum Archives.)

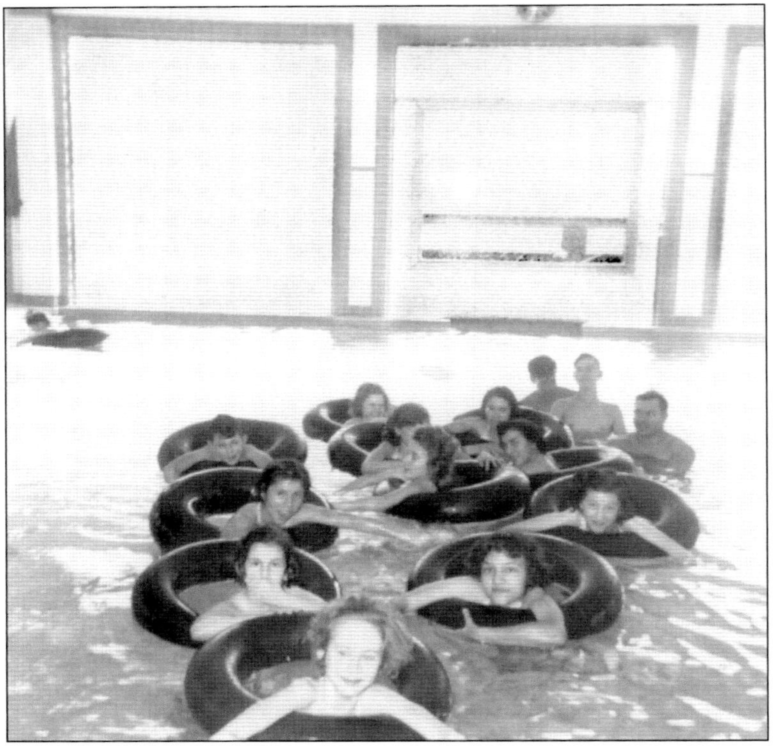

The hospital had two pools containing 70,000 gallons of water. The water was designed to recirculate continuously. The outdoor pool could be closed off from the indoor pool during inclement weather. The indoor-outdoor pool was designed to provide the heliotherapy and hydrotherapy treatments. The children received their water massages and then could rest around the pool or in the two courtyards that lay within the building's wings. The leading treatments were table exercises, massages, walking, pool, and hydrotherapy. Located under the hospital were refrigerated vaults, storage, and transformers. The heating, plumbing, and the main electric lines were contained in a 4-foot-square tunnel that ran three-quarters of a mile in length under the hospital.

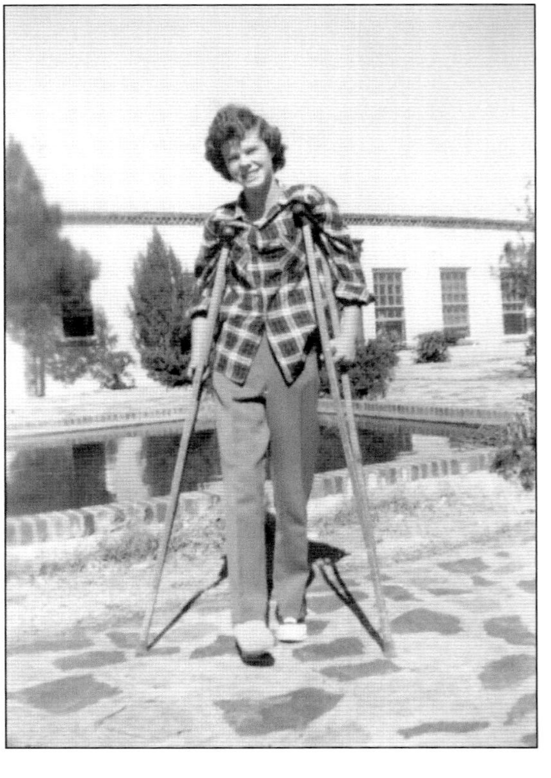

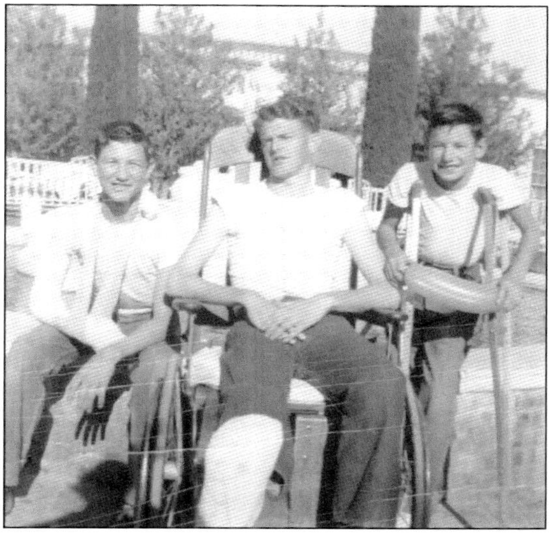

Between the years of 1937 and 1943, some 2,260 children with some form of paralysis were examined at Carrie Tingley. Of those 2,260 children examined, 933 were admitted to the hospital. The hospital's 300 windows had an estimated total of 19,500 panes of glass in order to let in the healing sunshine. With the beautiful weather of this small New Mexico town, a big part of the healing process included time in the sun for all of the patients, whether in a wheelchair or a bed. (Both, courtesy of Geronimo Springs Museum Archives.)

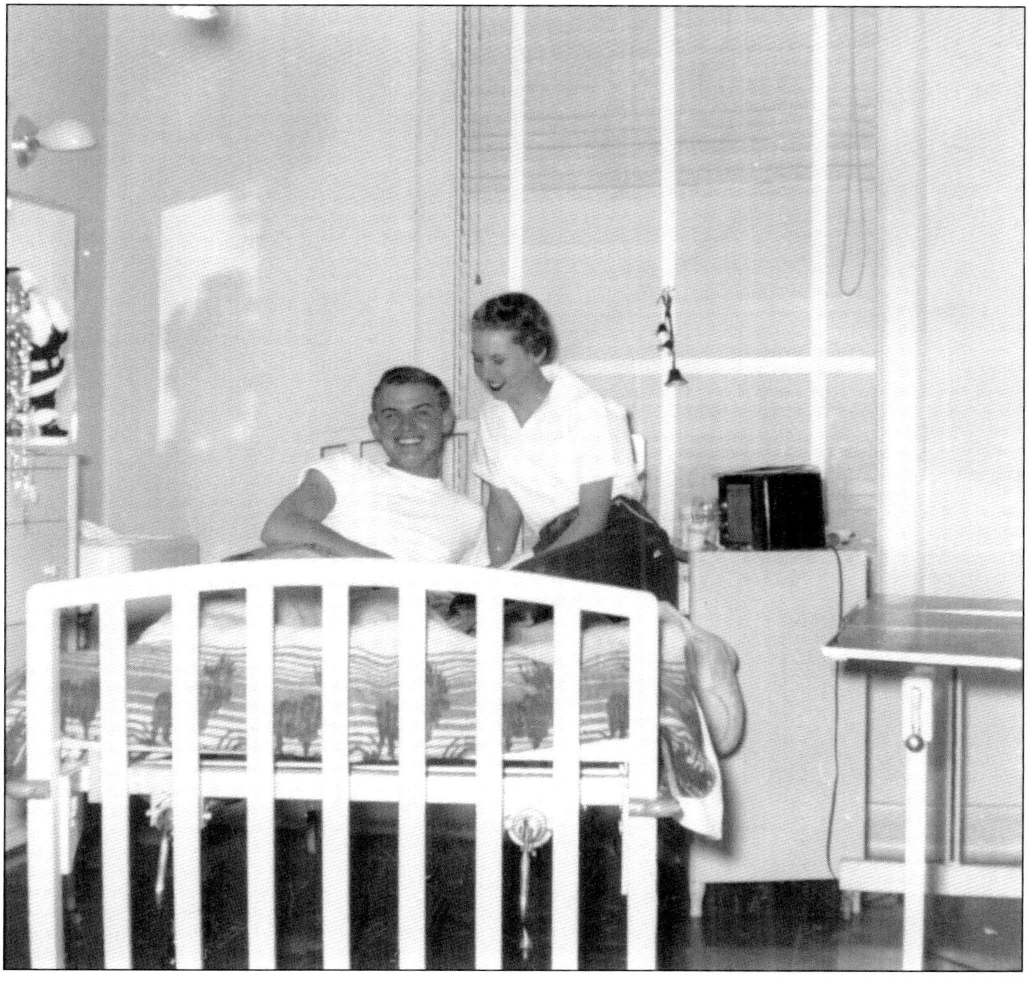

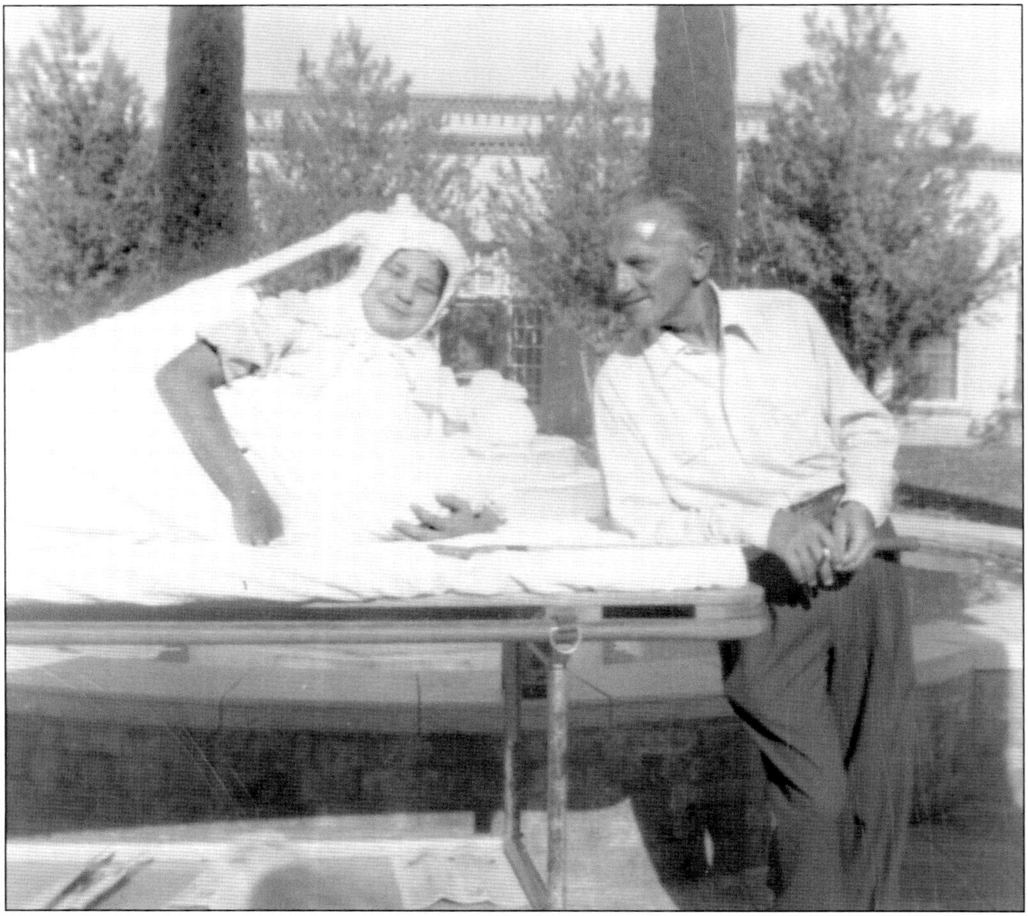

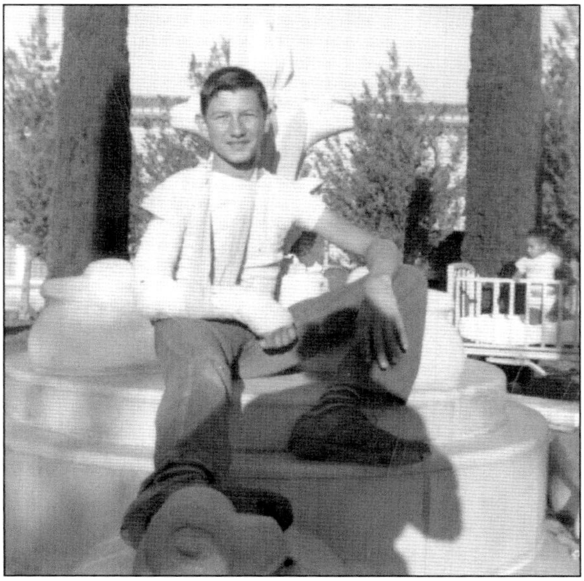

Governor Tingley made sure that the hospital was equipped with the best equipment that money could buy. The two operating rooms had been designed with the most powerful surgical lights available at that time. The operating table itself was equipped so that both the radiographic and the fluoroscopic work could continue even during an operation. A mobile X-ray unit was also available. A specialized sanitizing room was in place as well as departments of pathology, physical therapy, psychology, speech therapy, and hearing. Another department dealt with behavioral issues that might arise. (Both, courtesy of Geronimo Springs Museum Archives.)

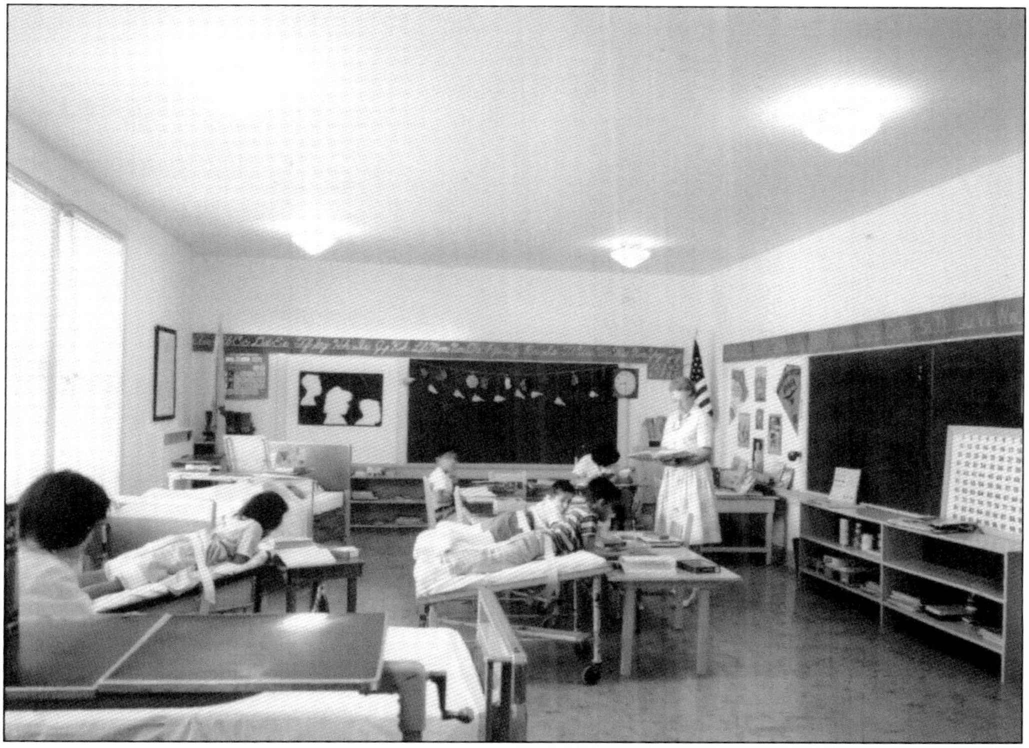

School-aged children were expected to attend classes, which were taught by special education teachers. They were not expected to do as much work as they would if they were in school, but there was no getting around having to attend classes. In November 1937, there were 78 children at the Carrie Tingley Hospital for Crippled Children. There were arts and crafts classes during the summer recesses. The days were designed to have games, music, and entertainment available to help the children stay upbeat and busy. Many times children were there without their parents being nearby to comfort them. These were trying times for both the small patients and their families.

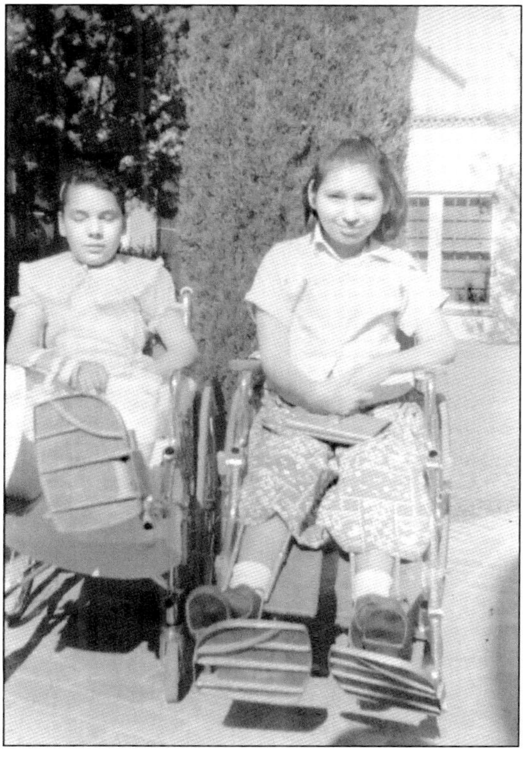

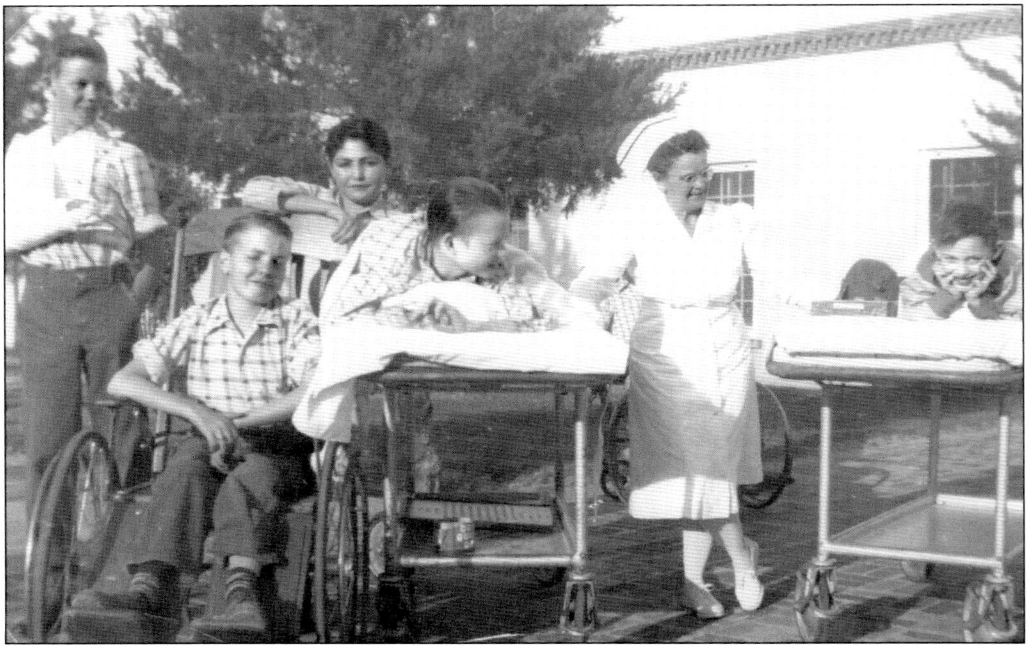

The hospital beds were designed to roll just as easily as the wheelchairs. Patients confined to a bed could easily be rolled out to the sunshine or to see a parade that passed by. Memories and friendships were made at the hospital with patients, nurses, and doctors.

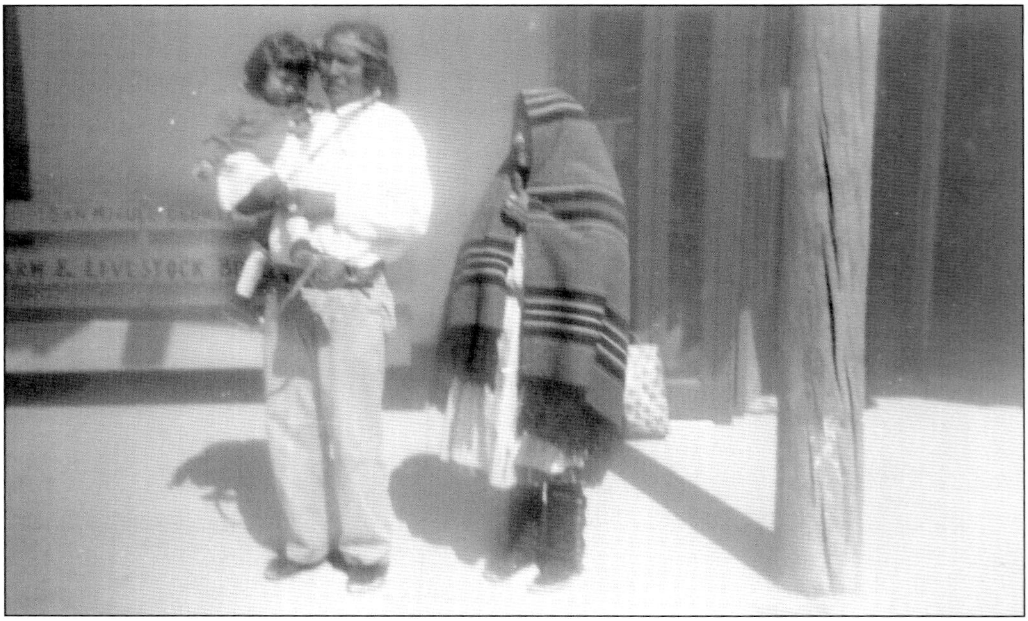

Governor Tingley had promised that the hospital would not be a place of discrimination, whether because of a patient's race, religion, or ability to pay. He kept his promise, and Carrie Tingley Hospital for Crippled Children did not show preferences due to color, economics, or any other social inequality. The promise was to help the children, and the hospital did, year after year. (Courtesy of Geronimo Springs Museum Archives.)

These two young women were employees of the Carrie Tingley Hospital for Crippled Children. On the left was Ms. Morgan, lab and X-ray technician, and on the right was physical therapist Ms. Welch. The hospital employed highly trained physical therapists as well as occupational therapists. All staff were certified and registered. (Courtesy of Geronimo Springs Museum Archives.)

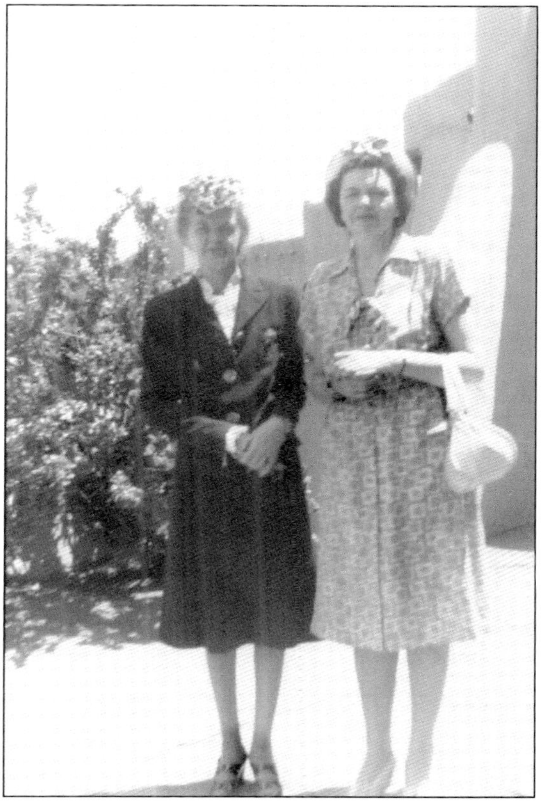

This particular piece of specialized equipment, a Hubbard tub, cost $1,100. The tub was made of stainless steel, and the thermostatically controlled water was designed to massage the patients' limbs. From the looks on these young patients' faces, the results must have been relaxing and enjoyable. With so many smiling faces, it is easy to forget that polio was a painful, debilitating disease.

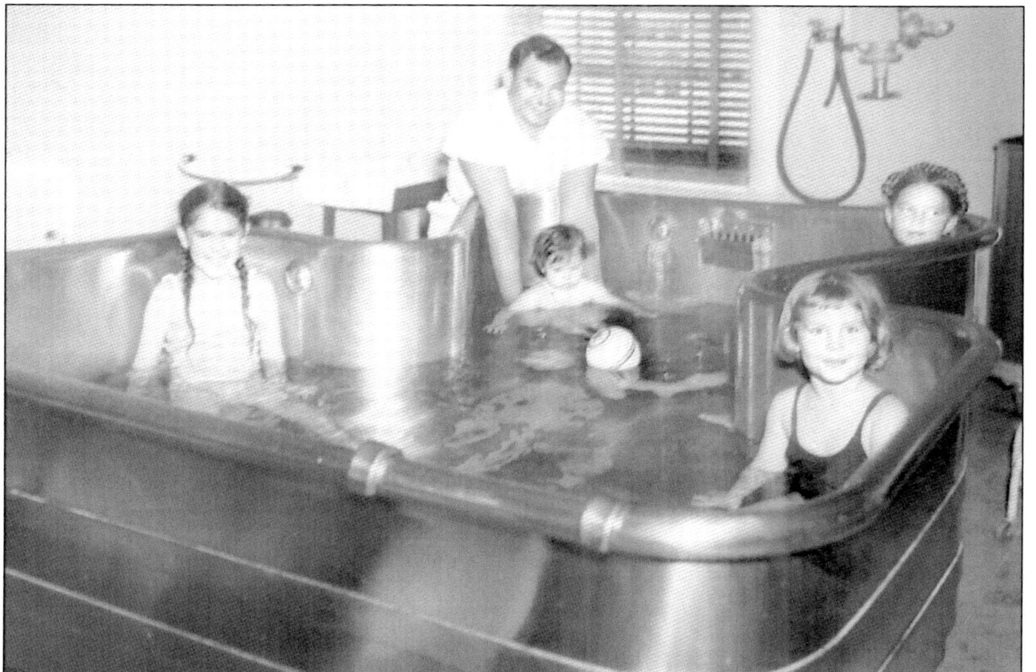

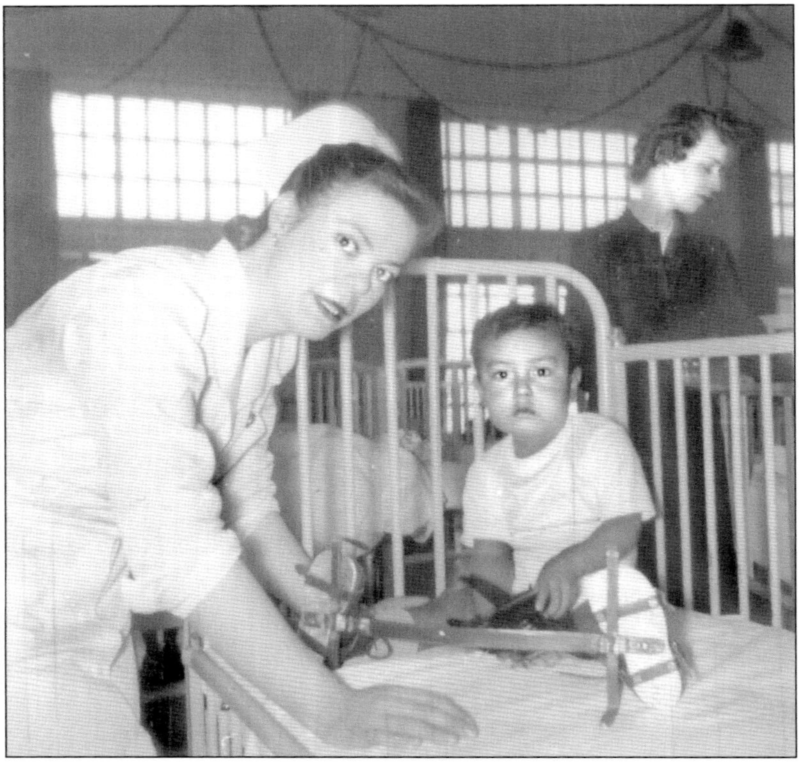

The walls of the rooms were a hard-finished plaster with corridors painted ivory and the rooms painted in varying shades of pastel. Two separate wings were designed to house the boys' and girls' dormitories. The patients had a three-button call system at each bed. As seen here, everybody received a lot of attention from the devoted nurses. (Courtesy of Geronimo Springs Museum Archives.)

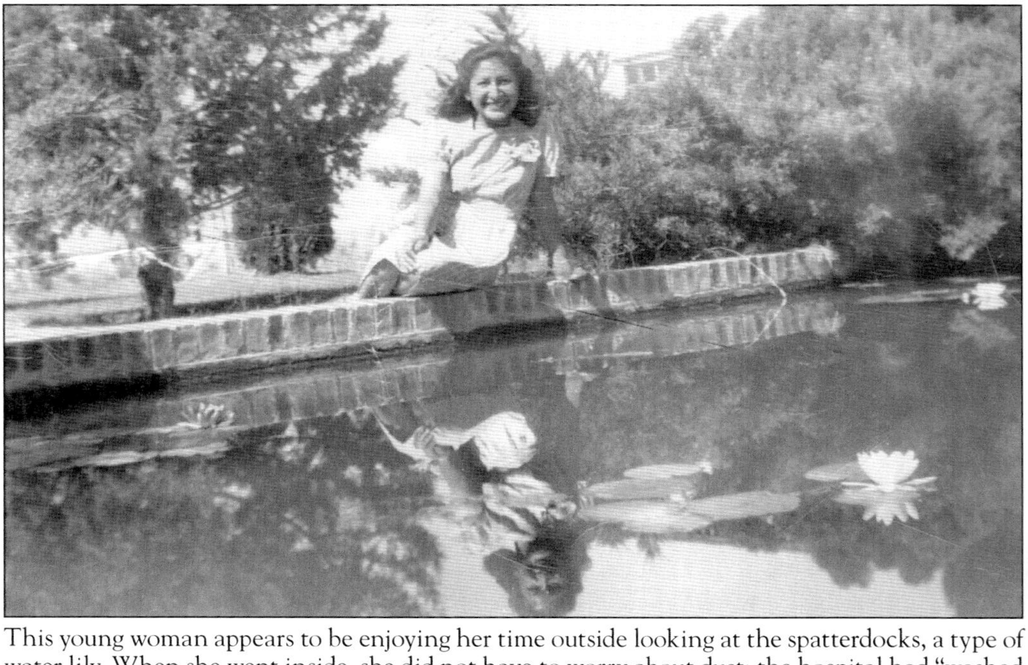

This young woman appears to be enjoying her time outside looking at the spatterdocks, a type of water lily. When she went inside, she did not have to worry about dust; the hospital had "washed air-conditioning" that was designed to ventilate and disinfect the hospital. Sanitization was of upmost priority. (Courtesy of Geronimo Springs Museum Archives.)

Puzzles, coloring books, and other activities were provided to the children to keep them occupied. It is not hard to imagine the homesickness and loneliness these young patients experienced as they spent months in this hospital without their parents. Parents that were financially able rented small apartments or a room in a car court in Hot Springs so that they could be near their children.

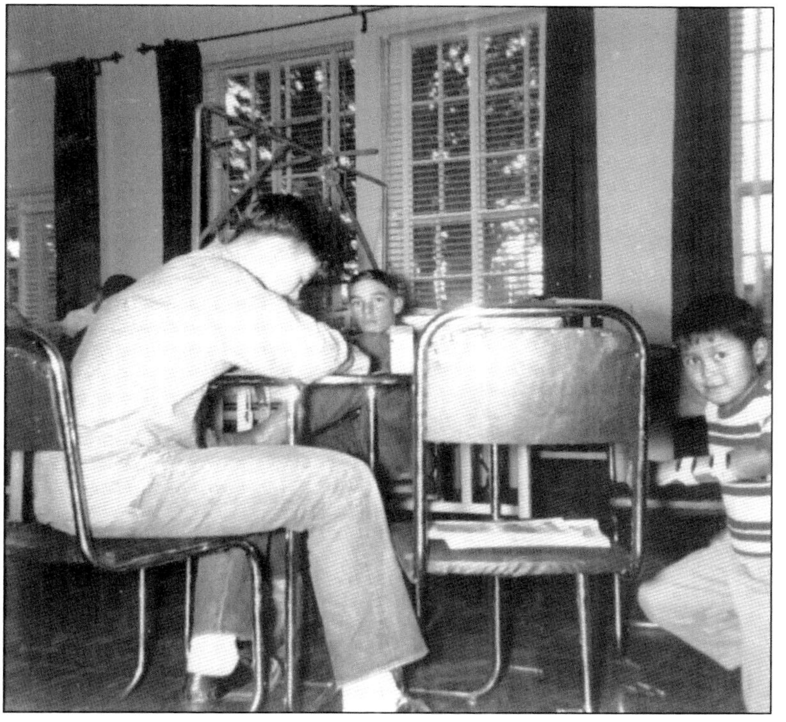

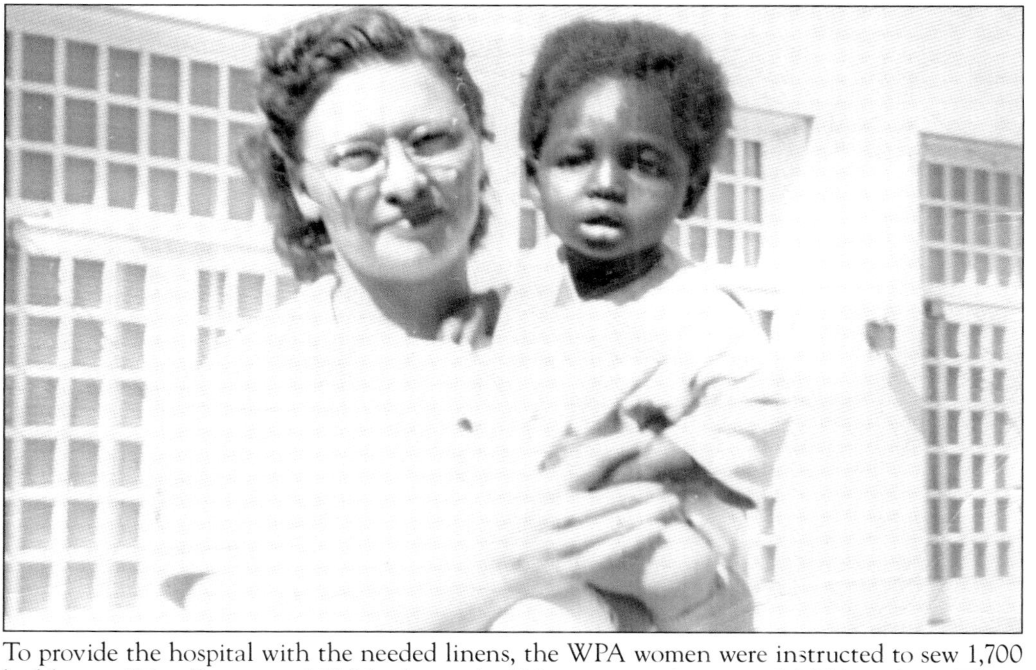

To provide the hospital with the needed linens, the WPA women were instructed to sew 1,700 bedsheets, 500 pillowcases, 1,300 bath towels, 100 operating sheets, and 1,500 napkins. There were no paper napkins at mealtime. Seamstresses also had their sewing machines running to turn 500 yards of checked muslin into night garments for the children, such as the one on this patient. (Courtesy of Geronimo Springs Museum Archives.)

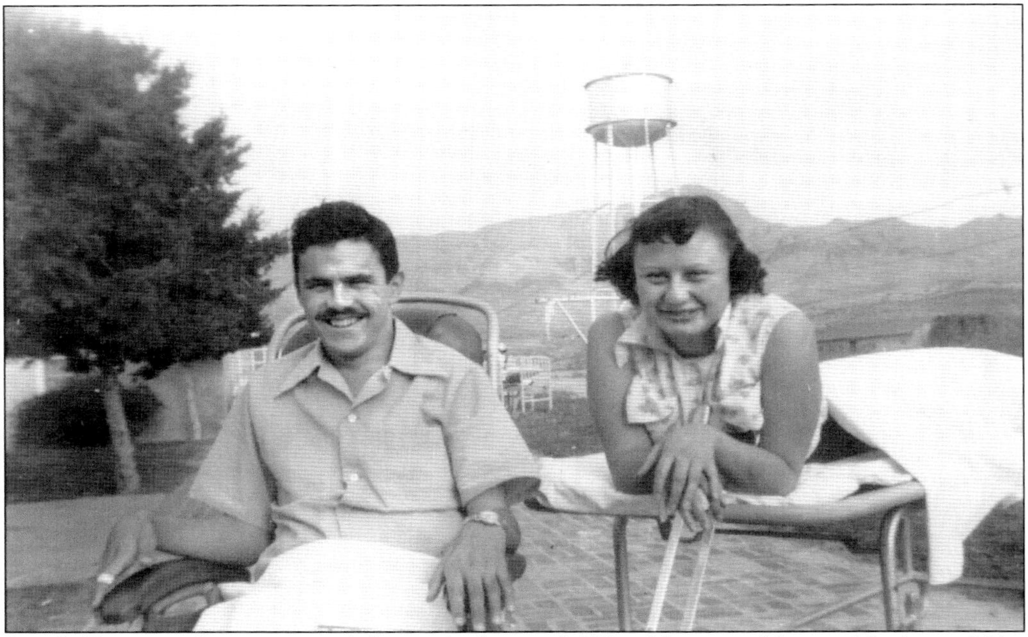

Parade Day was always a special day at the hospital. Wheelchairs and hospital beds would be parked on the curb next to the road, and the parade would go by. Nobody was left out. When Ralph Edwards began coming for the Truth or Consequences fiesta, he would bring celebrities out to the hospital to visit with the children. (Courtesy of Geronimo Springs Museum Archives.)

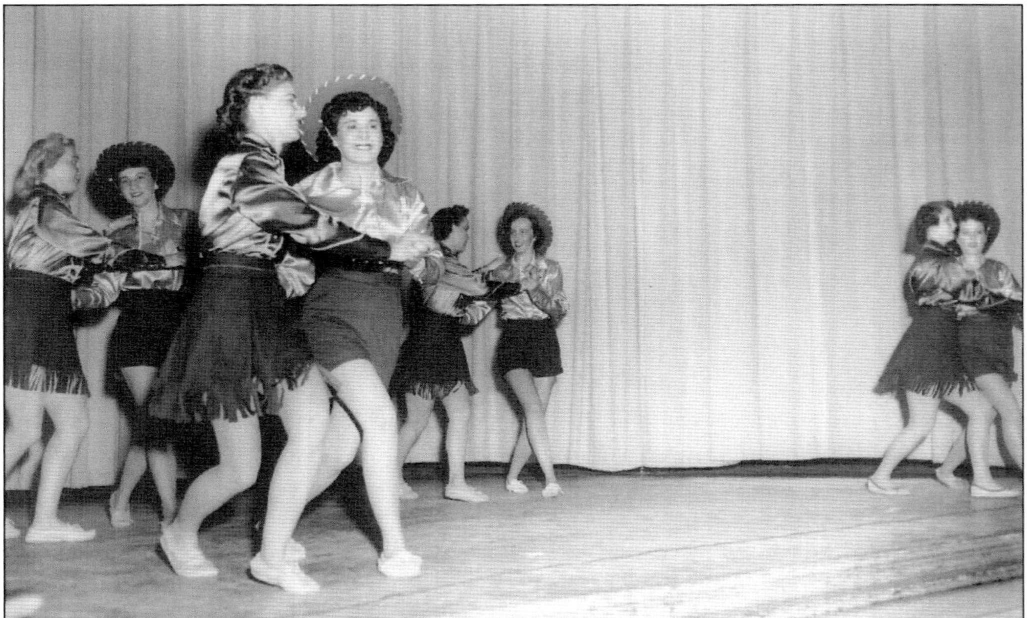

The dining room also functioned as a recreation room. It was equipped with a stage at the end and a motion picture "apparatus." Live entertainment was always a welcome treat for the kids. These young women (nurses?) appear to be having a Wild West time as they dance around the stage.

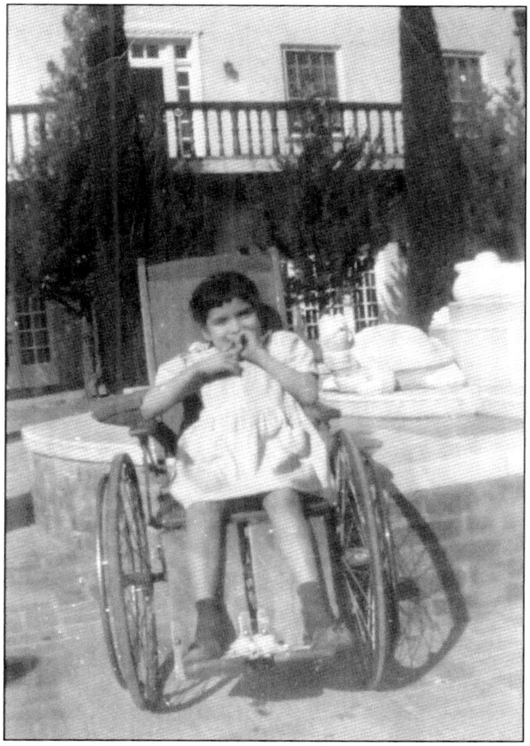

Sunshine and water were two of the best commodities that the Carrie Tingley Hospital for Crippled Children could offer its young patients. For the parents of children struggling with polio, the hospital was regarded as the best hope possible. Staff members came from all over the United States to work at Carrie Tingley. It was 1908 when Dr. Karl Landsteiner discovered that a virus caused infantile paralysis (polio). In 1916, the first major polio epidemic was documented in the United States. The National Foundation for Infantile Paralysis (known today as the March of Dimes) was founded by Pres. Franklin D. Roosevelt in 1938.

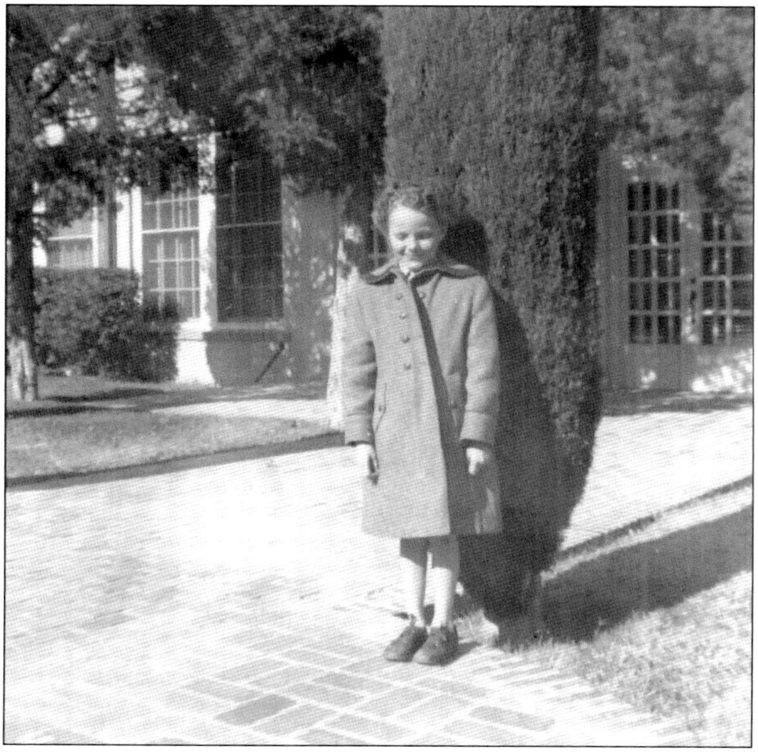

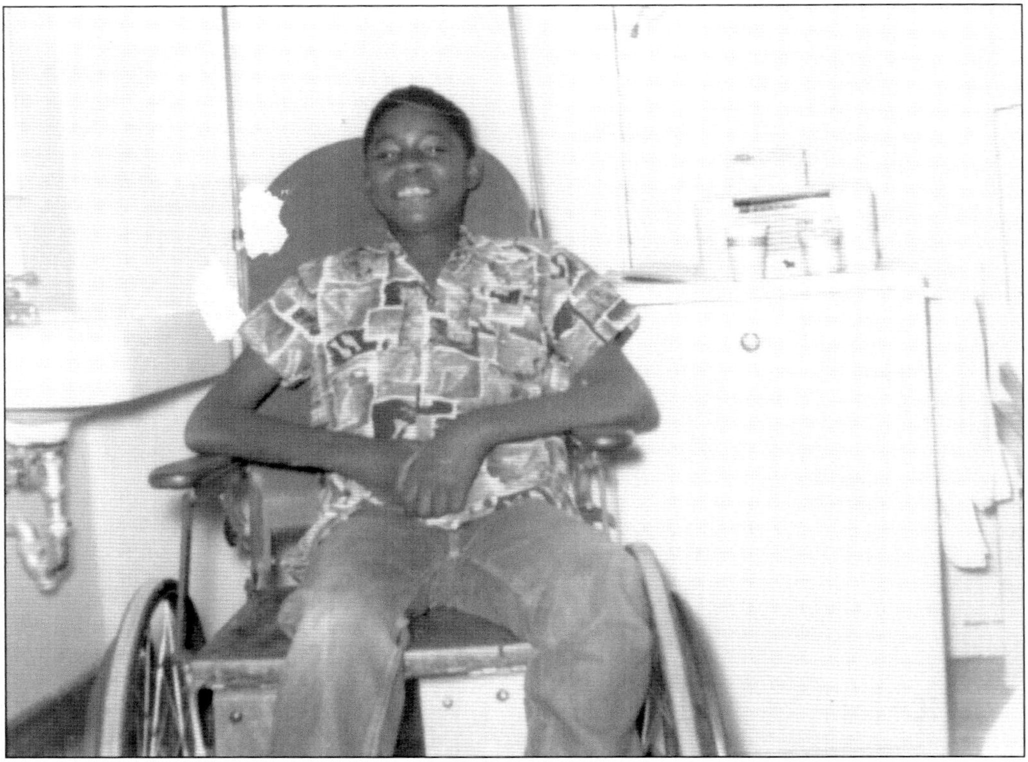

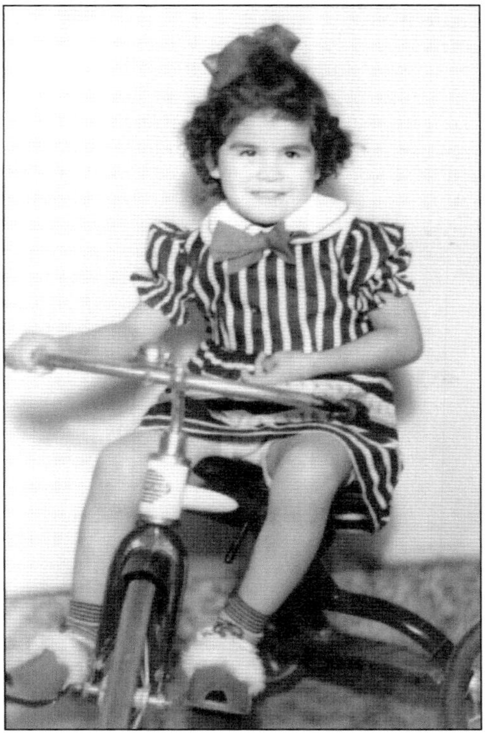

From 1937 to 1941, polio cases represented about 30 percent of the discharged patients of the Carrie Tingley Hospital for Crippled Children. The other major diseases treated at that time included congenital defects (17.3 percent), traumatic defects (12.4 percent), osteomyelitis (inflammation of bone and bone marrow, 7.8 percent), spastic paralysis (5.7 percent), arthritis (3.9 percent), and tuberculosis (21.4 percent). Any child, regardless of race, creed, national origin, or financial status, could be served at the Carrie Tingley Hospital for Crippled Children if they were less than 21 years of age and suffered from an orthopedic condition. The clinic area, x-ray department, and laboratory were remodeled in 1961. A hospital school was constructed on the site in 1972 and 1973. (Both, courtesy of Geronimo Springs Museum Archives.)

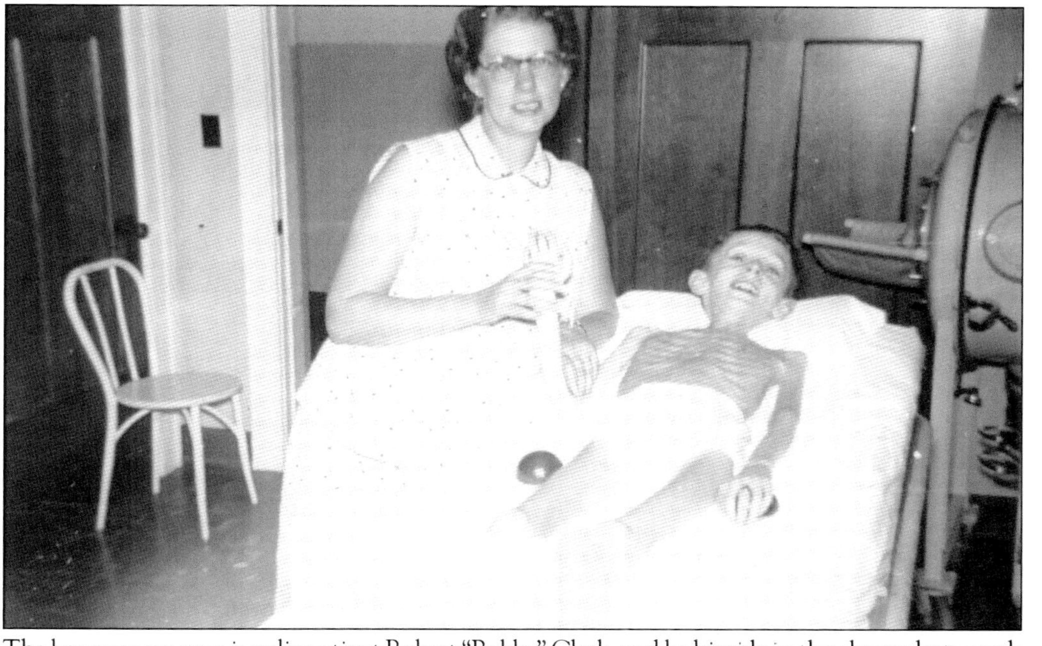

The brave young man is polio patient Robert "Bobby" Clark, and by his side in the above photograph is his mother. The photograph below shows Bobby, his nurse Mrs. Pearson, and his mother as he lies in the iron lung. The iron lung enabled Bobby to breathe by decreasing and increasing the air pressure in the airtight chamber, mimicking the physiological action of breathing. Polio would paralyze the muscle groups in the chest in children such as Bobby. In 1930, the iron lung cost about $1,500. Despite his polio, Clark would go on to be an attorney, according to childhood friend Ernestine Kipp, who recognized Bobby's picture at the 70th anniversary of the hospital.

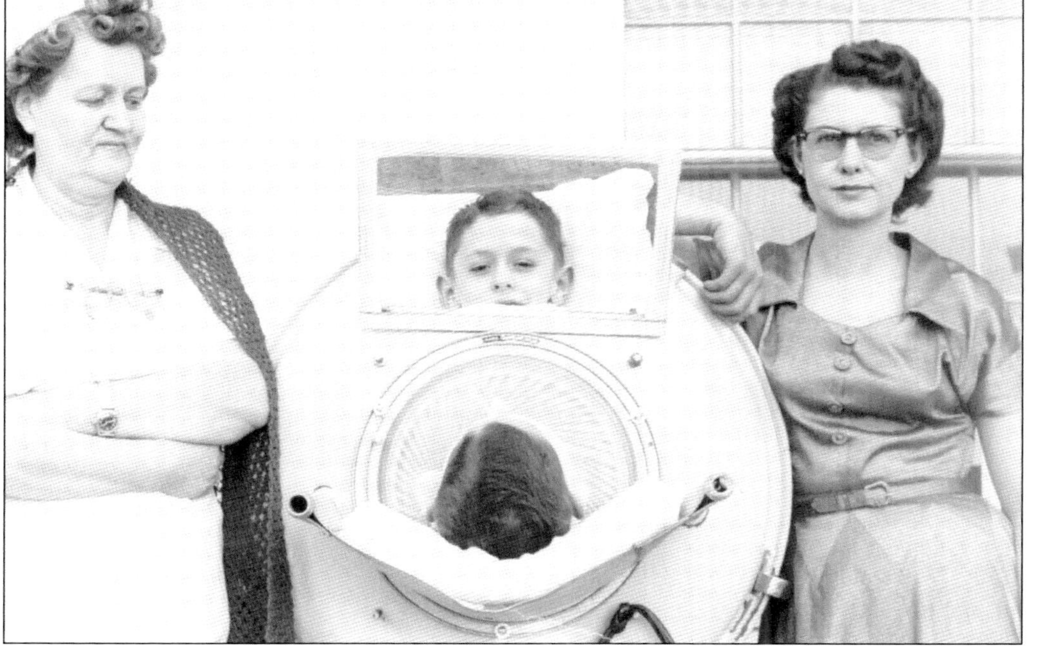

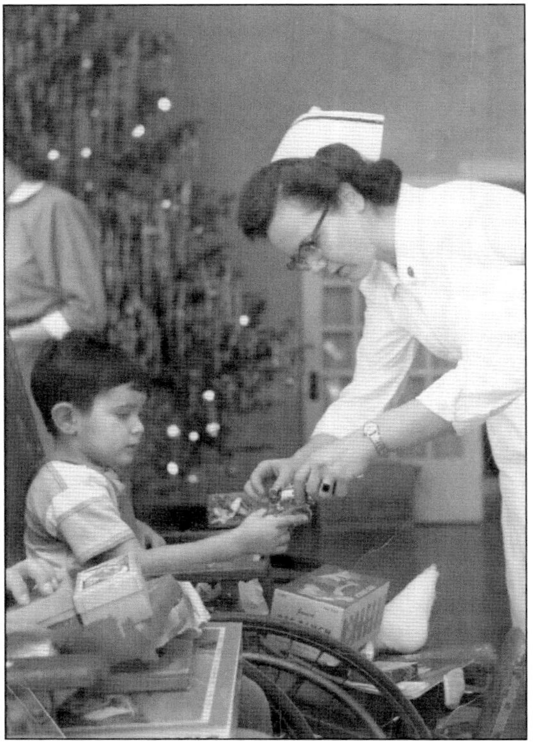

This nurse appears to be helping this young man unwrap a toy gun. The residents of Hot Springs were very generous at Christmastime with the children at Carrie Tingley. Not only did they give of their money, but they also gave generously of their time. Many community residents made a habit of going and visiting with the children in the hospital. (Courtesy of Geronimo Springs Museum Archives.)

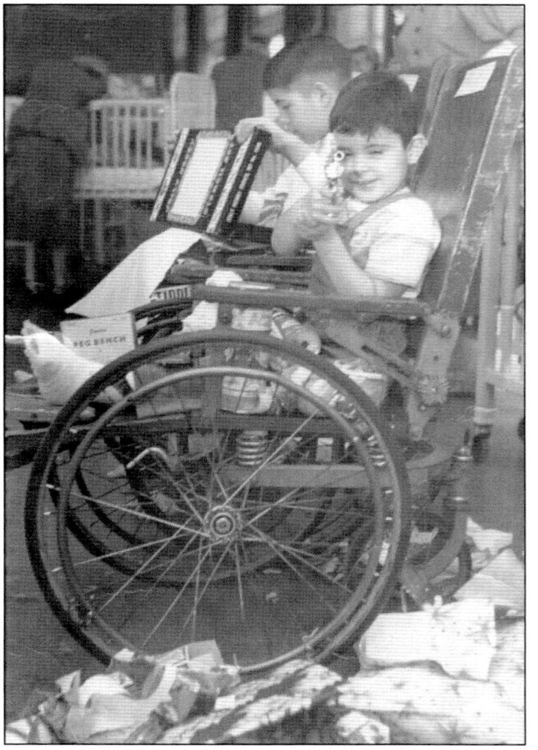

"No, you won't take my Christmas presents!" says this young man as he aims his new Christmas toy at the camera. Christmas was a special time at Carrie Tingley. All the Christmas wrapping in this photograph testifies to the fact that Santa Claus visited the hospital every year and was very generous with his presents. (Courtesy of Geronimo Springs Museum Archives.)

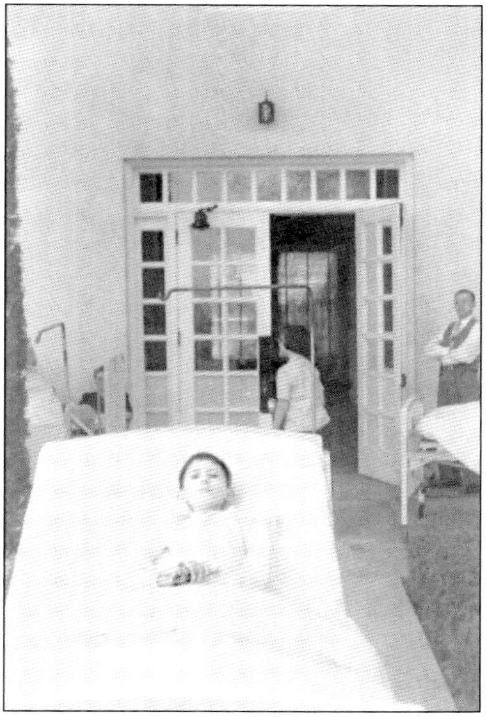

Mark Gentry arrived at Carrie Tingley on October 4, 1949, from the town of Watrous, New Mexico. He was tested and found to have bulbospinal poliomyelitis, a form of polio. He was placed in a Drinker-Collins iron lung, pictured below. Mark would be the longest admission ever to the Carrie Tingley Hospital for Crippled Children. In May 1950, he weighed only 36 pounds. At one point, he could attend school in a wheelchair, but exhaustion soon forced him back to bed with school services at his bedside. In January 1952, they attempted to give him a portable respirator that could be attached to his wheelchair, but he could not tolerate this. He would have to sleep in the iron lung every third or fourth night.

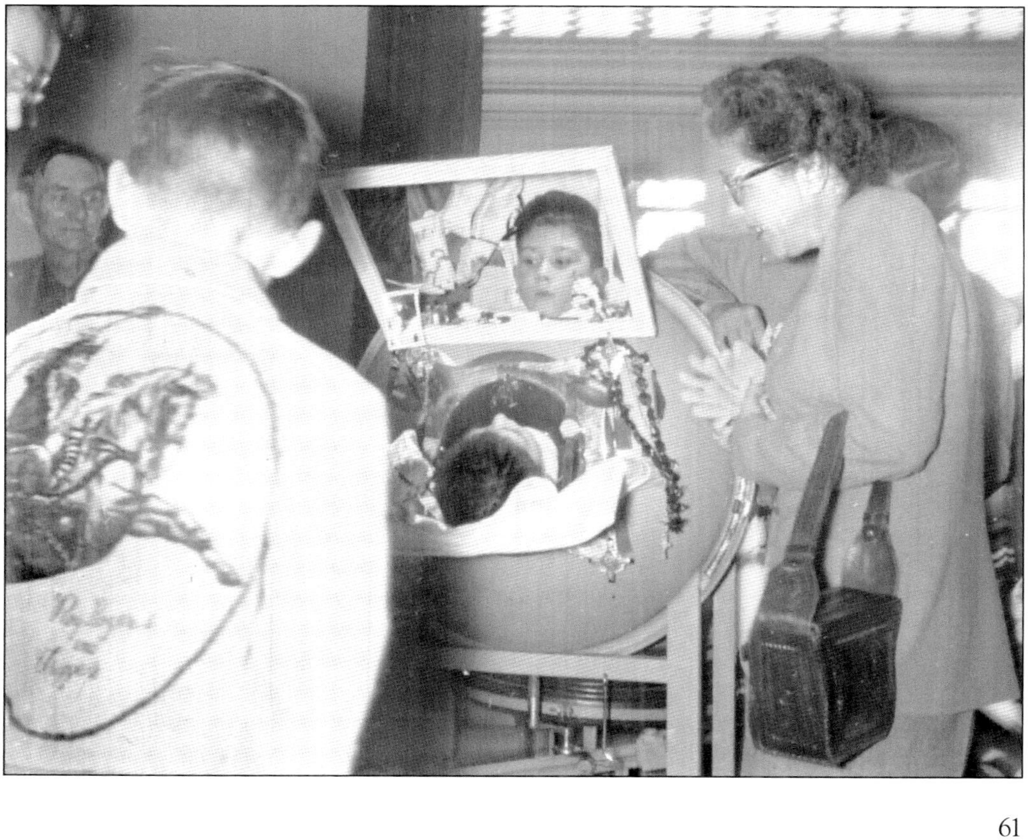

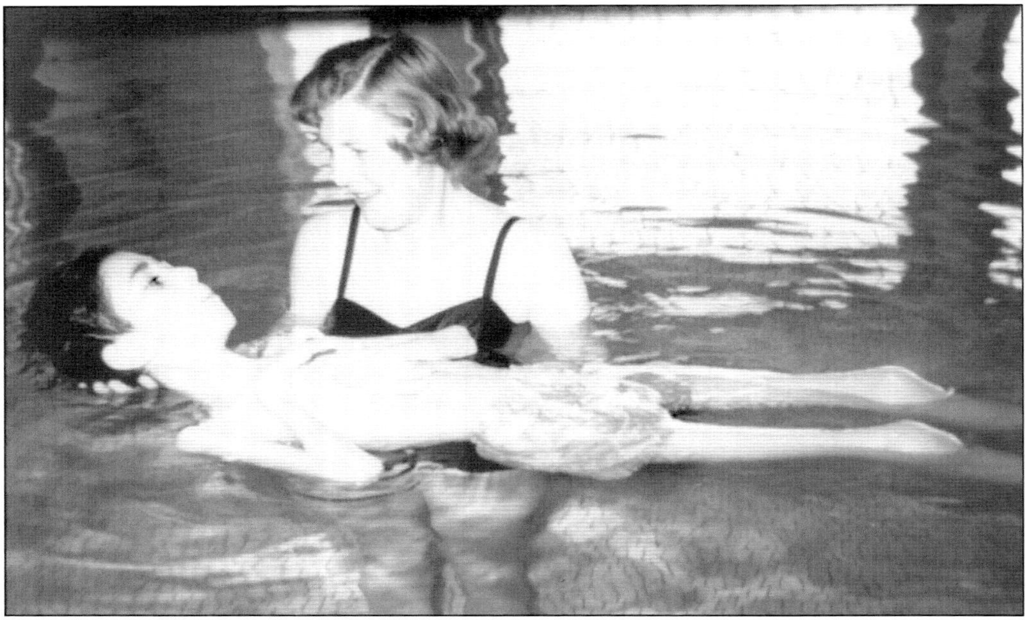

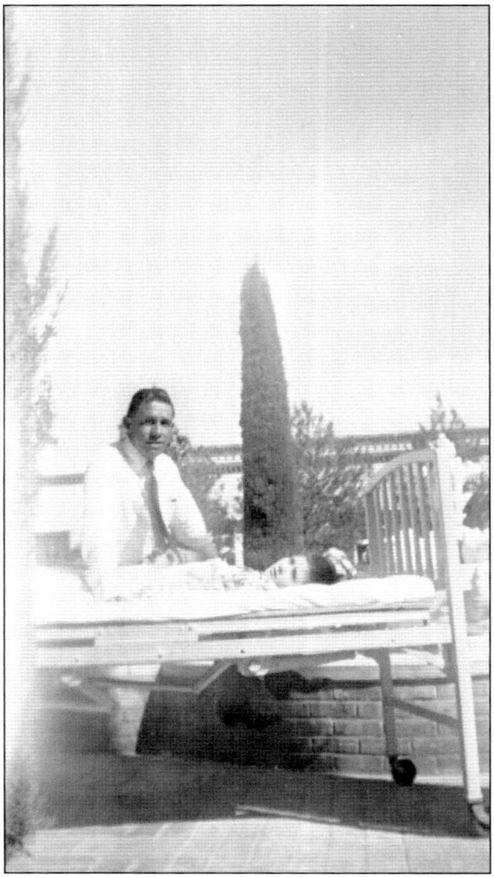

The picture above shows Mark Gentry in the pool. In February 1954, he started in the swimming pool, but at the end of the year he would be in bad shape again and have to sleep in the iron lung every other night. Mark graduated from the high school at Carrie Tingley on May 24, 1957. According to Daisy Wilson, R.N., Mark spent 2,893 days receiving care at Carrie Tingley. Looking at the picture at left, where Mark is with his father, it is hard to believe that he would be able to get around eventually in a wheelchair with a portable respirator, marry a former patient of Carrie Tingley, and have a child. He has since passed on but still lives in the hearts of many.

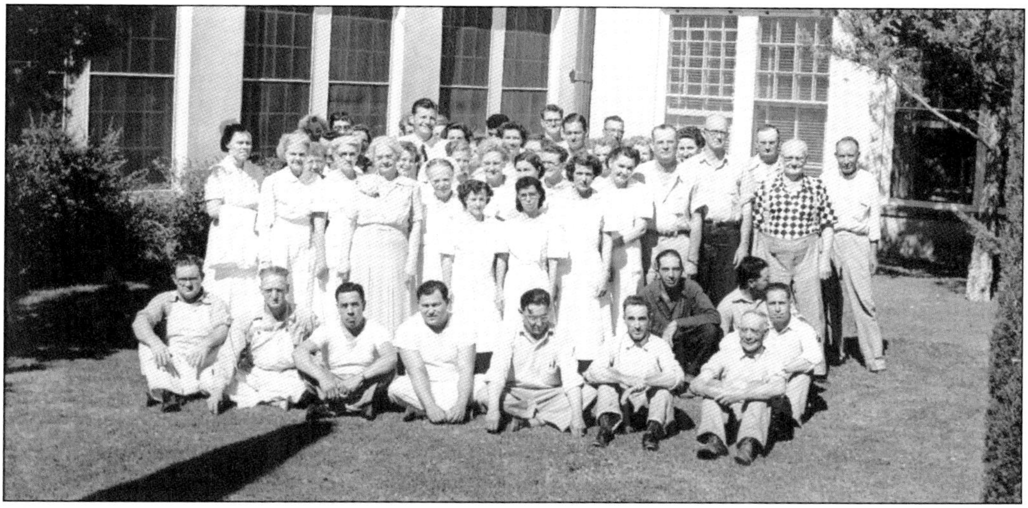

This is a group of Carrie Tingley staff members. For the 1941–1942 fiscal year, nursing salaries totaled $18,415.35, and administrative staff salaries totaled $8,151.50. In all, $74,547.33 was spent on salaries. Supplies for that year were estimated at $28,841.36, and travel expenses were only $1,364.53. (Courtesy of Geronimo Springs Museum Archives.)

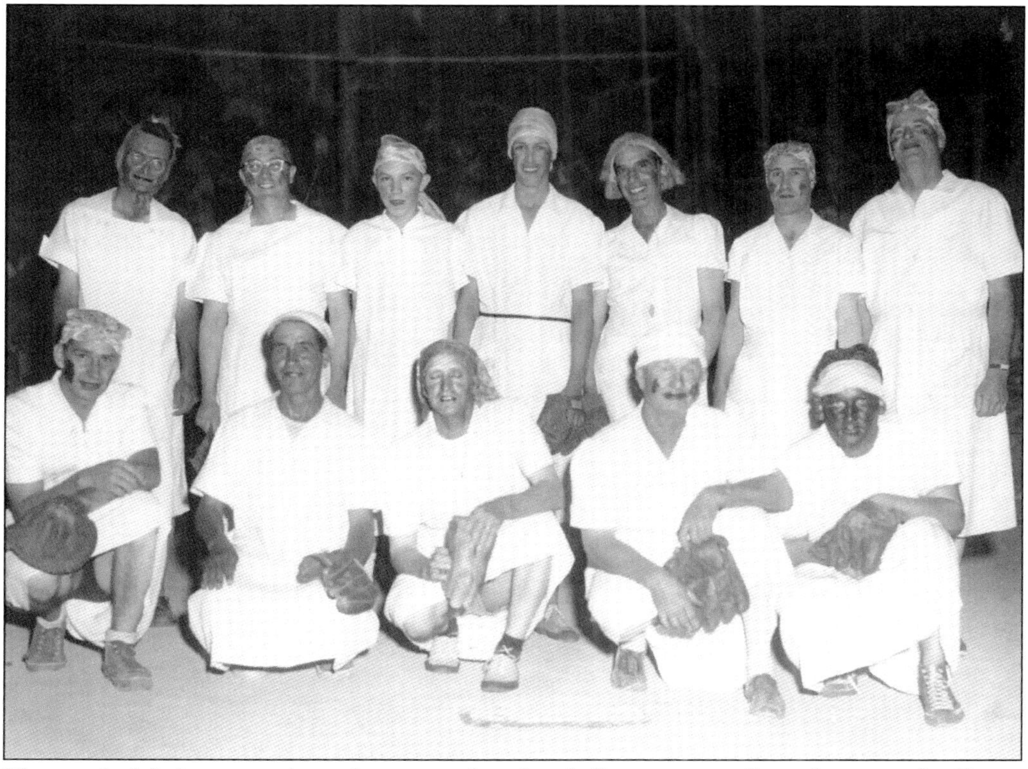

These colorful characters dressed as nurses for a baseball game were all employees at the Carrie Tingley Hospital for Crippled Children. In 1948, the American Medical Association approved Carrie Tingley for a 12-month residency-training program in pediatric orthopedics. (Courtesy of Geronimo Springs Museum Archives.)

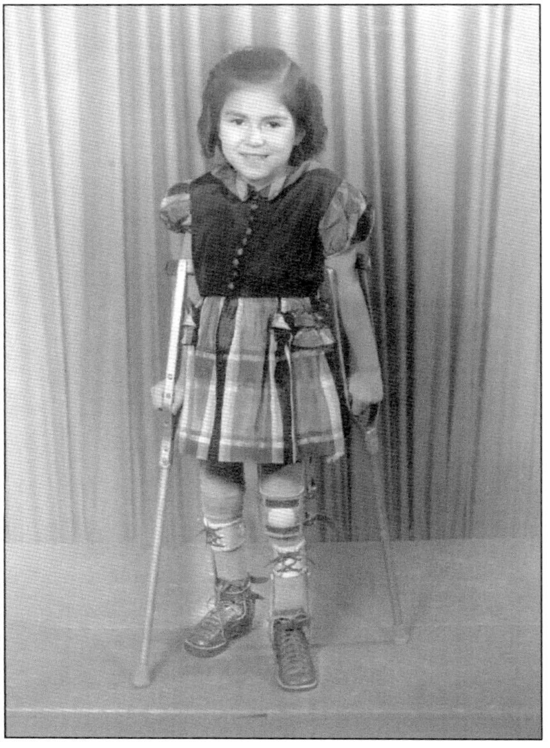

In 1954, the Salk vaccine was developed. The hospital's advisory board voted to move the hospital to the site of the University of New Mexico's School of Medicine in 1979. The move was completed in 1981. Two years later, the state legislature voted to turn the vacant state property over to the New Mexico Veterans' Center. The building still stands today, serving an older population.

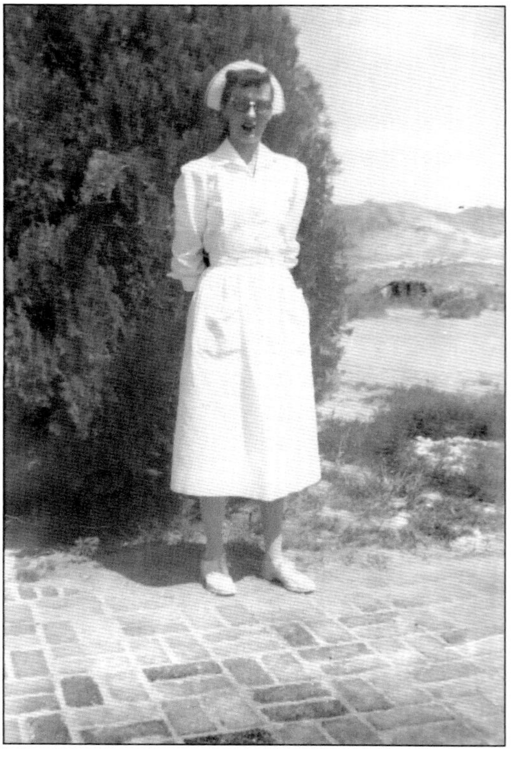

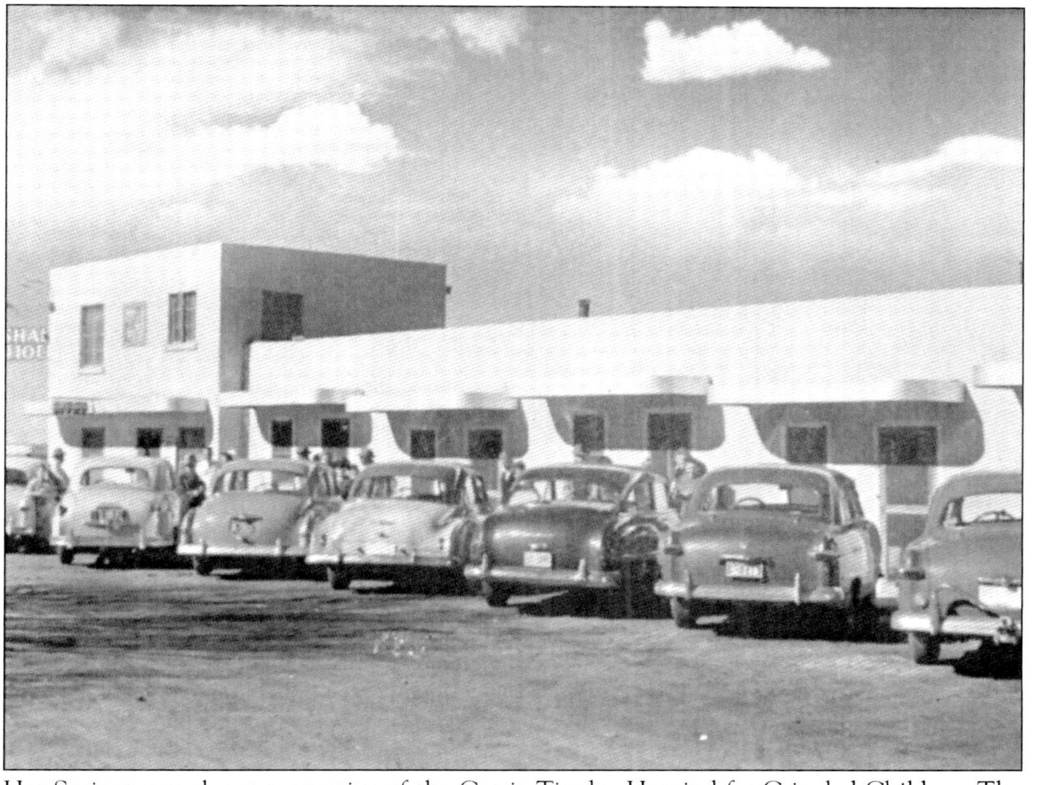

Hot Springs was always supportive of the Carrie Tingley Hospital for Crippled Children. The concept of the "car court" filled the need for parents to have a place to stay while their children were patients at the hospital. Many families were unable to afford to maintain a second residence in town while their little one was at the hospital, but for those who could, Hot Springs was ready. Hotels, motels, and car courts had rooms available for rent throughout the community. Car courts were unique in that they allowed guests to park just outside their rooms.

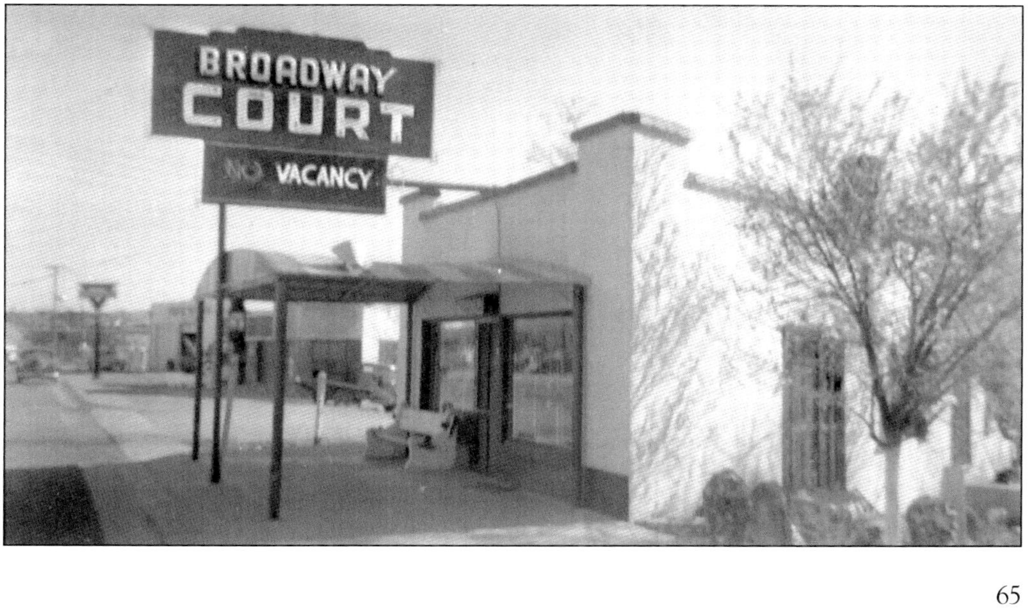

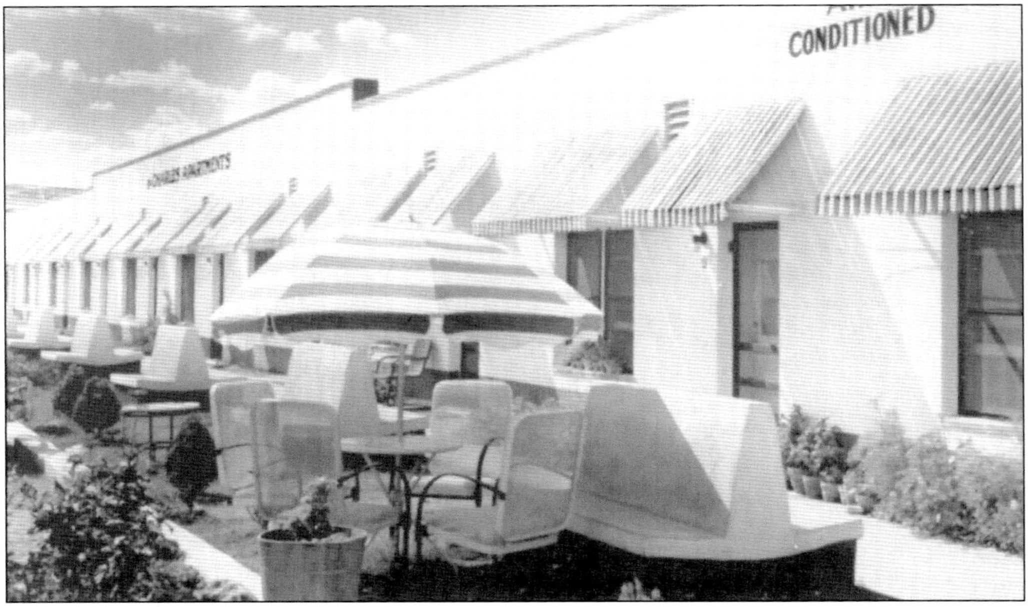

The Charles Apartments were advertised as completely modern but moderately priced. The rooms featured kitchenettes and televisions and were considered spacious. Advertisements also noted that the apartments were close to the business area but far away from the busy streets. Their bathhouse offered sauna baths, hot mineral water baths, Swedish massage, sitz (warm water) baths, colonic, and tubs. For long-term guests with children at Carrie Tingley, the kitchenette was a big draw because it allowed them to fix their own meals in the rooms.

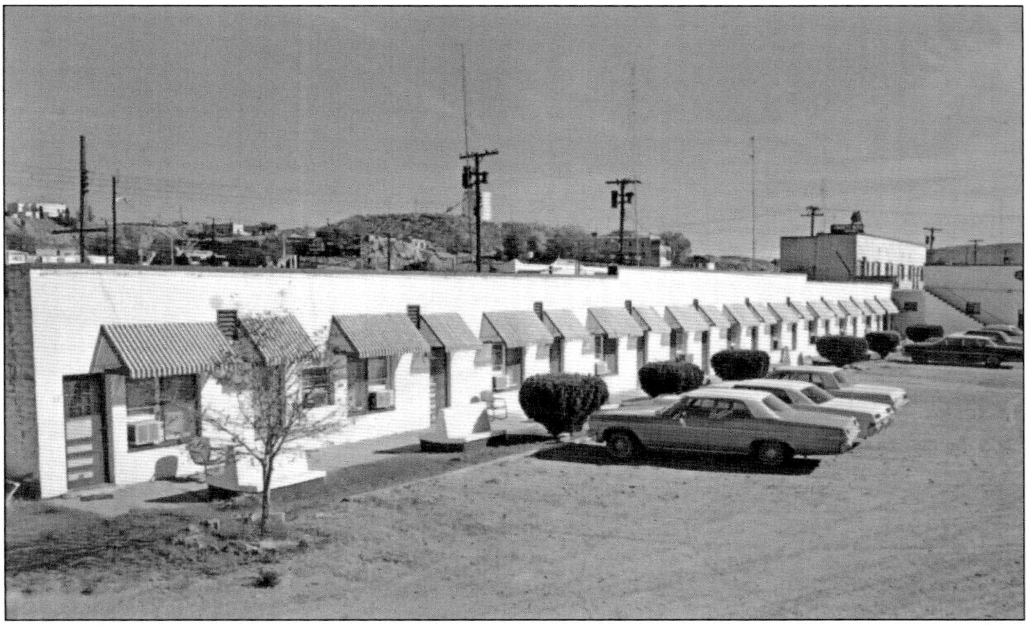

Four

CONSTRUCTION AND COMMERCE

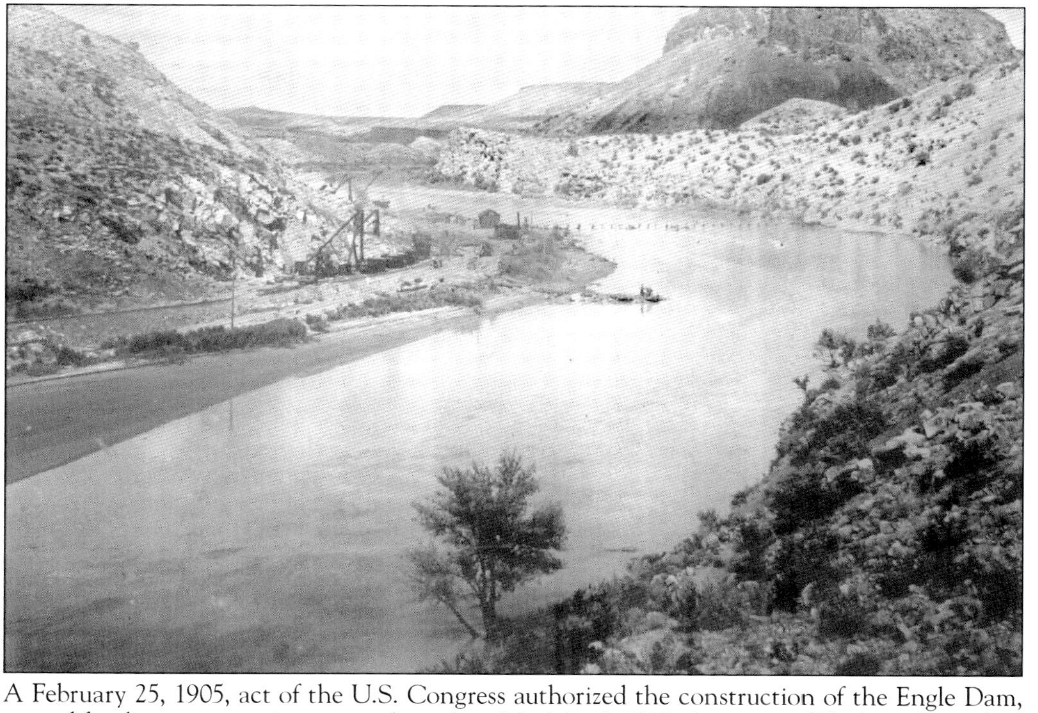

A February 25, 1905, act of the U.S. Congress authorized the construction of the Engle Dam, named for the nearest train stop on the railroad. In March 1911, the name of Elephant Butte had been given to the post office established at the dam site. The branch railroad was not complete, so the supplies came 12 miles from Engle by wagon. History was being made. (Courtesy of Dam Site Resort.)

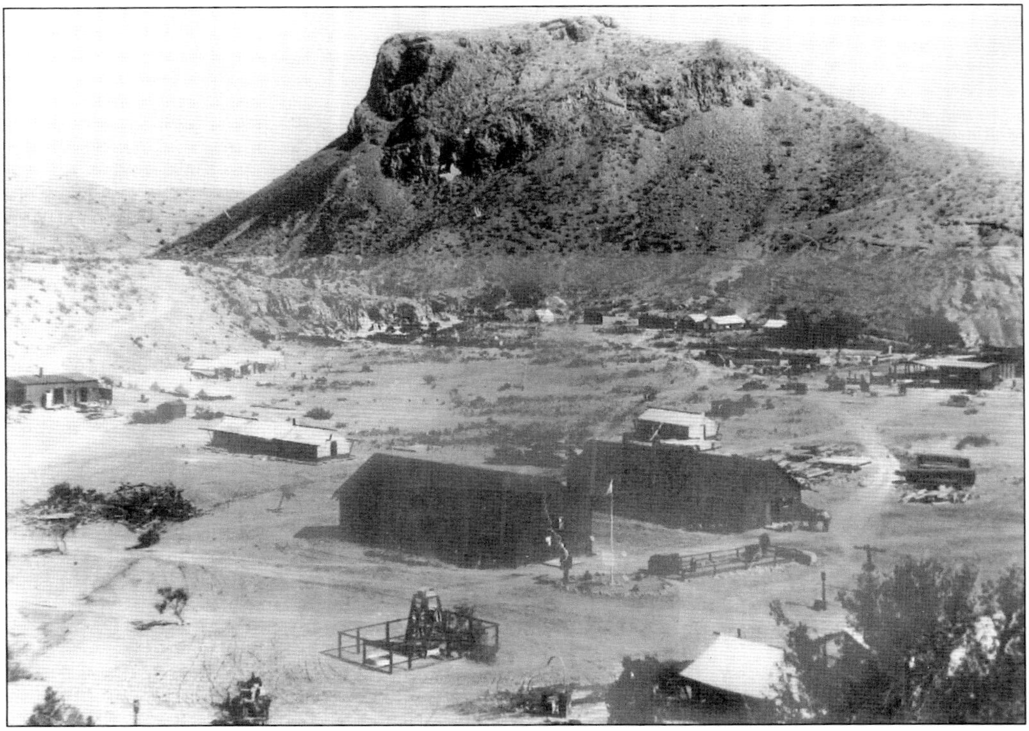

As people arrived, the camp started to assume the appearance of a working construction camp. Workers were a little crowded in their living quarters, but that was remedied quickly as new buildings were constructed. The "upper town" camp housed the construction offices, warehouses, labs, and the quarters for the engineering and office staff. The lower camp had barracks and mess halls to house and feed the laborers. The U.S. Reclamation Service also built a hospital with a cottage next to it where the camp physician could live. Sixteen cottages would be built on the hill to house the officials and their families. (Both, courtesy of Dam Site Resort.)

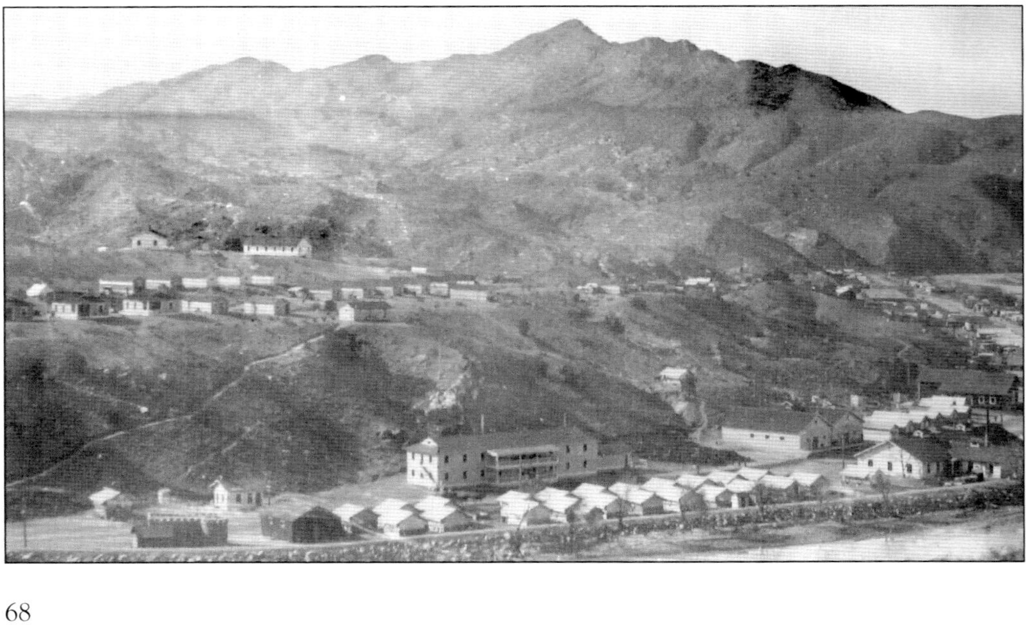

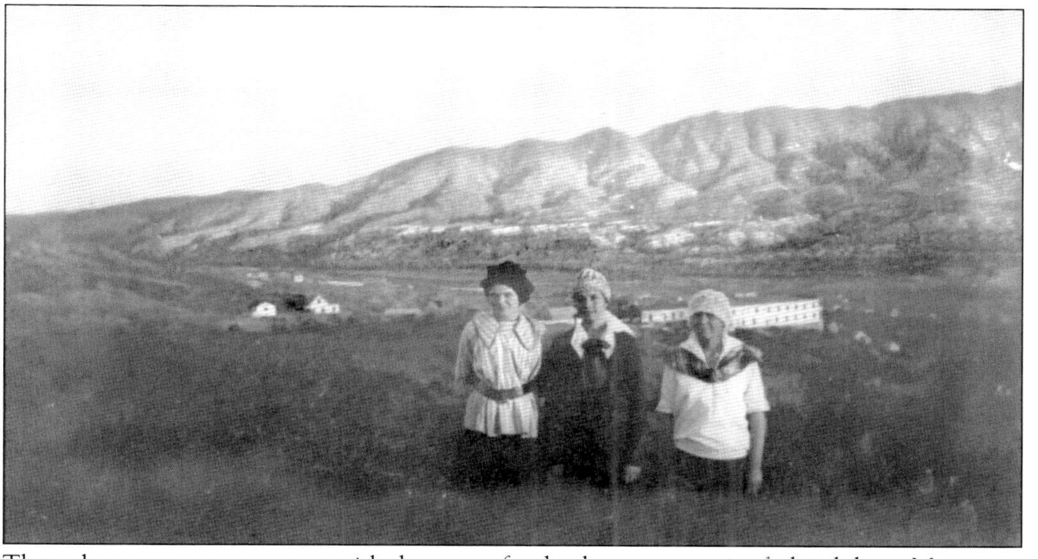

These three young women pose with the camps for the dam construction behind them. Marriages, births, romances, and other normal routine activities went on as the U.S. Bureau of Reclamation developed the town site below the dam. (Courtesy of Dam Site Resort.)

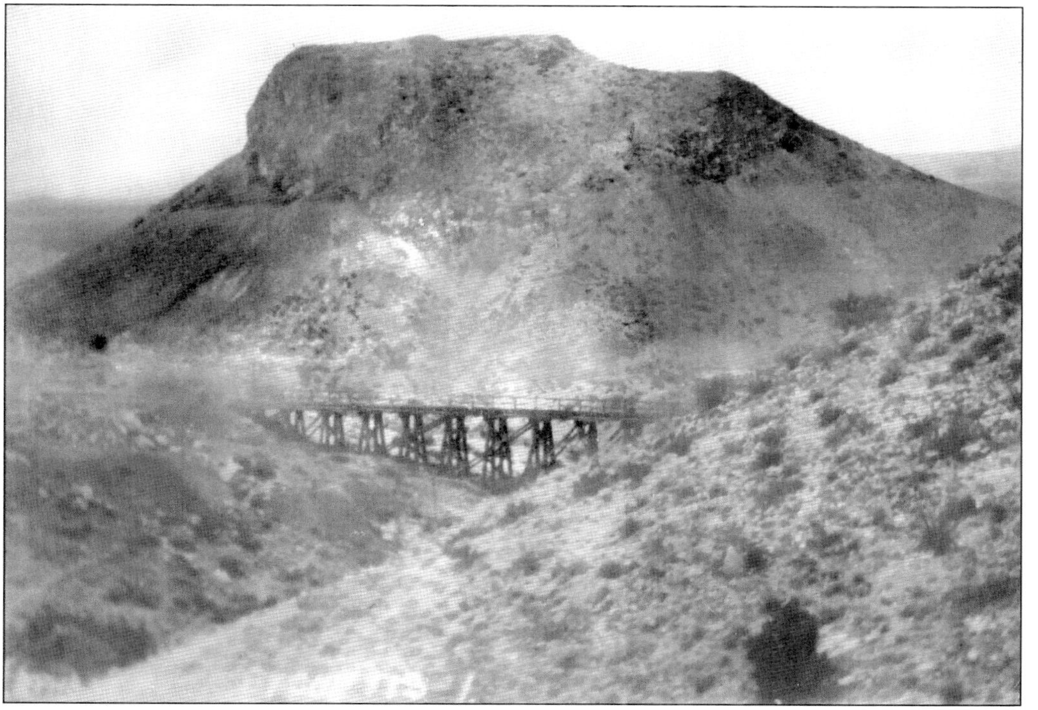

The railroad spur was 10 miles long and would be the link to the Santa Fe Railway between Engle and Cutter. Before the railroad was laid, supplies were delivered by horse and wagon. At first the railroad would only transport supplies. Later, however, it started to bring in passengers. (Courtesy of Dam Site Resort.)

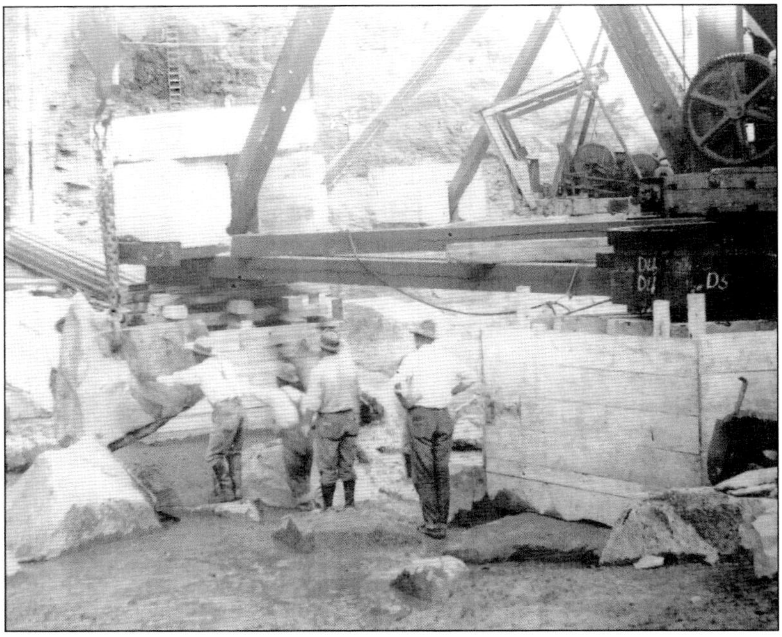

Men who worked at concrete mixing, placing, and finishing were paid $1.25 to $1.50 a day. Skilled laborers could earn from $2 to $2.50 a day. On every day of the week but Sunday, dam workers toiled around the clock in shifts. The men who worked in various departments (e.g. construction) were collectively called a "gang." (Courtesy of Dam Site Resort.)

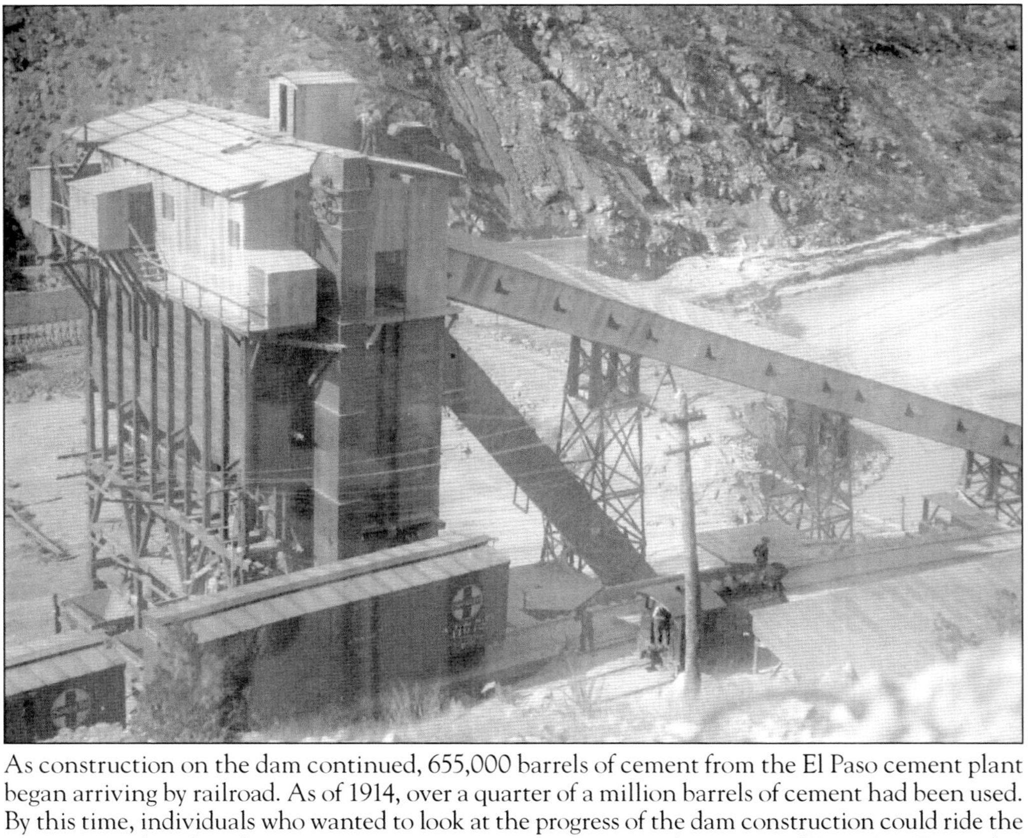

As construction on the dam continued, 655,000 barrels of cement from the El Paso cement plant began arriving by railroad. As of 1914, over a quarter of a million barrels of cement had been used. By this time, individuals who wanted to look at the progress of the dam construction could ride the Santa Fe Railroad to the construction site to see the progress. (Courtesy of Dam Site Resort.)

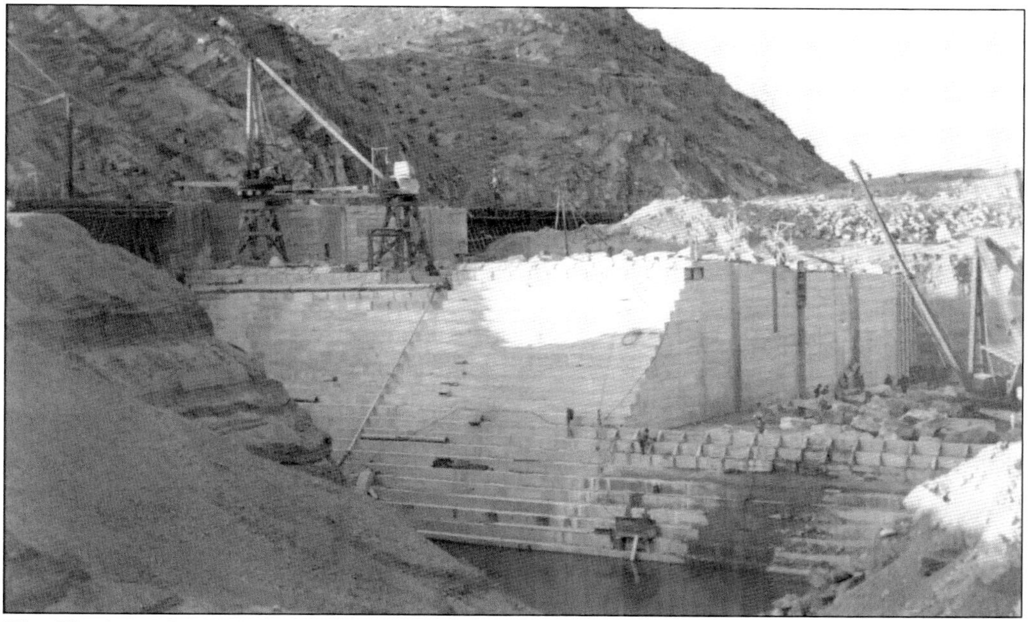

The Elephant Butte Dam was part of the Rio Grande project that was designed to provide irrigation to the south-central part of New Mexico and western Texas. The width at the top of the dam was 18 feet, and the base was 228 feet. The March 7, 1911, *Albuquerque Morning Journal* reported big possibilities for using water for electricity for Sierra County. Seventy-three years after its completion, the dam was named a National Historic Civil Engineering Landmark. It was the first civil engineering project designed to distribute water internationally (to Mexico). The dam was set into steeply dipping and highly fractured Cretaceous rocks that required highly technical engineering and a large amount of grouping to stabilize the dam's footing. (Both, courtesy of Dam Site Resort.)

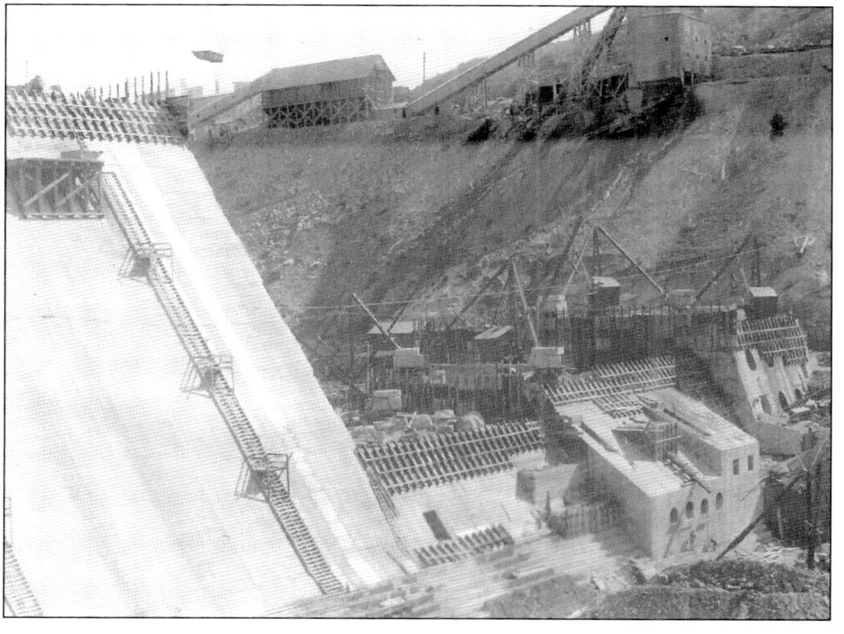

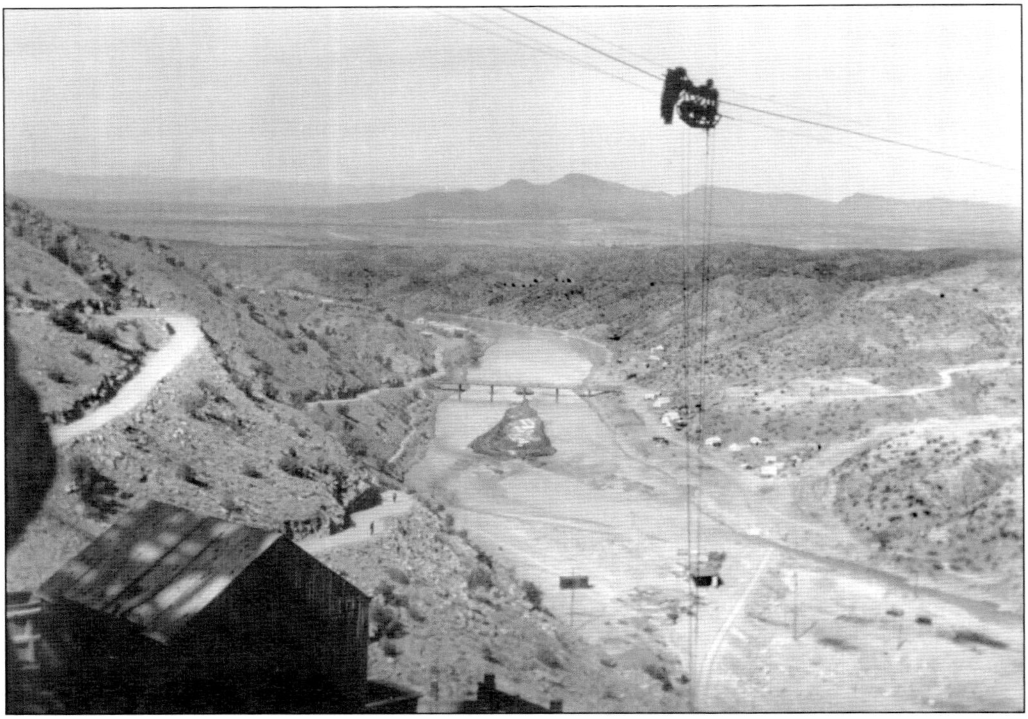

June 13, 1913, the first batch of concrete was poured. Each end of the dam had three towers that stood 350 feet above the riverbed. These towers supported a 1,400-foot-long triple cable powered by a 300-horsepower electric motor. The cables were so strong that once they were used to lower a locomotive over a bluff. Workers used plum stones (boulders) in the pour to help tie the layers together and reduce the amount of concrete needed. The plum stones were transported from the quarry by the railroad. In all, plum stones accounted for about 15 percent of the dam's total volume. They were imbedded by teams of men who also shoveled the concrete up against the forms.

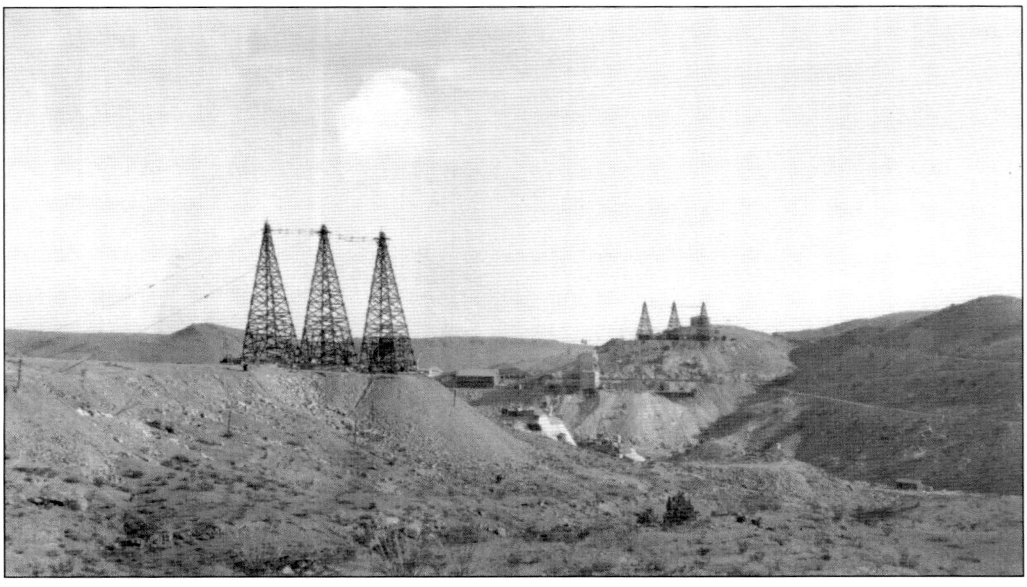

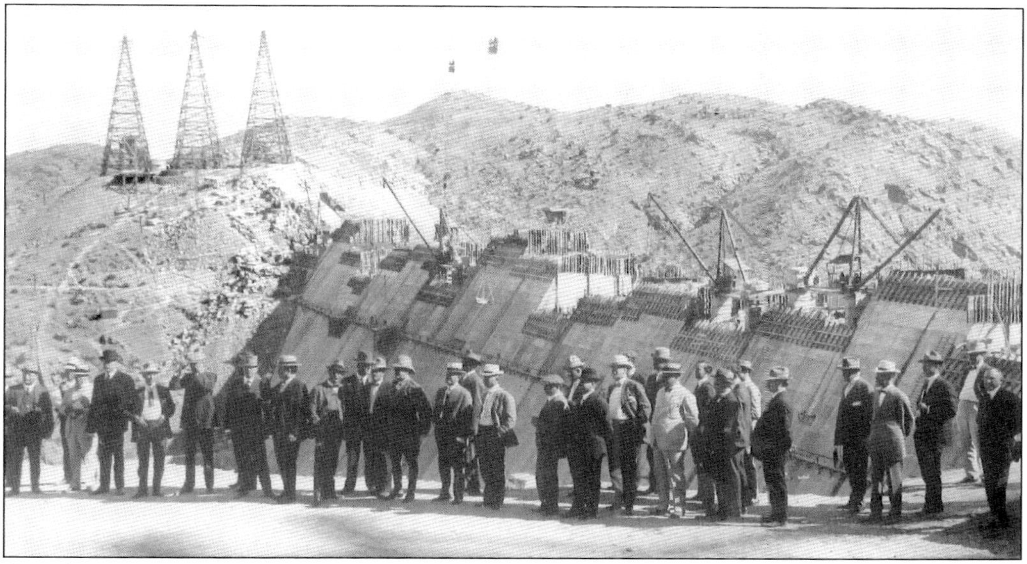

On July 10, 1914, the *Deming Headlight* ran an article saying the latest proposal to change the name of Elephant Butte Dam to something else was a "foolish idea" and declared that the dam would always be known as "Elephant Butte and nothing else." On December 7, 1951, the *Albuquerque Tribune* reported that Sen. Dennis Chavez wanted to change the name of Elephant Butte Lake to Martinez-Courchesne Lake. (Courtesy of Dam Site Resort.)

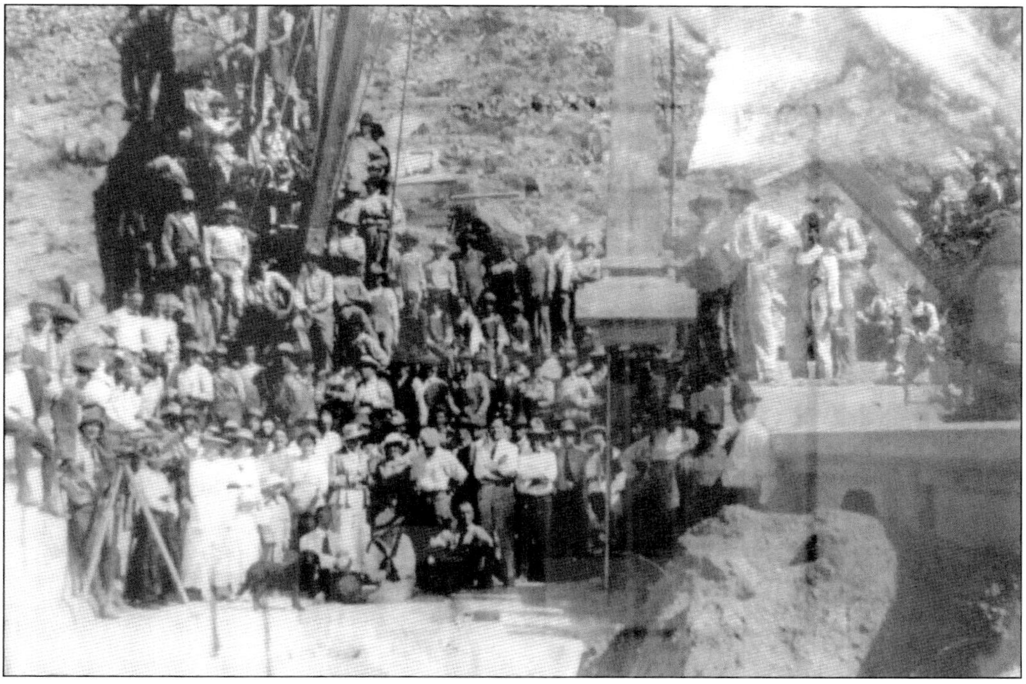

This picture represents the unofficial dedication of the dam by the workers who built it. The "official" dedication for the dam took place October 19, 1916. Pres. Woodrow Wilson sent acting secretary of the interior of the United States, A. A. Jones, as his representative along with brigadier generals George Bell Jr. and G. Morton. (Courtesy of Dam Site Resort.)

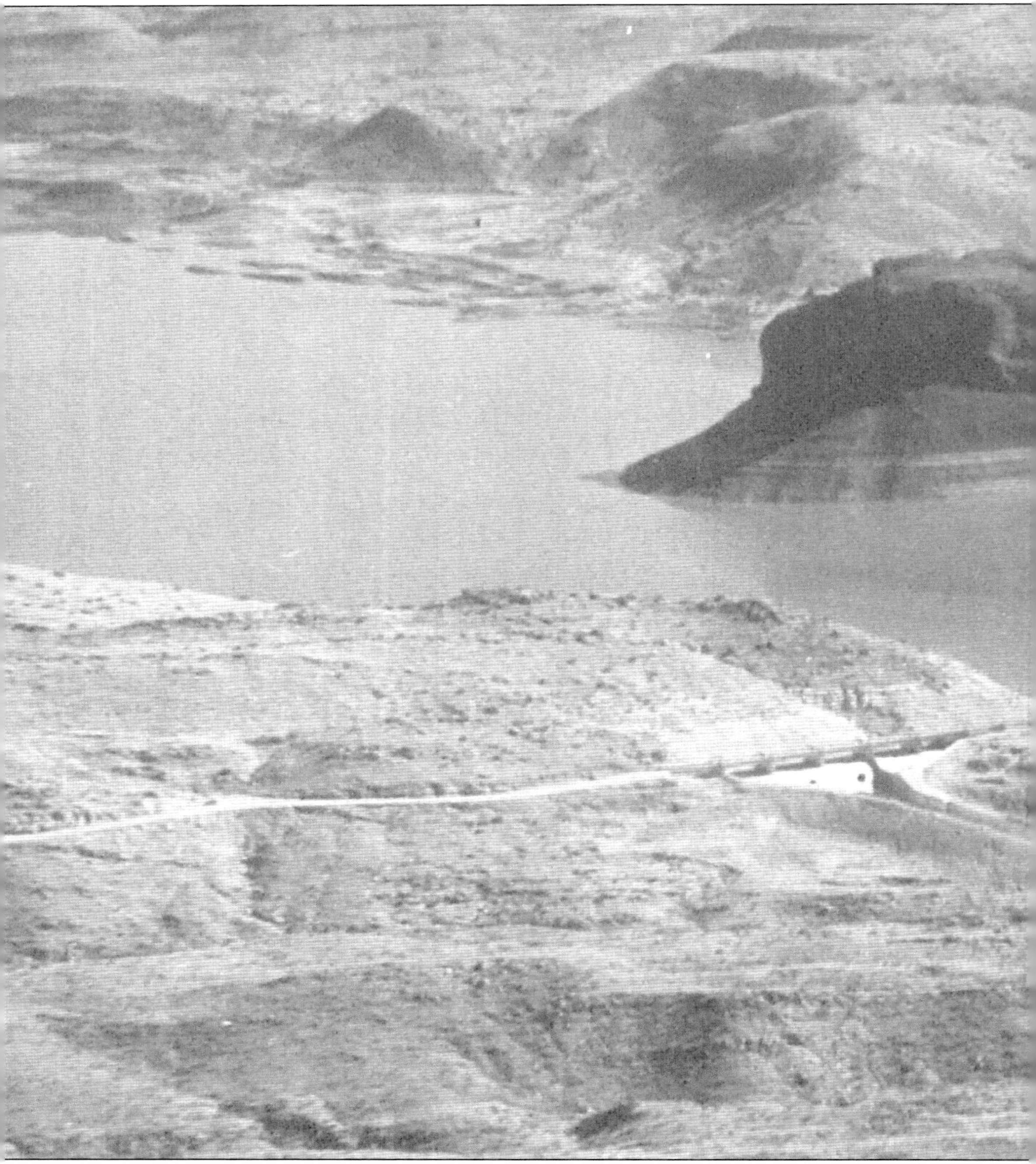

In 1915, the dam construction was far enough along that water could be impounded into a large reservoir. That was the same year that the first water deliveries were made to farmers. The reservoir had a 2,638,860-acre-foot water capacity, making it the largest reservoir in the world in 1916. W. S. Hopewell appeared at the official dedication on October 19, 1916, representing the governor of New Mexico. The downstream diversion dams, channels, and other structures ended up costing the government millions of dollars more than expected. These included the Percha,

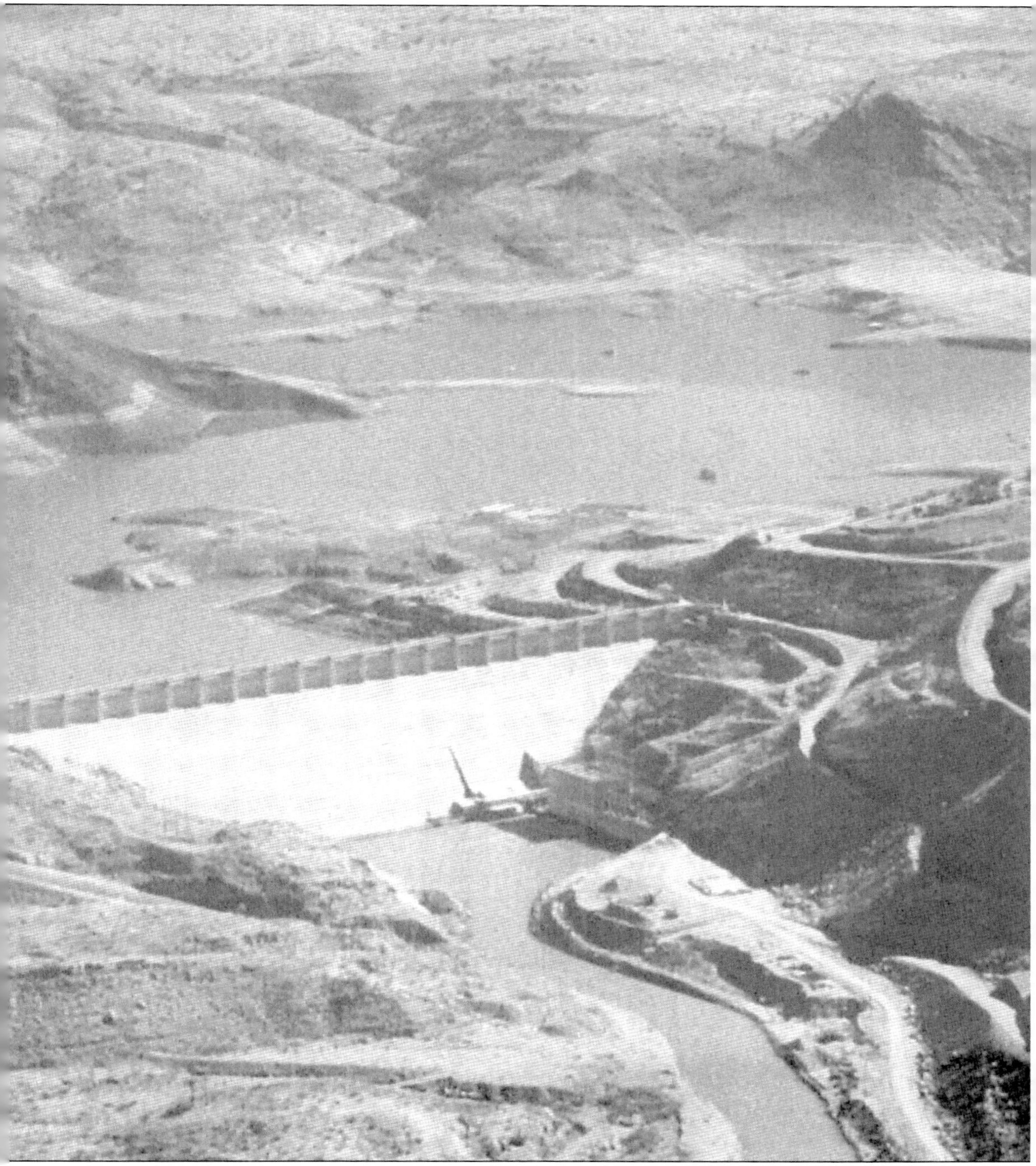

Leasburg, Mesilla, and Riverside diversion dams. There were 152 miles of main canals with two flumes and three siphons crossing the Rio Grande. The total cost for the reservoir and dam was $8,194,025, and would submerge more than 42,000 acres of land, extending to a maximum length of 45 miles. The project was designed to irrigate and enable the intensive cultivation of 180,000 acres of land. (Courtesy of Dam Site Resort.)

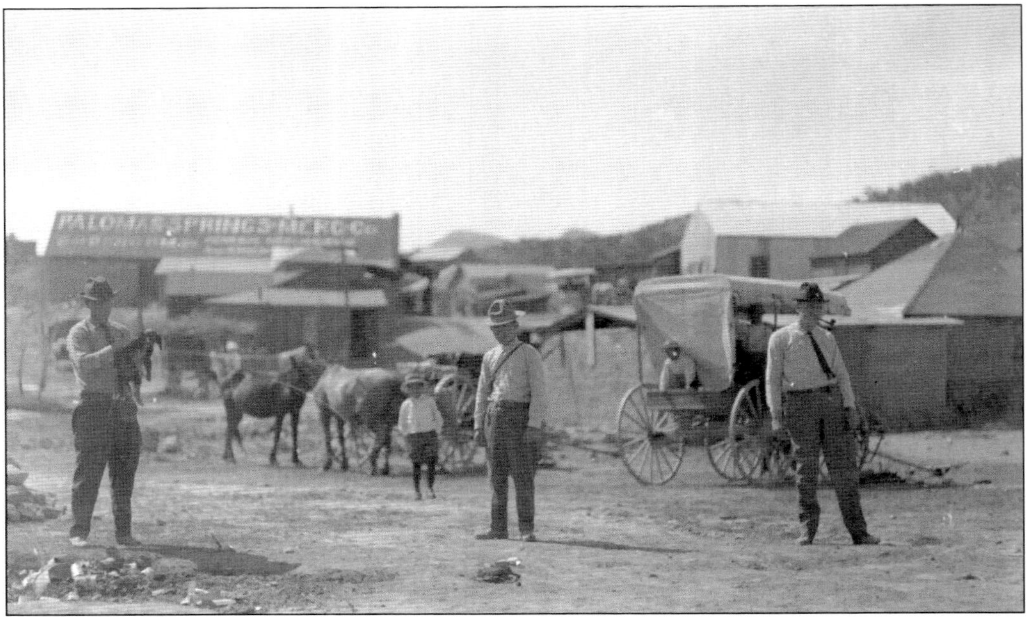

One popular business in Palomas Hot Springs was the Palomas Springs Mercantile. In 1918, the government surveyed the land, and anyone who lived on the land at that time could file and get a patent from the federal government. The patent featured the signature of Pres. Woodrow Wilson and the governmental seal of the United States. (Courtesy of Geronimo Springs Museum Archives.)

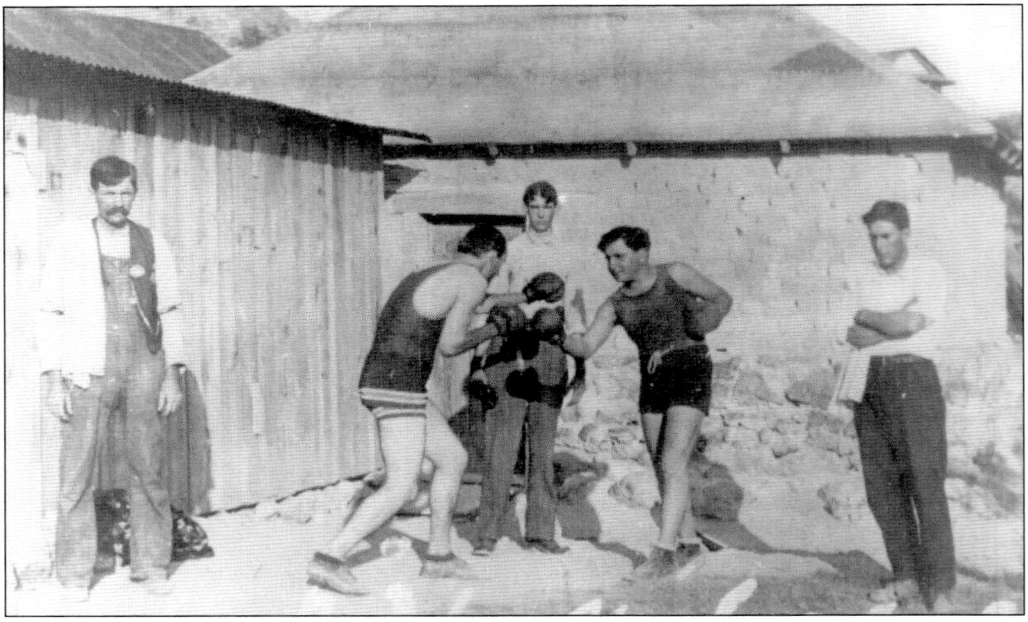

Seen here from left to right at the Geronimo Bathhouse in 1912 are Jim Hartley, an unidentified boxer, Clabe Van Winkle, another unidentified boxer, and Bill Graham. Graham opened up the first barbershop in Palomas Hot Springs. It must have been a slow day for him. (Courtesy of Geronimo Springs Museum Archives.)

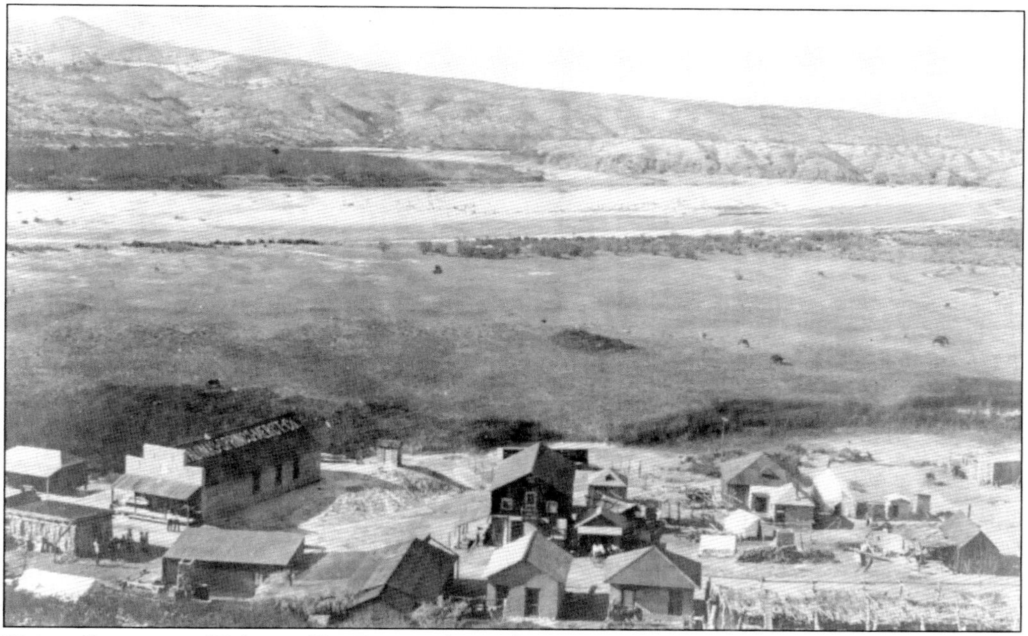

This early picture of Palomas Hot Springs shows the Rio Grande River and the Caballo Mountains in the background. A 1907 flood shifted the river to its present, more northerly course. The southern portion of the district was a grassy wetland, which provided grazing for livestock. (Courtesy of Geronimo Springs Museum Archives.)

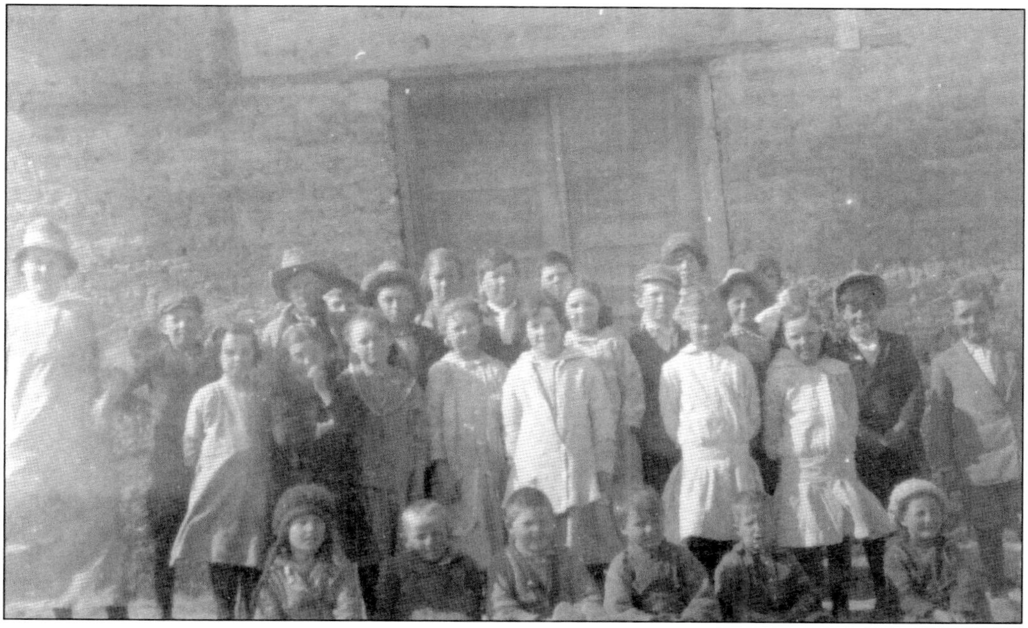

The first grade school was built at Palomas Hot Springs in 1914. This group of youngsters and their teacher, Mae Graham, posed for the camera in front of the adobe building. Before this school was built, school was held in a tent. Education was valued, and these youngsters look as though they are ready to learn. (Courtesy of Geronimo Springs Museum Archives.)

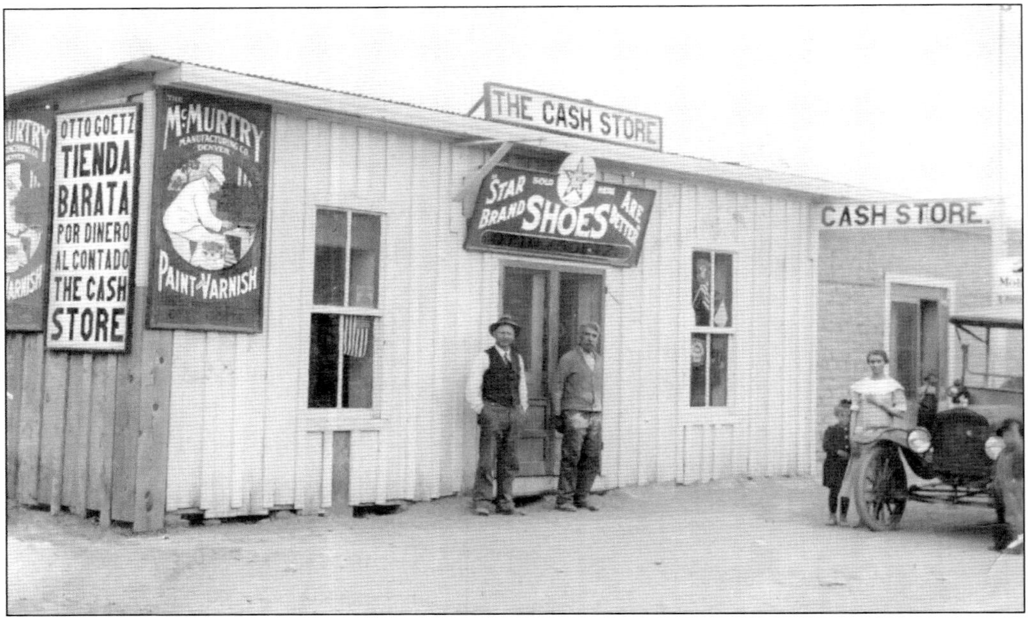

German-born Otto Goetz, on the left, became the first mayor of Palomas Hot Springs. He was credited with helping to obtain appropriations for the State Bathhouse, which precipitated sanitary regulations for bathing places that used the hot mineral spring water. He is shown here in front of his store. He was also credited with organizing the Bethesda Masonic Lodge. (Courtesy of Geronimo Springs Museum Archives.)

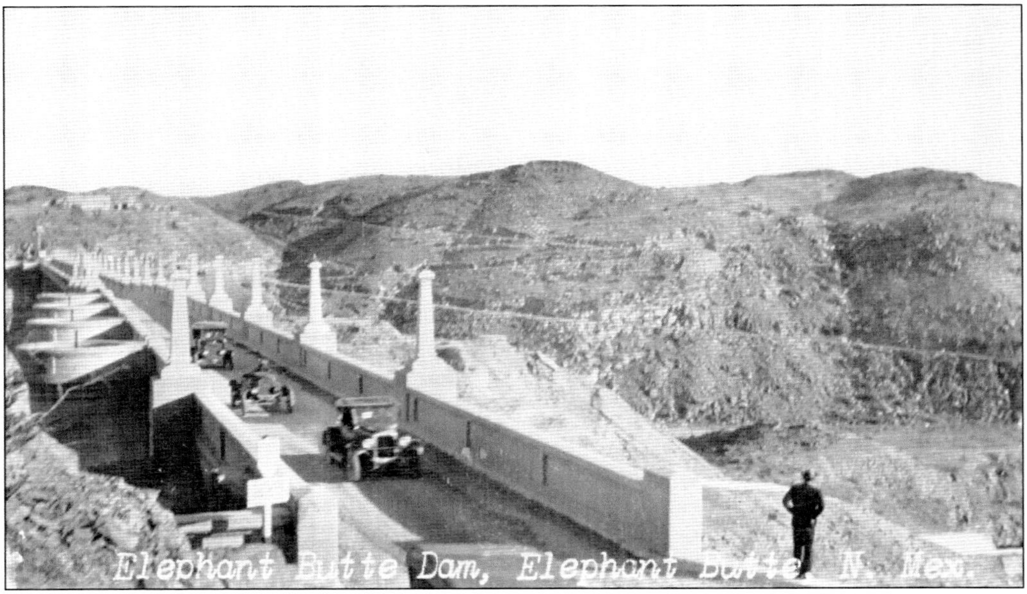

The U.S. Department of Homeland Security (DHS) prohibits travel across Elephant Butte Dam today. In 1916, Pres. Woodrow Wilson sent Gen. John J. Pershing with a force of 10,000 men into Mexico to capture Pancho Villa in what was called the "Punitive Expedition." There were rumors that the dam was to be dynamited, so on July 3, 1916, the New Mexico National Guard was sent to protect the dam.

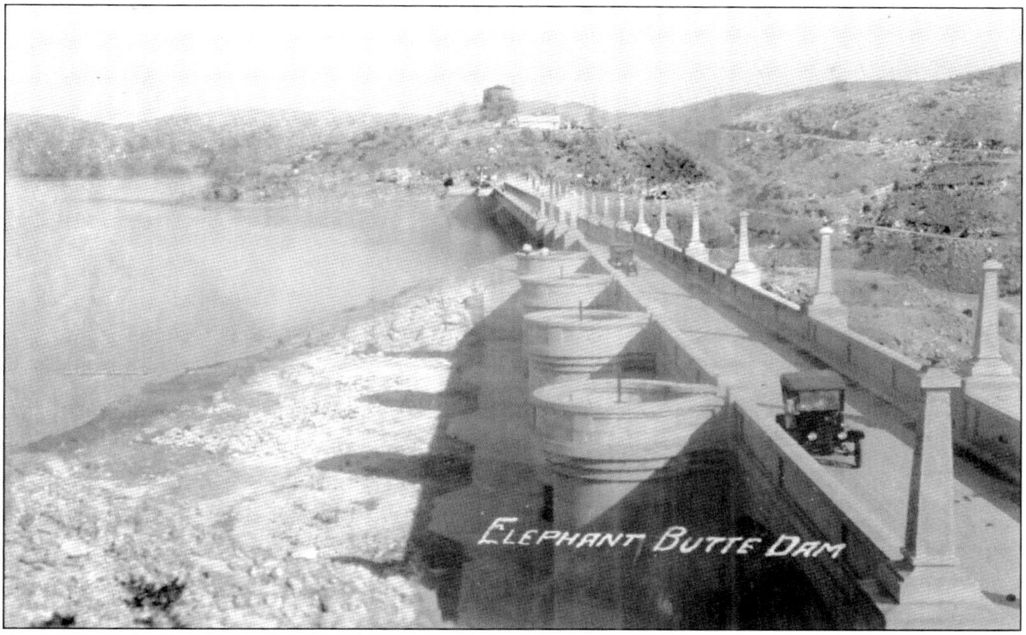

A story in the *Rio Grande Republic* of October 20, 1916, claimed that the Elephant Butte Dam would be named after Pres. Woodrow Wilson. Earlier newspapers had called the dam the Engle Dam. Evidently there were several considerations for the dam's name before it officially became known as Elephant Butte Dam.

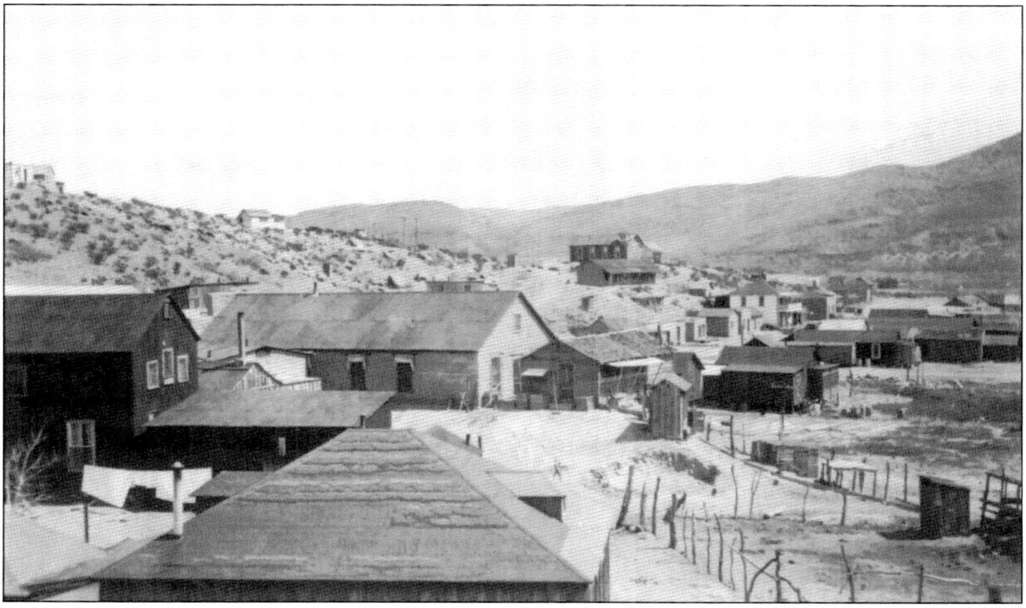

Adobe was the major building material in early Hot Springs as everything needed to make adobe blocks could be found nearby. Supplies taken from the dam's construction provided a surplus of materials with which to construct buildings in Hot Springs. The town was still attracting health seekers, and buildings began cropping up all over town. (Courtesy of Geronimo Springs Museum Archives.)

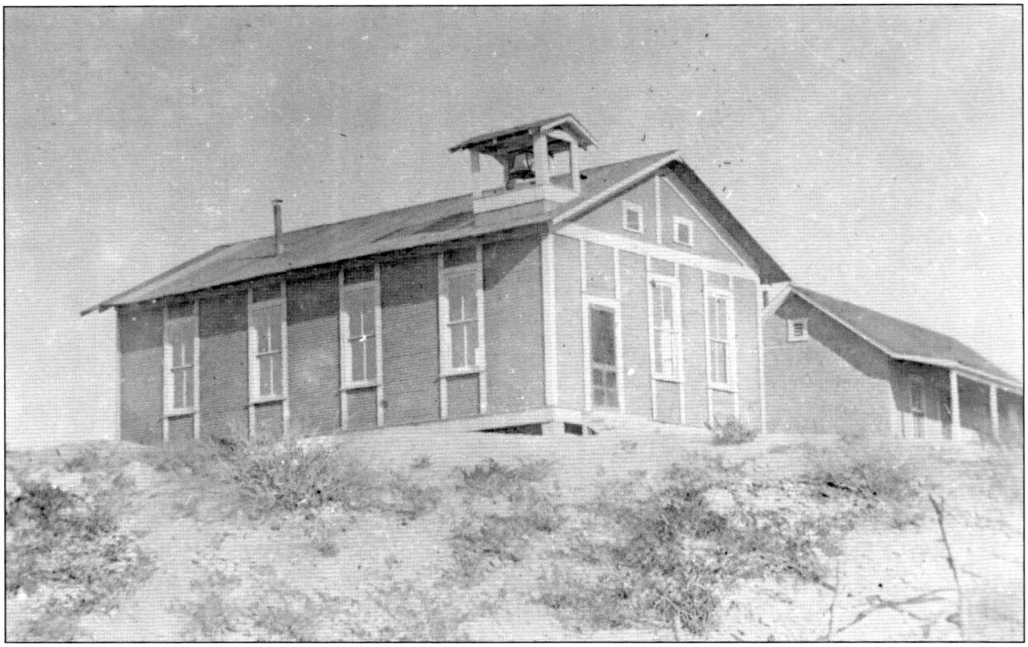

The Union Church, shown above, was moved in from the construction site of Elephant Butte Dam after the project's completion. Preacher Hunter Lewis, based out of Las Cruces, rode the train to Engle and visited various sites in Sierra County, including Hot Springs. He would walk and knit the hats he would give to babies when he christened them. A man of true faith, he truly walked many miles to bring the gospel to the people of Sierra County. Hot Springs would not have a Catholic church until after 1921, but Baptists organized a congregation in 1920. Faith and houses of worship have always been and will continue to be an important aspect of life in present-day Truth or Consequences. (Both, courtesy of Geronimo Springs Museum Archives.)

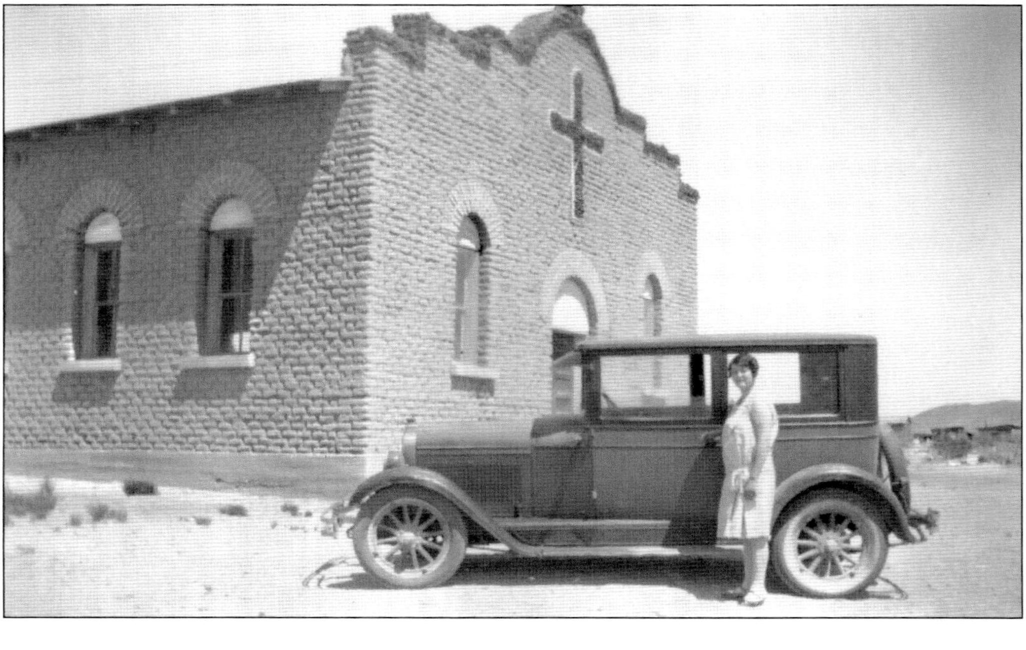

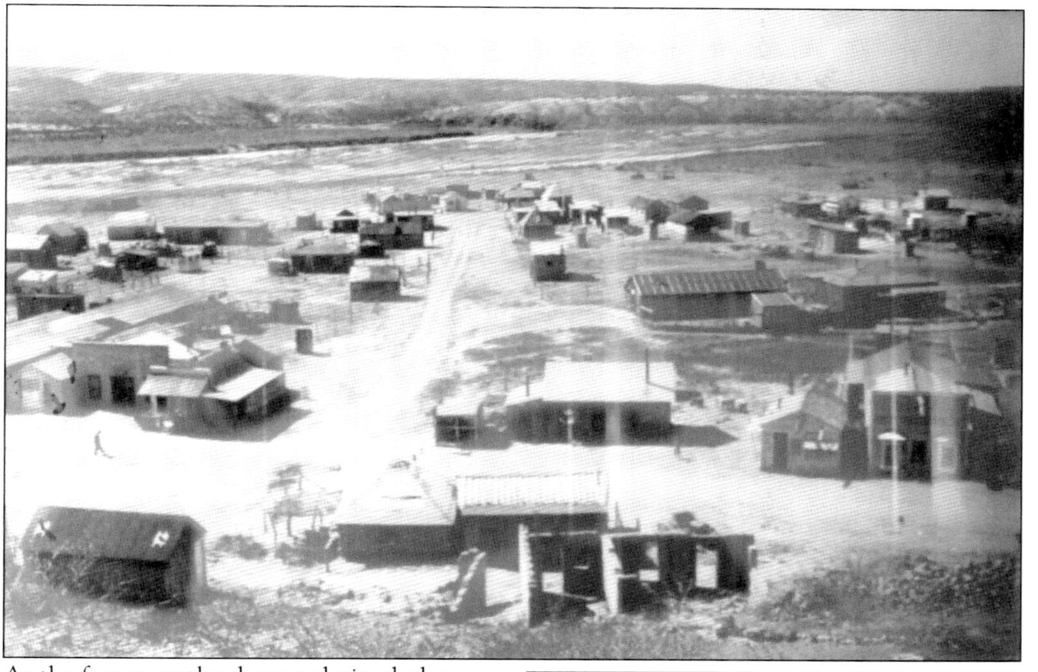

As the former wetlands were drained, the area began opening to development. Main Street was located along a contour marking the higher, northerly edge of the floodplain. The thermal water table was so close to the surface that the water pooled into a low-lying area, creating a need for drainage, so the Hot Springs ditch was dug to use the waters of the bathhouses, sewers, and hot springs for irrigation of the lands southwest of the ditch. Produce was grown using the irrigated water, including the watermelon shown at right. The remnants of the ditch are visible today at the Hay-Yo-Kay Hot Springs Bathhouse, located at 300 Austin Avenue. (Both, courtesy of Geronimo Springs Museum Archives.)

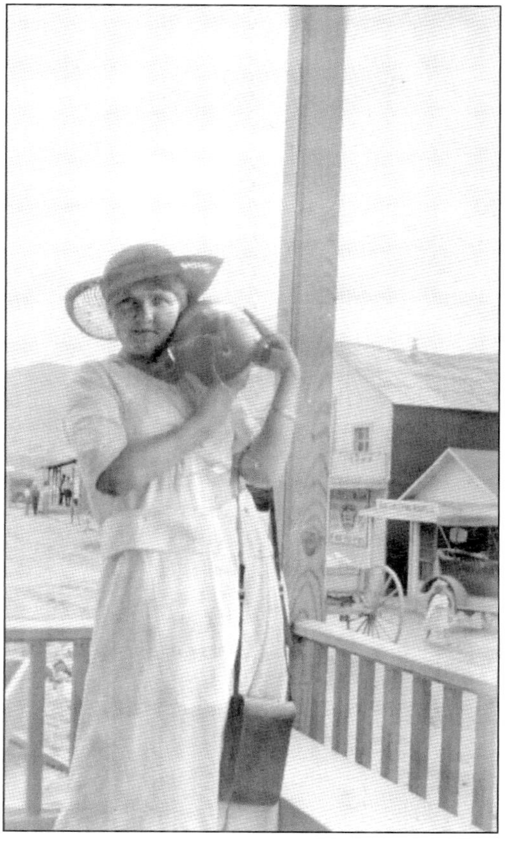

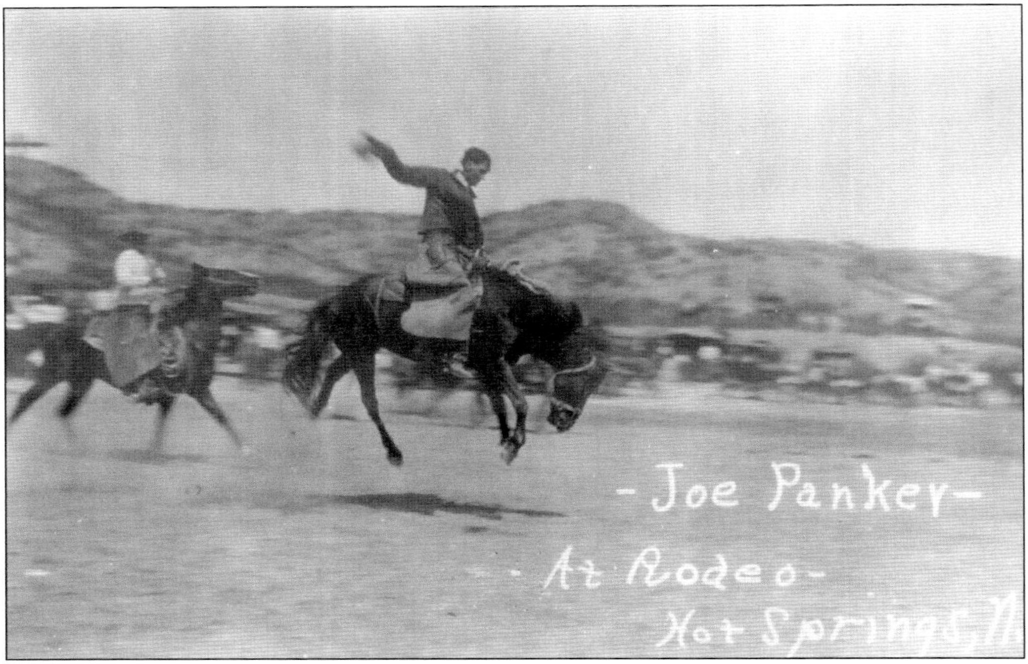

Cowboy Joe Pankey (above) loved to rodeo. Perhaps that is what attracted Edith Armer to this robust young man. Edith Armer would marry Pankey, and together they would build their ranch at the foothills of the San Mateo Mountains. Edith's mother had her own legacy of raising Angora goats. She became known as the "Angora Goat Queen of the United States," raising her goats in nearby Kingston, New Mexico. It was said that Joe was given his first cow and calf at his birth in 1892. On March 31, 1967, he received the New Mexico Cattle Growers' Association Cattleman of the Year Award. (Both, courtesy of Geronimo Springs Museum Archives.)

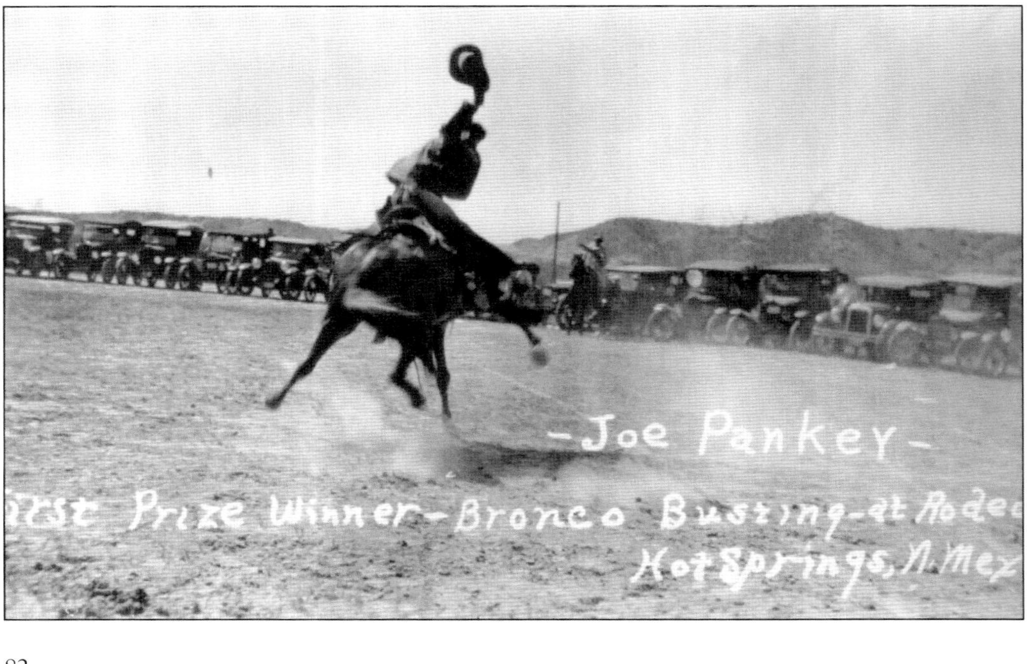

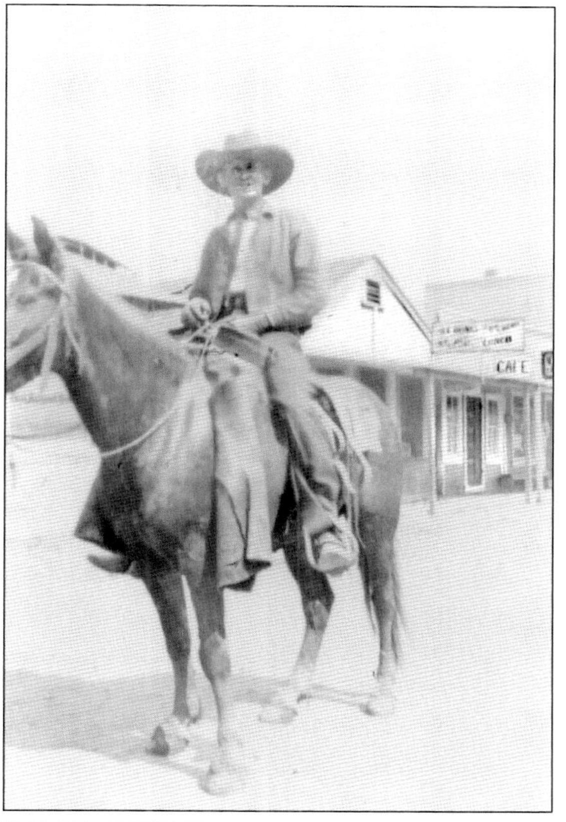

This picture shows Joe Pankey at a rodeo on Main Street in Hot Springs. In 1930, Joe owned the LM Bar Ranch in the Black Range with his brothers Bill, Lee, and Hugh. Joe had been born in Doña Ana County but started his ranch 27 miles north of Hot Springs in 1922. (Courtesy of Geronimo Springs Museum Archives.)

Not many people believe that cattle actually crossed Elephant Butte Dam, but the proof is in the picture. This is a very rare photograph that paints a scene depicting changing centuries. This is an event that will most likely never occur again, and people today can only speculate as to why the cattle were being driven across the dam.

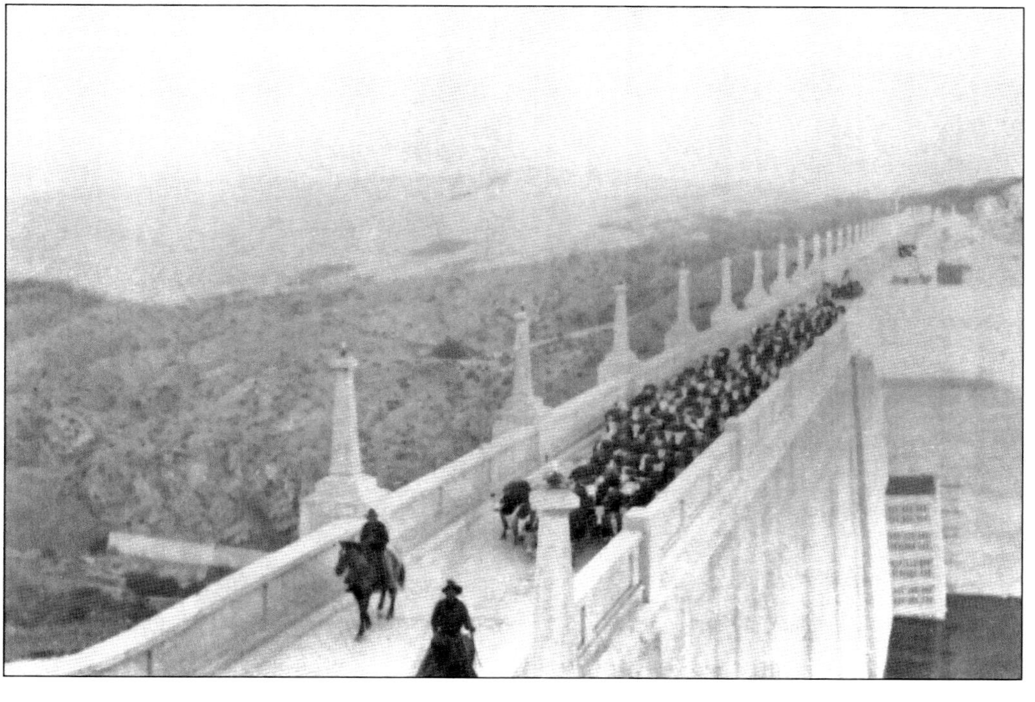

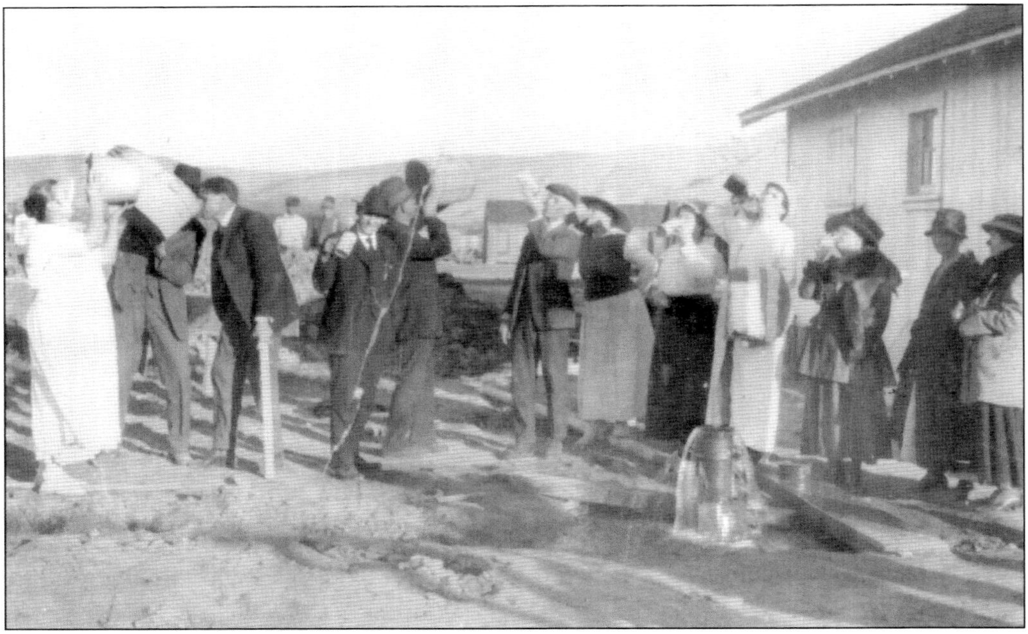

Around 1920, these individuals are drinking water from this hot spring "drinking well" by the cup, the bucket, and the bottle at the James Apartments. Reported to cure anything from rheumatism, arthritis, stomach, blood, and skin diseases, the hot springs attracted health seekers from all over, and the managers of the James Apartments were more than willing to rent them a room. (Courtesy of Geronimo Springs Museum Archives.)

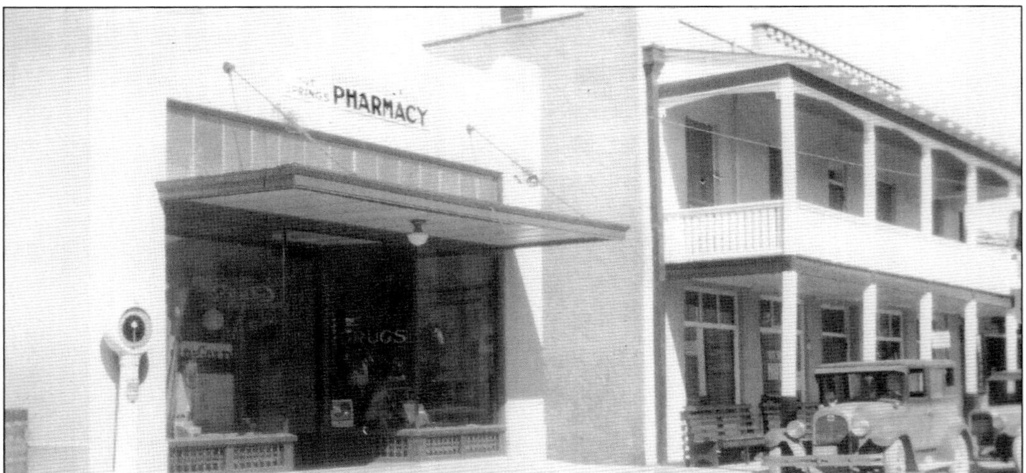

The left side of this 1926 picture shows the Hot Springs Pharmacy, and to the right is the Hot Springs Hotel. An item in the *Gallup Independent* of April 4, 1926, noted that Mrs. George Kraker and Mrs. Joe Asten were leaving at the end of the week for Hot Springs, New Mexico, and would be gone for one month. Perhaps they stayed in this hotel.

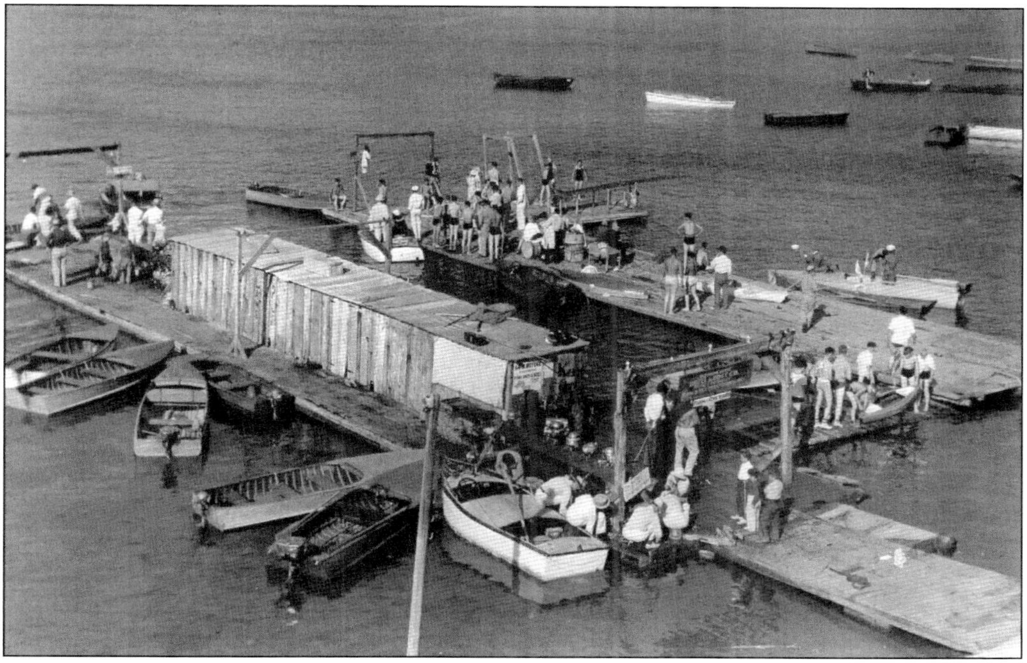

In the *Rio Grande Republican* of March 10, 1921, game warden J. F. O'Leary is quoted as saying that the bass are so thick in the lower end of Elephant Butte Lake that they are "fighting for places." The bass could be found in the shallow water, but they were rumored to practically disappear during fishing season. Who said that bass were not smart fish? George Sickles had the first and second concessions for fishing and boating after the dam was completed in 1916. In the *Albuquerque Journal* on March 18, 1952, Sickle noted that the Elephant Butte Lake had formerly been known as Lake M. B. Hall in honor of the engineer in charge of the Elephant Butte project.

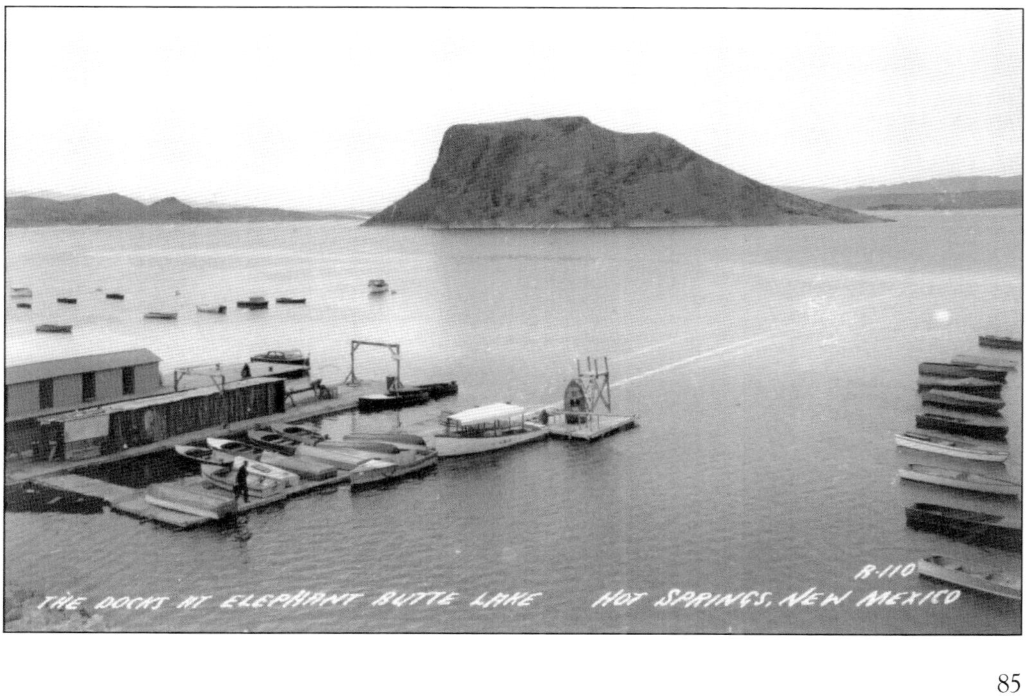

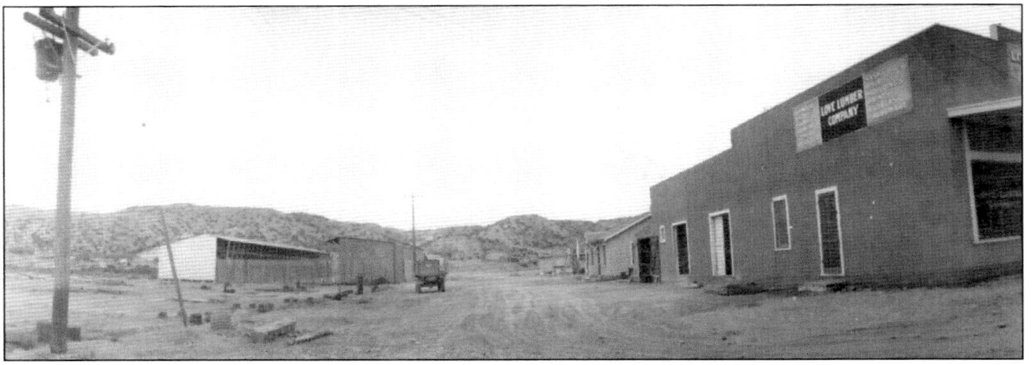

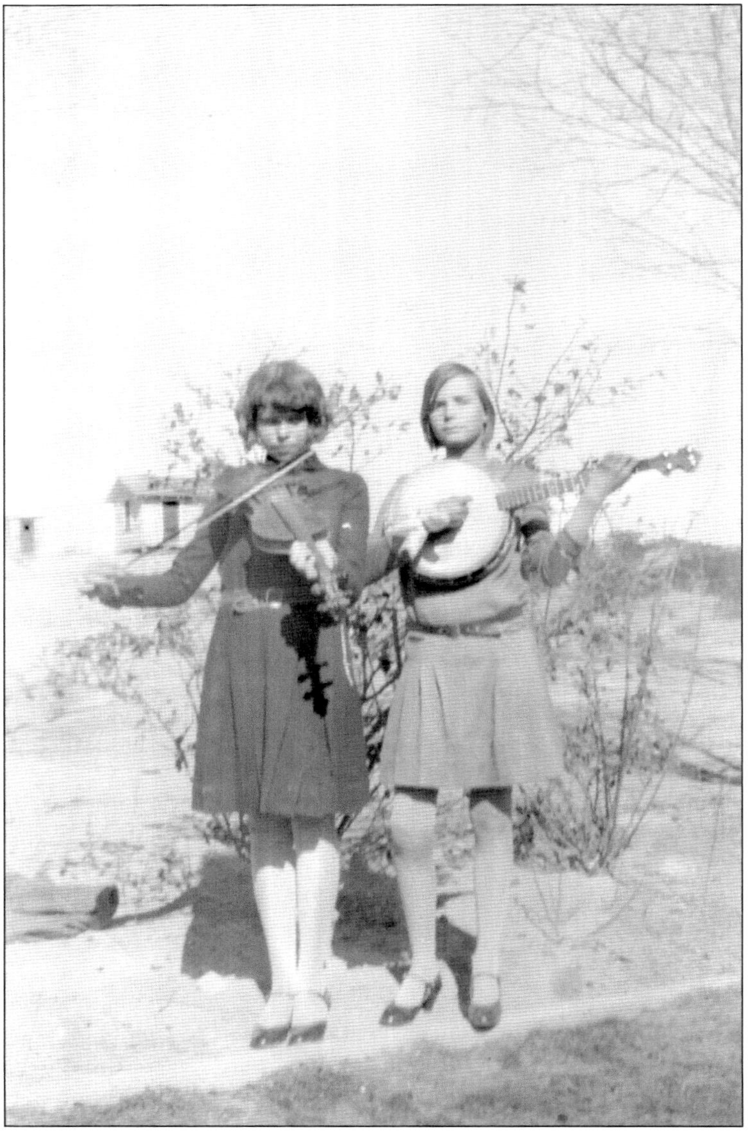

The above picture depicts the front of John E. Love's lumber company in Hot Springs. Charles C. Martin and his wife, Jennie, moved to Hot Springs in 1931 to work with John E. Love at the Love Lumber Company. Love passed away in 1934. (Courtesy of Charles "Chuck" Martin.)

Annette Smith and her friend Ruby are pictured here posing with their instruments. Annette Smith is responsible for both written and oral history of the early days of Hot Springs. As a young girl, she bathed in the water of the hot springs, noting that people were not allowed to bring soap, which would have made it an "official" bath.

These two young men, Ken and Frank Umberson, pose with their girlfriends on Main Street in the 1930s. As this was the period of the Great Depression, the mothers of these two girls were probably very happy that they had picked employed men with whom to run around. (Courtesy of Geronimo Springs Museum Archives.)

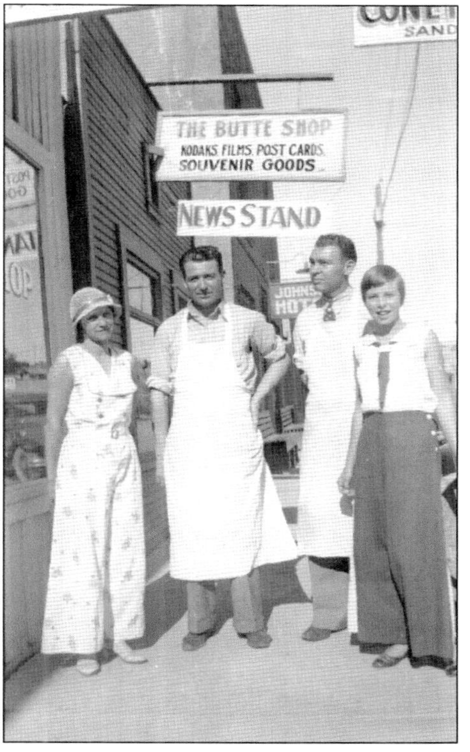

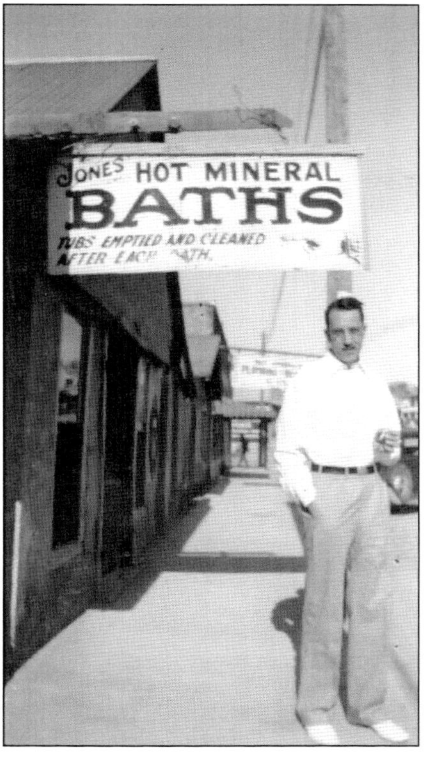

What is interesting about this picture is the sign that says, "Tubs emptied and cleaned after each bath." The bath owners were beginning to understand the idea of sanitation, which this young man and all of the other individuals that took a bath after him must have appreciated. (Courtesy of Geronimo Springs Museum Archives.)

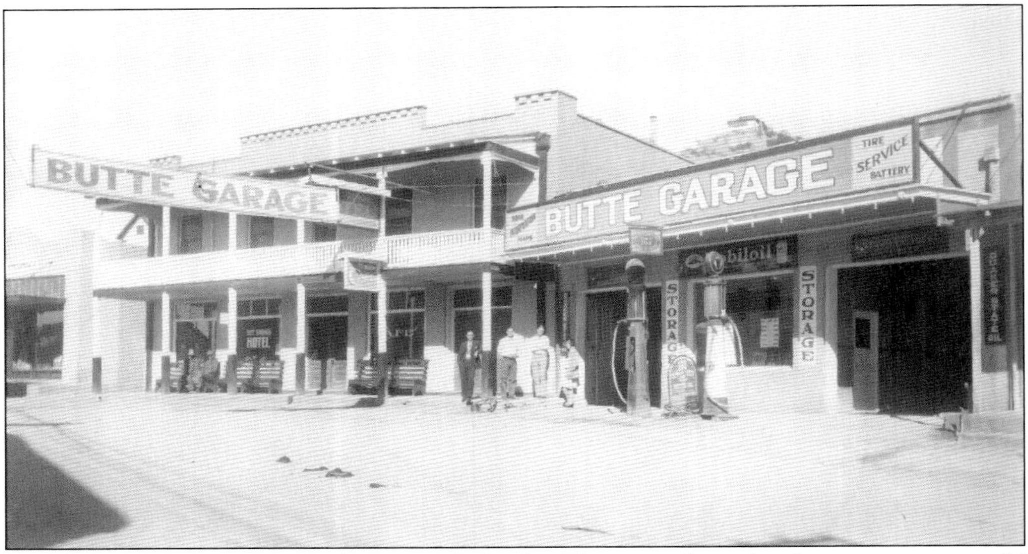

Butte Garage was built in 1919 by Grover Bolander. The tin-and-wooden-frame structure would be sold to Cecil Wilson in 1934 and operated as a garage as well as the first fire station in Hot Springs. It would become a Firestone Store in 1949 after it was sold to the Sullivans. (Courtesy of Geronimo Springs Museum Archives.)

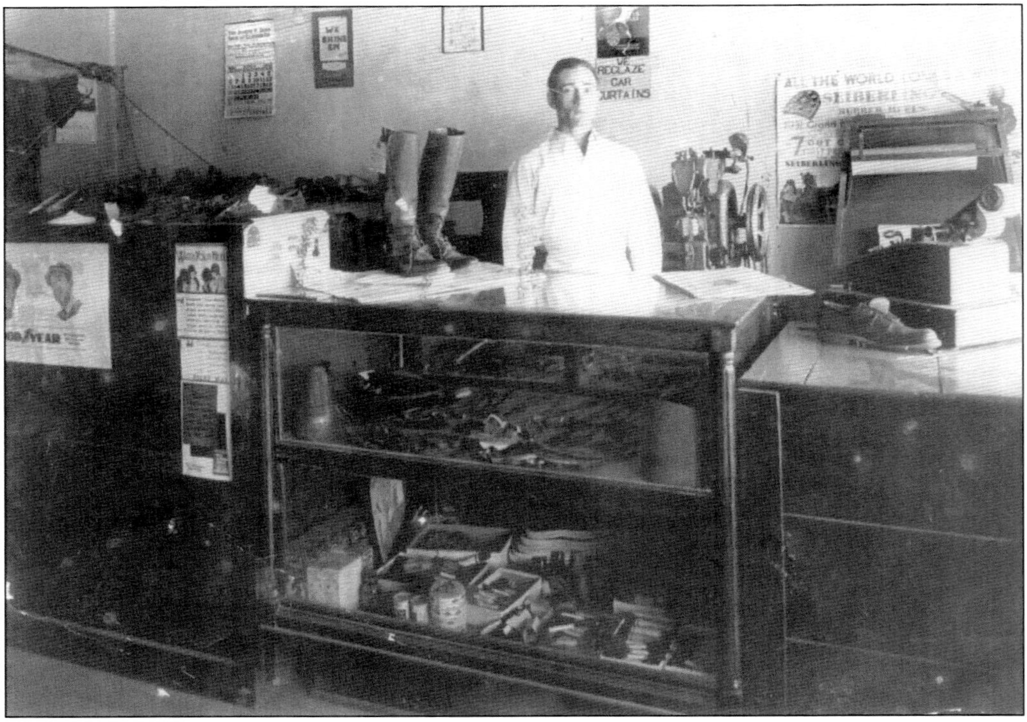

This picture shows Elmer Swinson in his shoe shop around 1932. The shop started out with no electricity but later became known as the Electric Shoe Shop. Hot Springs had many entrepreneurs that created businesses to fill a need for the residents and visitors of the area. (Courtesy of Geronimo Springs Museum Archives.)

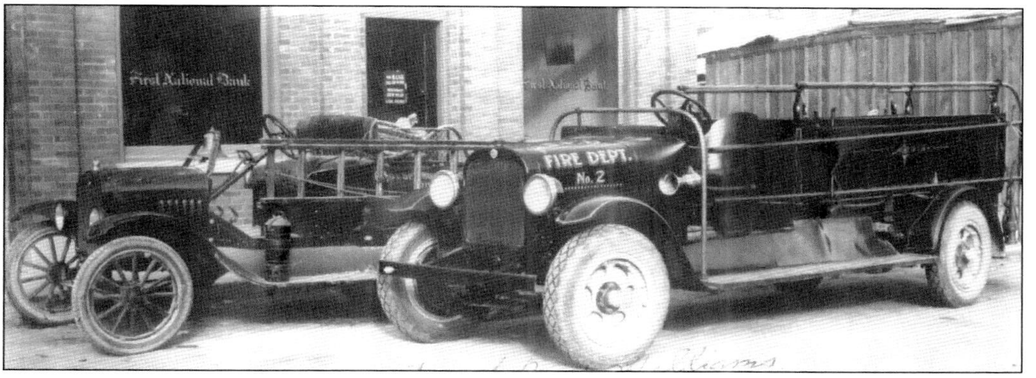

On the left is a 1923 Ford fire wagon, and on the right is a 1927 Dodge half-ton. In 1926, Leo Smith resigned as the fire chief of Hot Springs to become the mayor. Evidently he had a big influence in the building of a firehouse in 1927. (Courtesy of Geronimo Springs Museum Archives.)

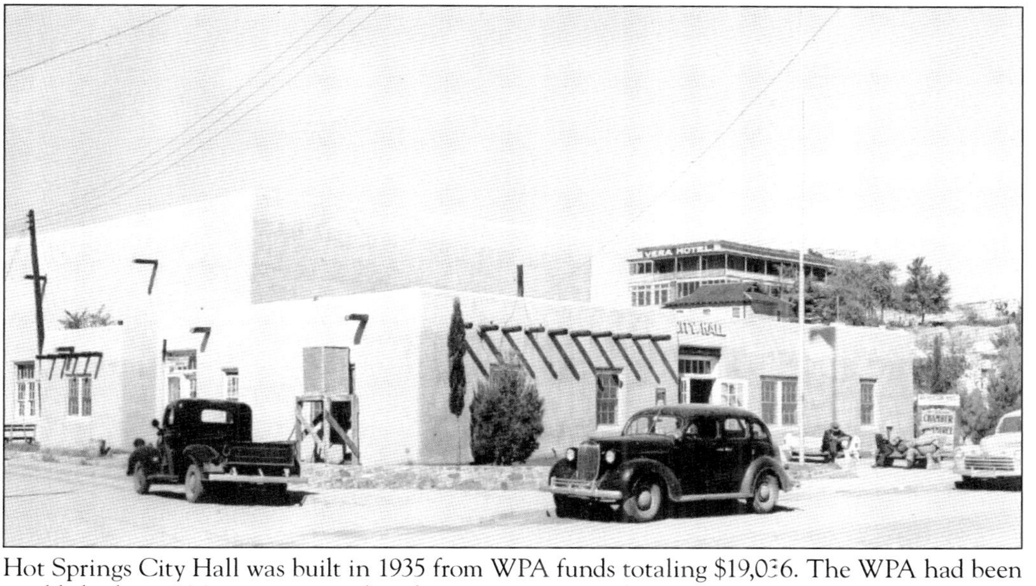

Hot Springs City Hall was built in 1935 from WPA funds totaling $19,036. The WPA had been established in 1935 to put unemployed Americans to work on public projects that would have lasting value to their communities. The architectural style shown here is called Pueblo Revival. Truth or Consequences City Hall was moved to another location in the early 1950s.

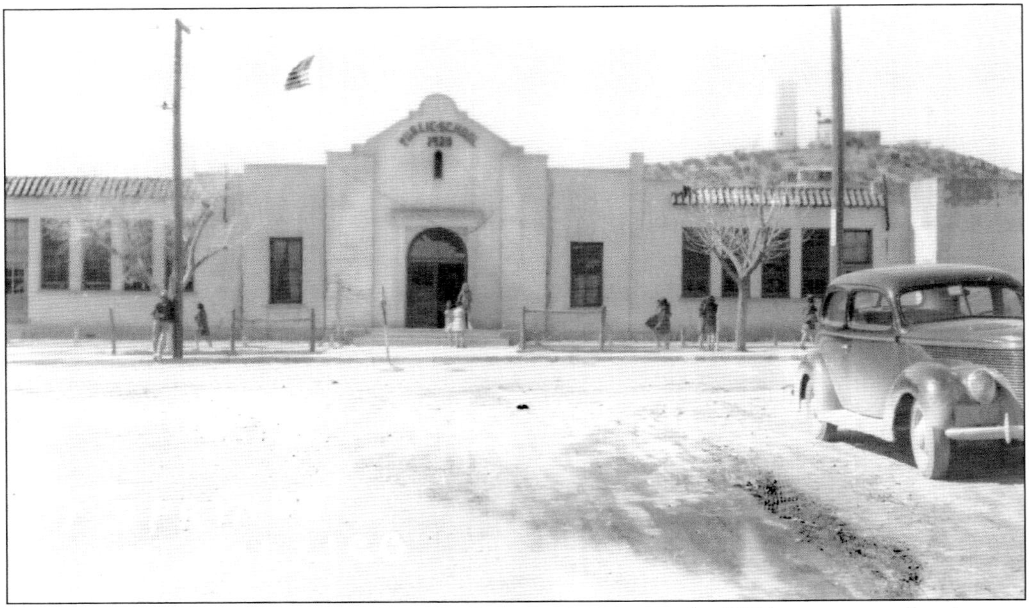

The town's first elementary school was built in 1923. During the WPA projects, schools were remodeled. These two photographs show the school after renowned architect Henry Trost renovated the building into the Pueblo Revival architectural style in 1937 and 1938. The building sat on Highway 85, which today is known as Date Street. This was the main highway connecting Socorro and Las Cruces through the town of Hot Springs. Eventually a tunnel was built under the busy highway, and a fence enclosed the school. The students would cross under the highway through the tunnel; the fence kept any wayward students from getting run over. Trost was able to keep the cost of the 10,233-square-foot building to $19,036, paid for by WPA funds.

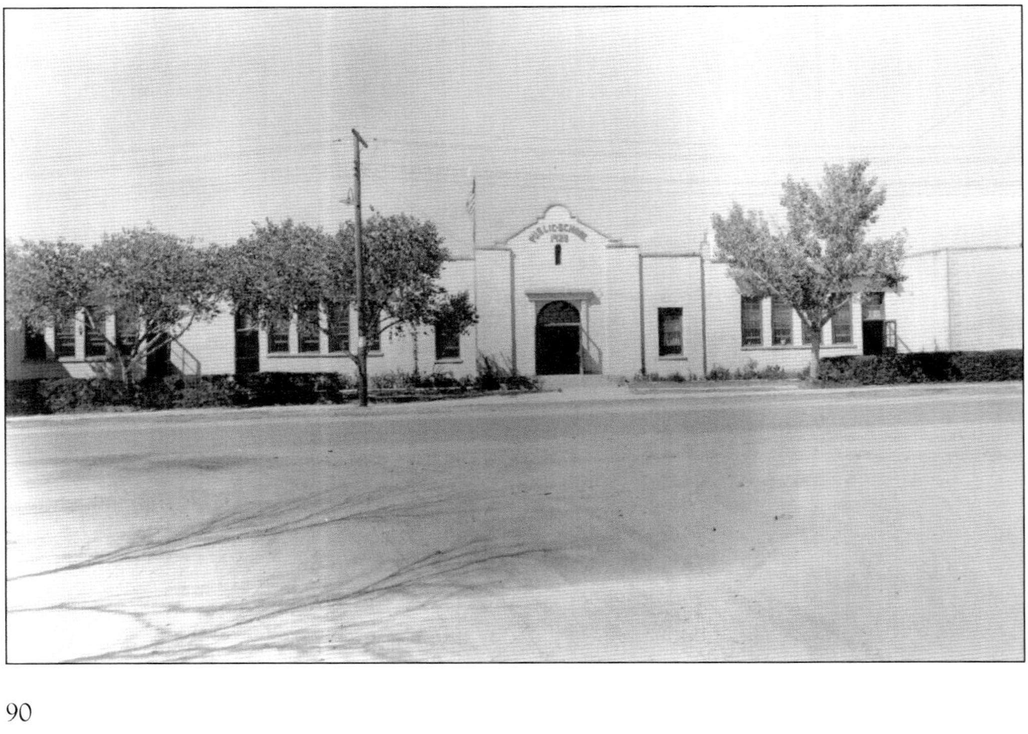

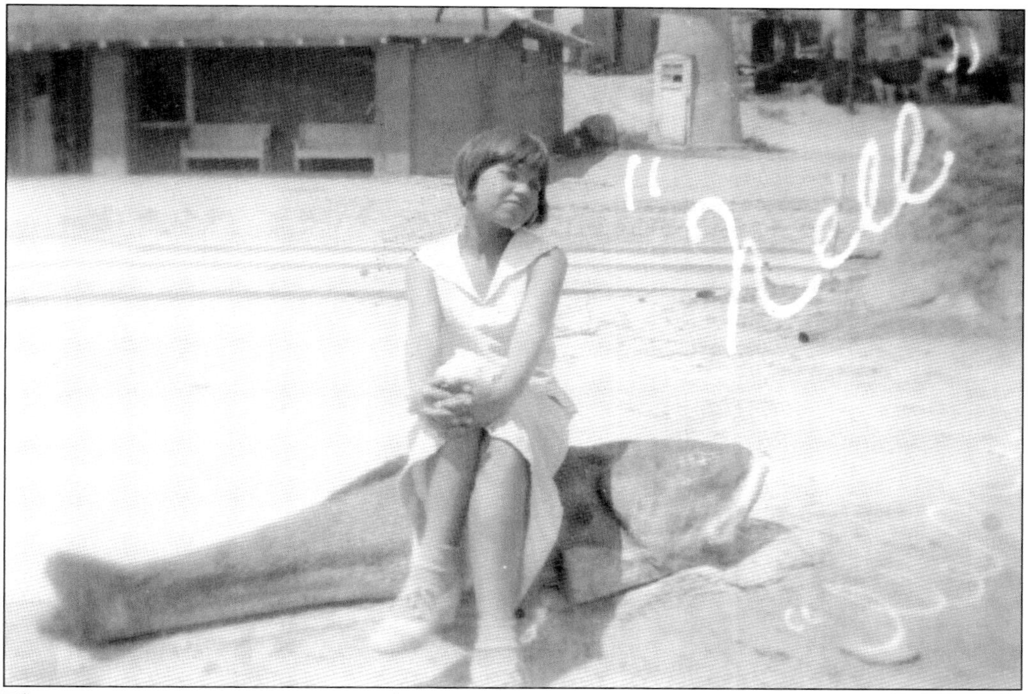

This sassy young woman appears to be enjoying herself as she poses for the camera sitting on a gigantic catfish. Reports still circulate today of giant catfish lurking beneath the waters of Elephant Butte Lake. There must have been quite a fish fry when this specimen was cut up and cooked.

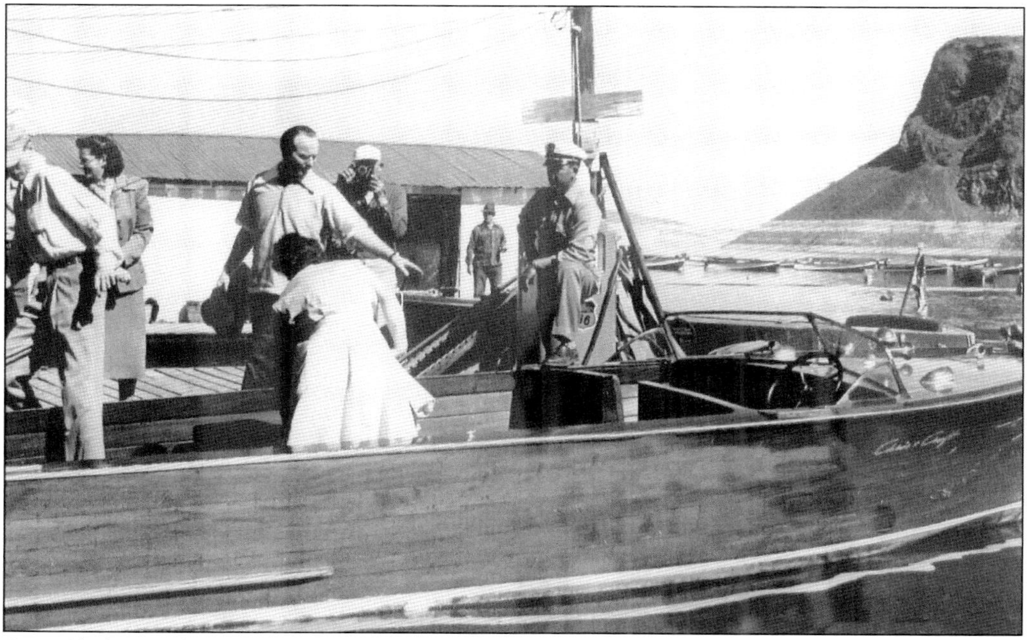

Gov. Clyde Tingley owned a Chris-Craft that he stored at Elephant Butte Lake. He would often come down and take some of the children from the Carrie Tingley Hospital for Crippled Children out for a boat ride or to go fishing for the day. (Courtesy of Dam Site Resort.)

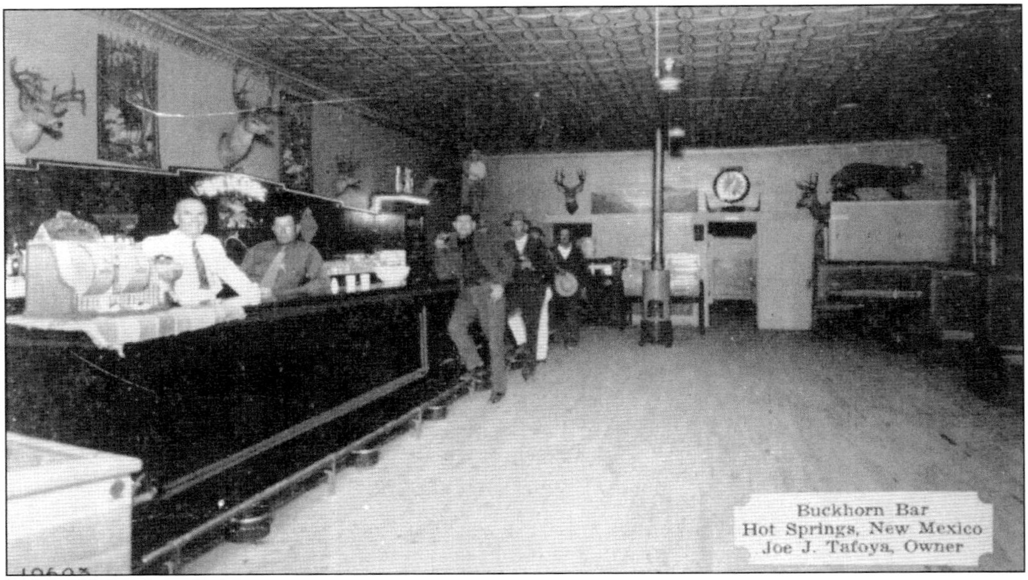

The Buckhorn Bar was owned by Joe Tafoya. It was inevitable that bars, gambling, and prostitution would be present in the small town of Hot Springs. The Buckhorn Bar was a popular bar for those wanting to talk about the fish, get a game of cards going, or simply dance to the music. (Courtesy of Charles "Chuck" Martin.)

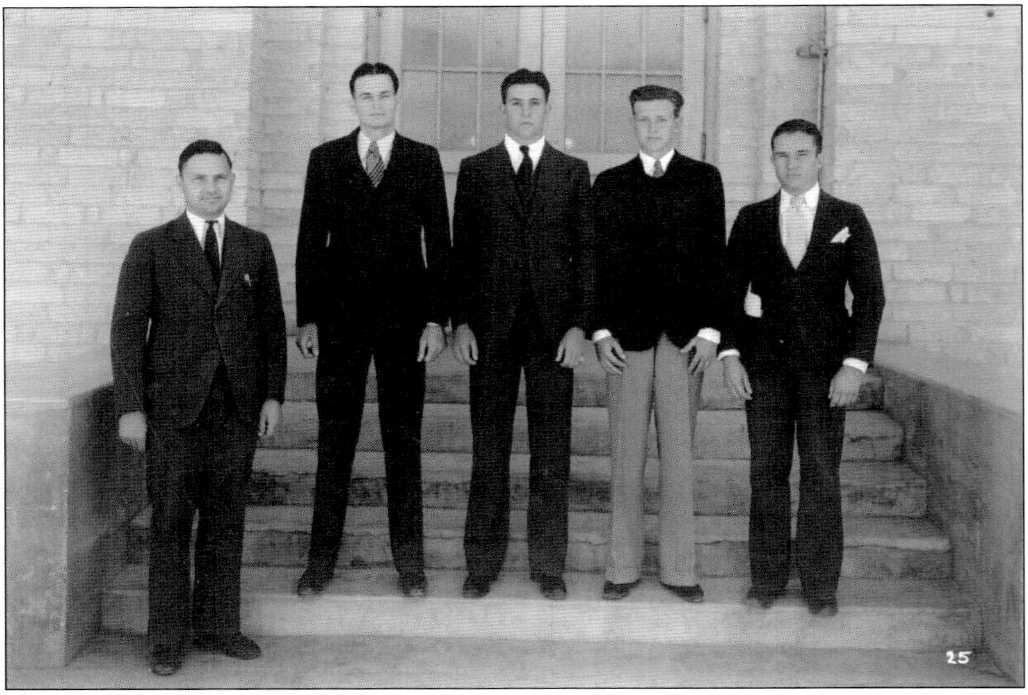

The 1934 Hot Springs High School male quartet was directed by a Mr. Robbins. Pictured from left to right are Robbins, Pete Taylor, Raymond Keithly, Pat Rea, and Wallace Darr. The 1934 class motto was "Be on the Square." Despite hard times of the Depression, these young men were dressed for success.

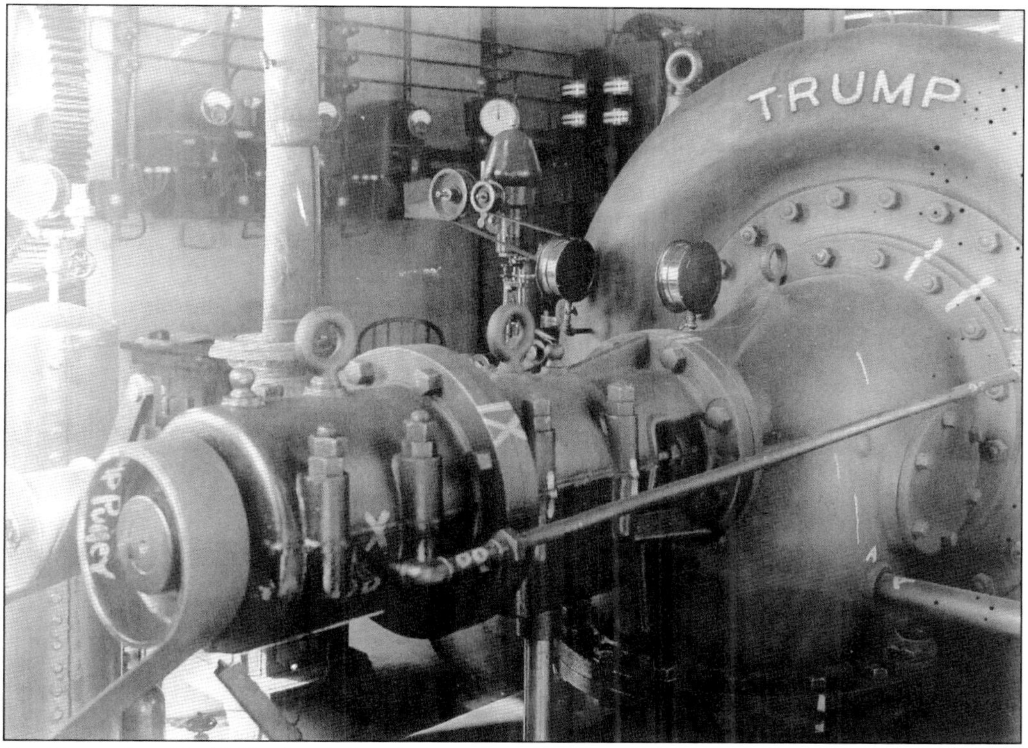

On November 22, 1940, the *Gallup Independent* told its readers that when the turbines at the Elephant Butte Dam power plant began to hum, cheap electricity would become a reality. More than half of the power up for sale would go to the El Paso Electric Company, which served customers in Texas and New Mexico. The U.S. Department of the Interior had drawn up contracts with the El Paso firm and the other utility firms in the area to distribute half of the dam's power output to Texas and half to New Mexico. The plant was estimated to have an average output of eight million kilowatt hours up for sale.

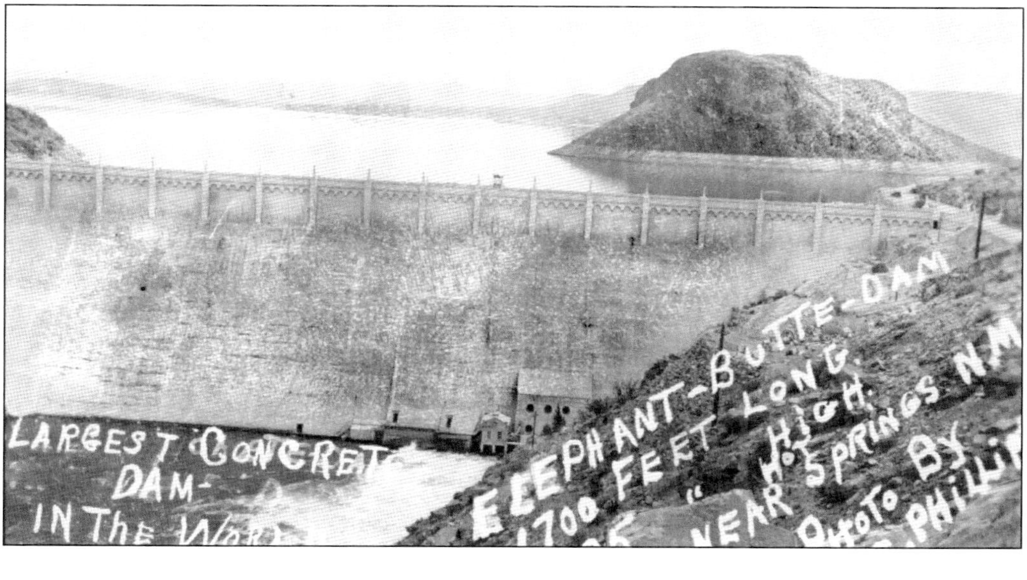

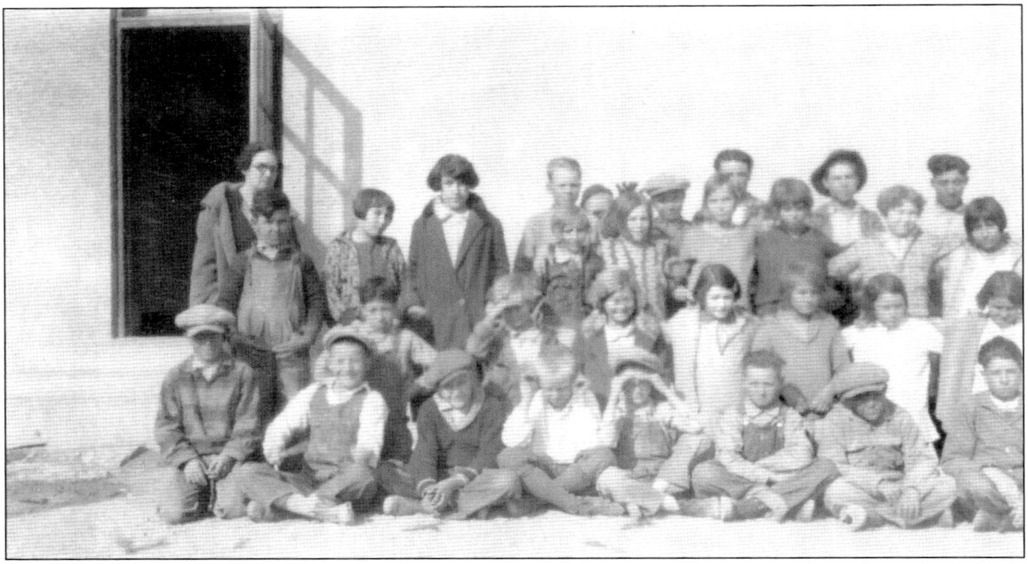

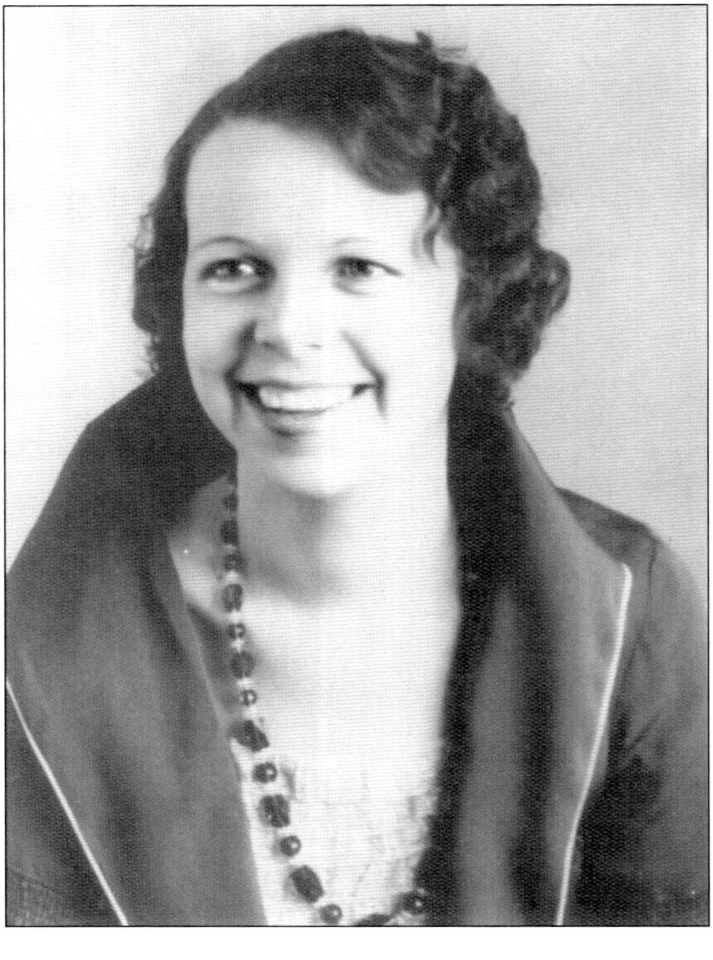

These youngsters are in the fifth grade. By 1925, it was mandated that all schools had to be open for eight months out of the year. Before this time, schools were only open seven months a year, which allowed students to help out during the planting seasons.

Marie Landers was the Hot Springs High School librarian. She claimed to have read every book in the school's library. She was married to school superintendent G. V. Landers and was also the sponsor of the senior class. In 1934, she directed the senior play, *Big Business*.

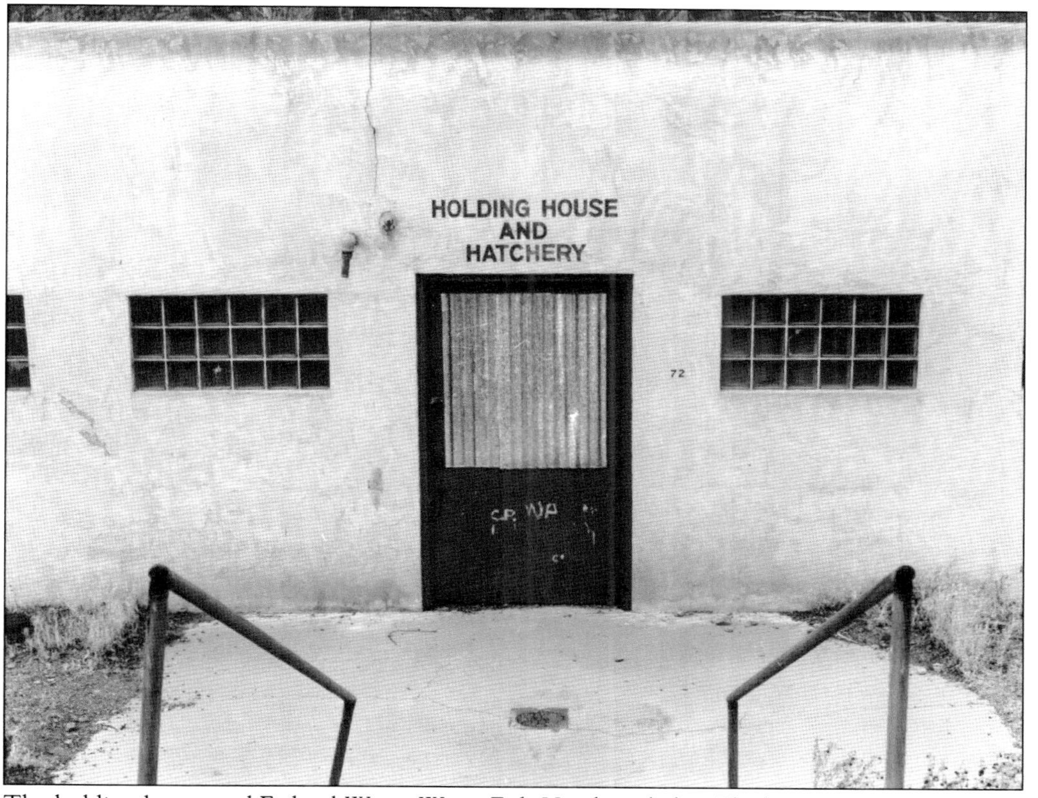

The holding house and Federal Warm Water Fish Hatchery below Elephant Butte were built by the men of the Civilian Conservation Corps (CCC) under the supervision of Thomas F. Nelson. Nelson worked as the facility's first superintendent. Although now closed, the hatchery reared trout and warm-water fish that included channel catfish, blue gill, largemouth bass, sunfish, walleye, northern pike, white bass, crappie, and more.

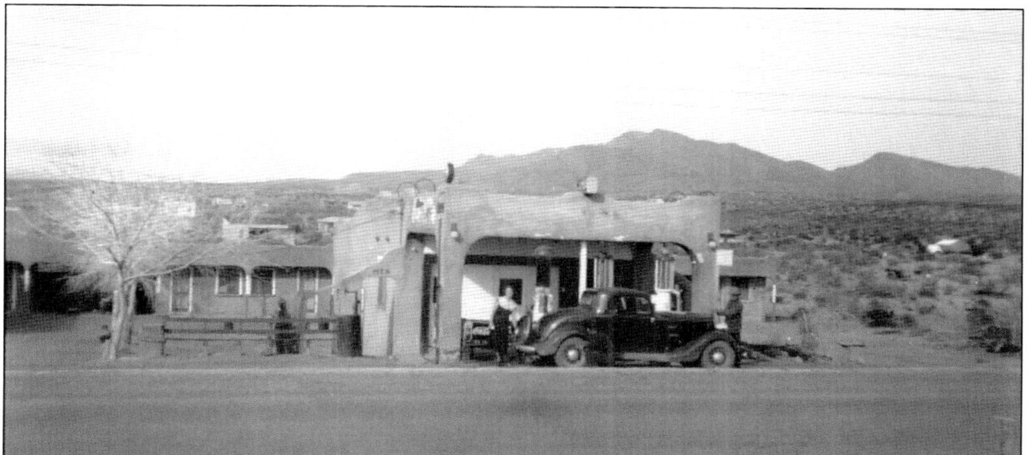

Le Grande Court, shown here, stood at 700 North Date Street in the 1930s. Pearl Wallace is seen at the back of the car. Car courts as well as hotels and motels were plentiful in the town during the 1930s and 1940s. (Courtesy of Geronimo Springs Museum Archives.)

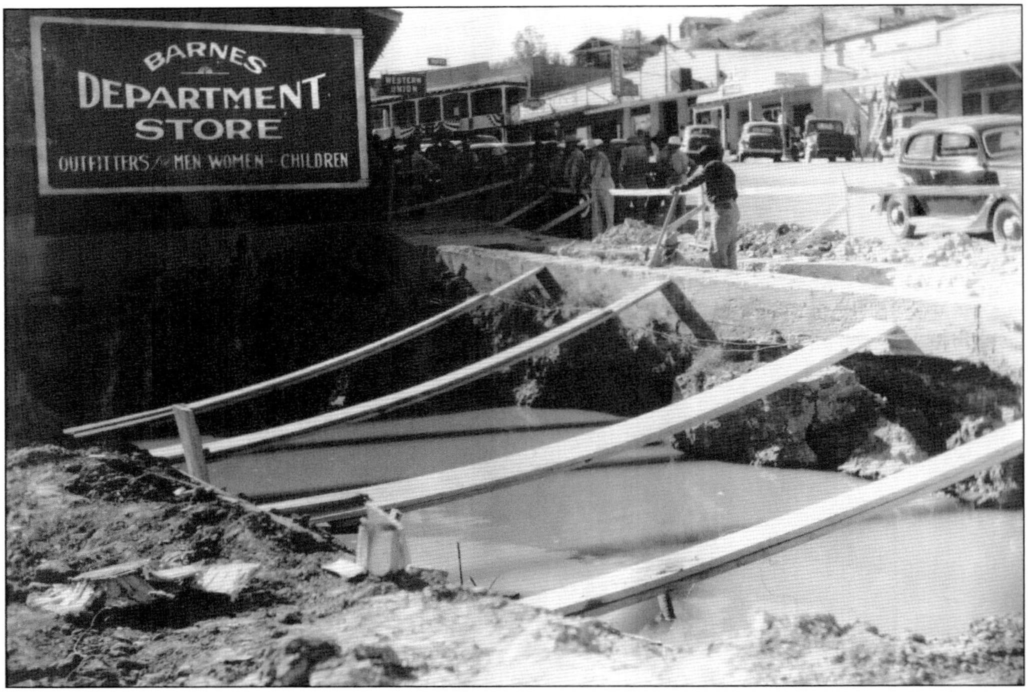

As seen in this photograph, the water of the hot springs below the construction site for the post office necessitated the structure being built on a raised-concrete platform. The Government Springs, later renamed Geronimo Springs, was located directly across from the post office. The post office was built in 1937 from funds and labor under the WPA. (Courtesy of Geronimo Springs Museum Archives.)

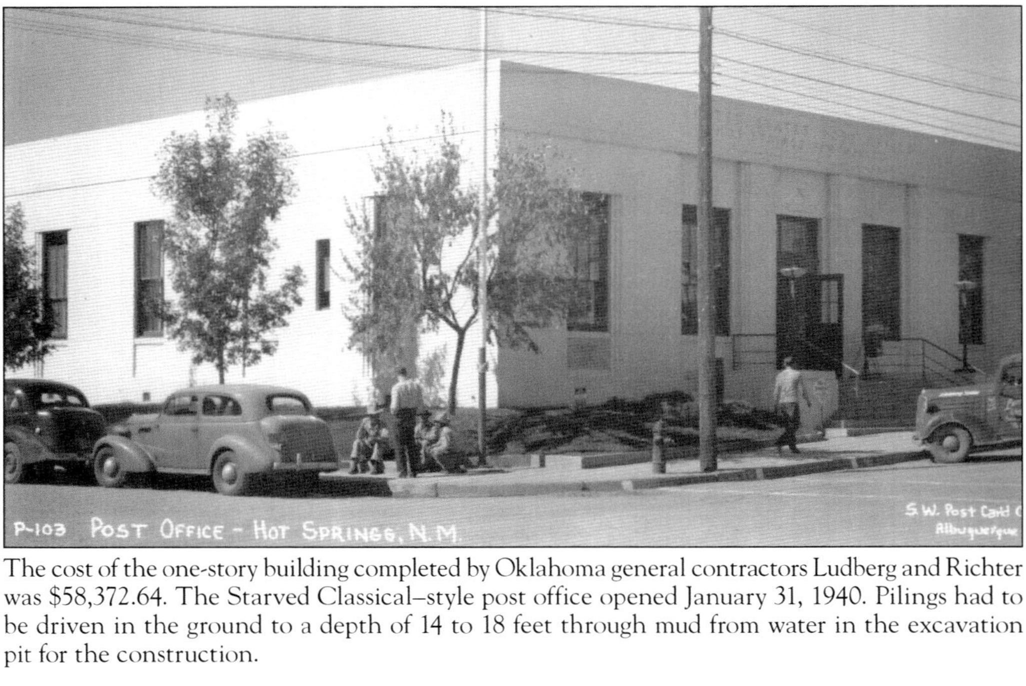

The cost of the one-story building completed by Oklahoma general contractors Ludberg and Richter was $58,372.64. The Starved Classical–style post office opened January 31, 1940. Pilings had to be driven in the ground to a depth of 14 to 18 feet through mud from water in the excavation pit for the construction.

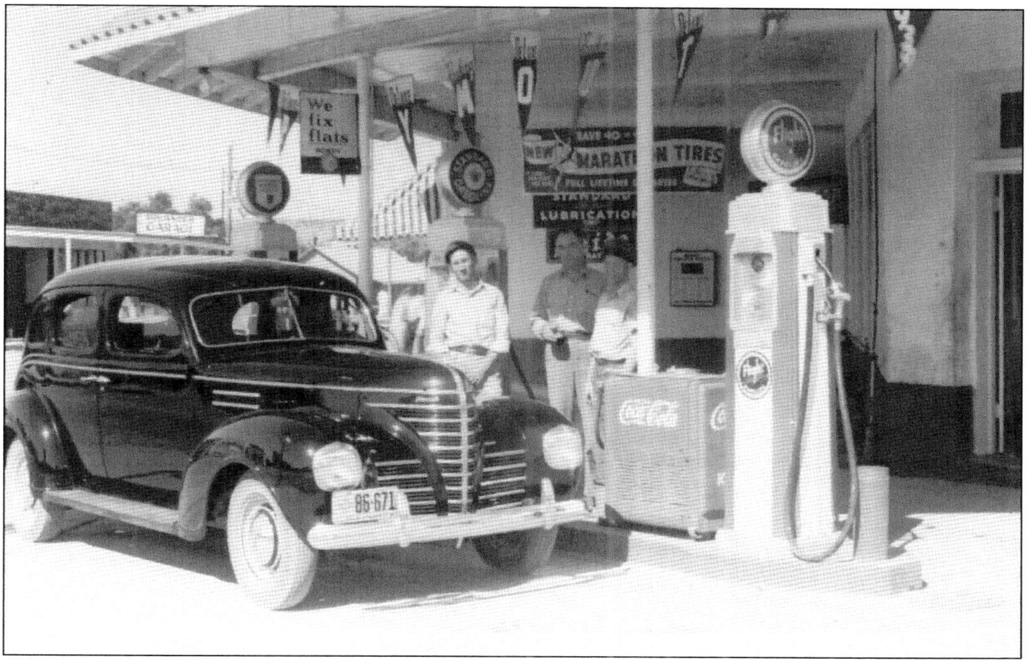

Wilson's Motor Company could be reached by dialing the number 33. In 1932, Flight gasoline, sold at Wilson's Motor Company, cost 13¢ a gallon. Wilson Motor Company also fixed flats. Notice the man in the middle holding a bottle of soda. Soda bottles were made of glass in 1932. The men on both sides of the gentleman in the middle appear to be the service station attendants. These young men would not only pump customers' gas but also would also wash their windshields and take their money. (Both, courtesy of Geronimo Springs Museum Archives.)

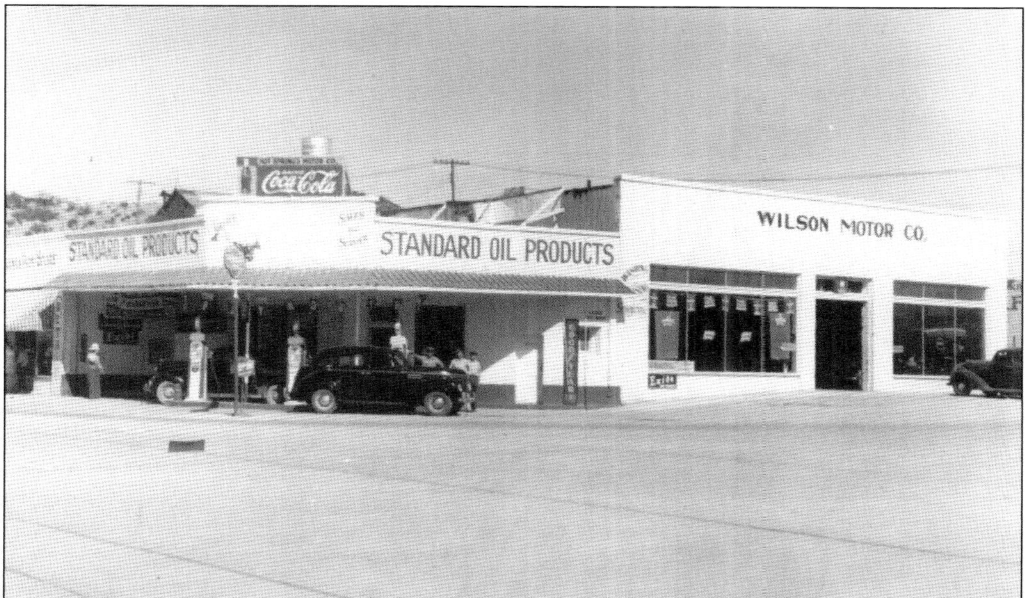

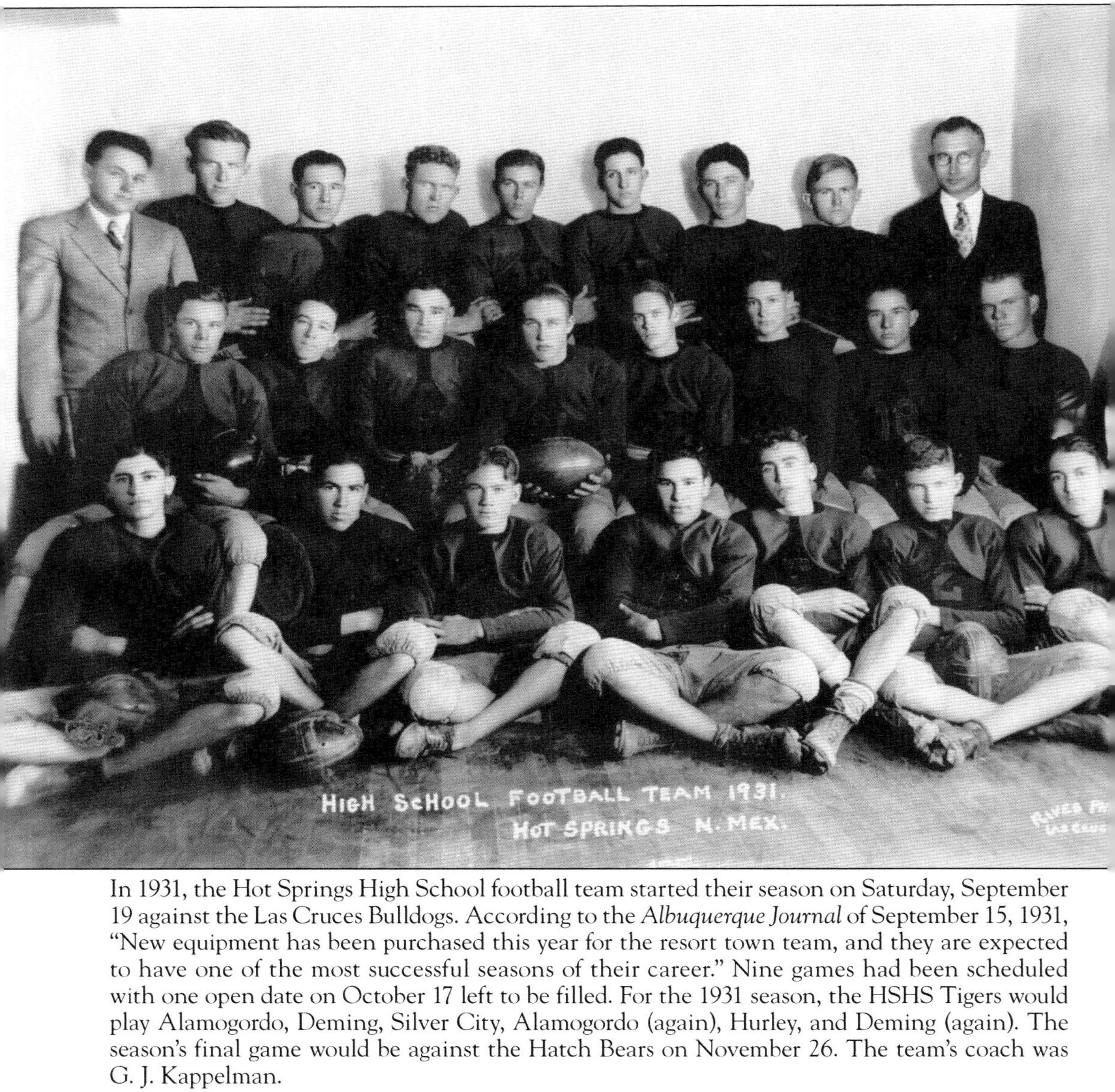

In 1931, the Hot Springs High School football team started their season on Saturday, September 19 against the Las Cruces Bulldogs. According to the *Albuquerque Journal* of September 15, 1931, "New equipment has been purchased this year for the resort town team, and they are expected to have one of the most successful seasons of their career." Nine games had been scheduled with one open date on October 17 left to be filled. For the 1931 season, the HSHS Tigers would play Alamogordo, Deming, Silver City, Alamogordo (again), Hurley, and Deming (again). The season's final game would be against the Hatch Bears on November 26. The team's coach was G. J. Kappelman.

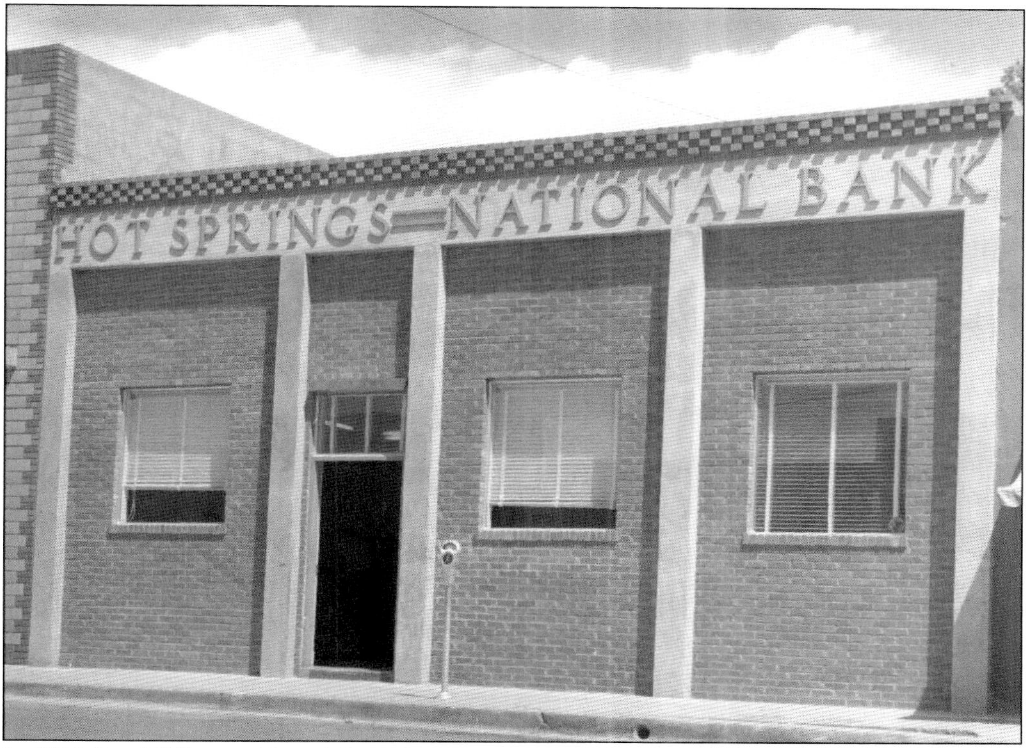

In 1934, Rex Williams, 19, and Otto Cox, 20, robbed the Hot Springs National Bank, above. Williams had been a Hot Springs football star, and Cox was a former HSHS student. The only motive given by the boys was that "they needed the money." Residents of Hot Springs were shocked as it was said that Williams came from a good family. (Courtesy of Geronimo Springs Museum Archives.)

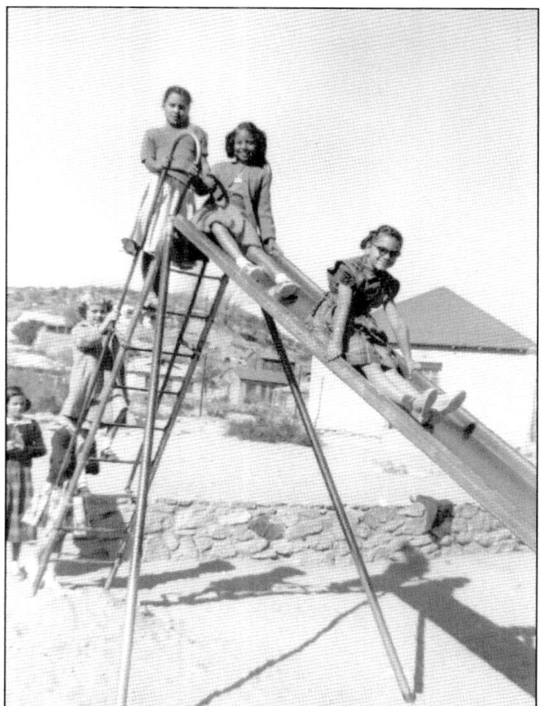

These young women are enjoying the slide at the elementary school that was located on Date Street. In the background is Water Tank Hill. The building was the music room. The school district had been supporting music in their curriculum since 1918. No wonder the yearly fiddler's contest is held in Truth or Consequences. (Courtesy of Geronimo Springs Museum Archives.)

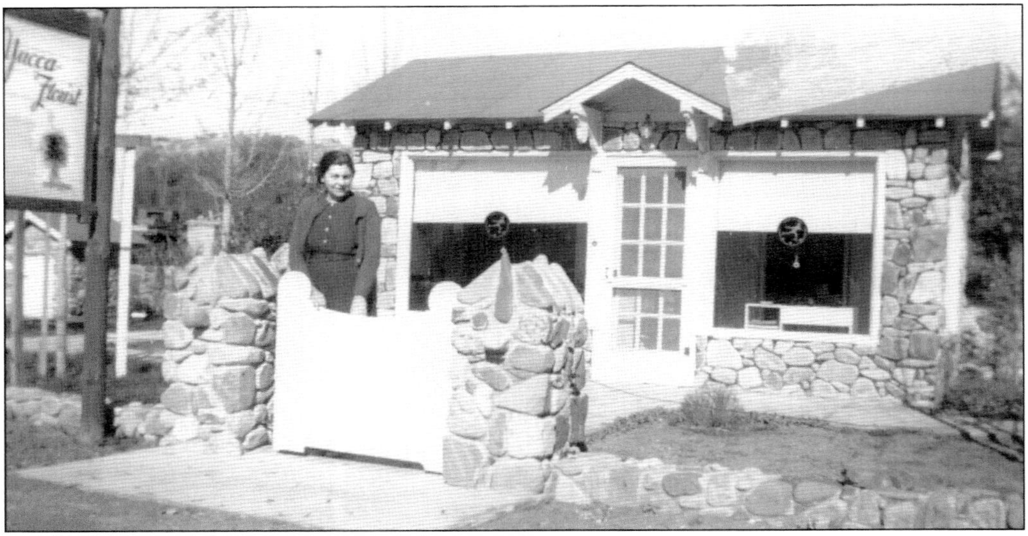

Helen Watson-Morgan was both the owner and the operator of the Yucca Florist. The shop, seen here in 1937, was located on East Riverside Drive. Jewell Glenn Mims built the old dike road, which would eventually become Riverside Drive, because he did not want to drive by the Pine Knot Bar. (Courtesy of Geronimo Springs Museum Archives.)

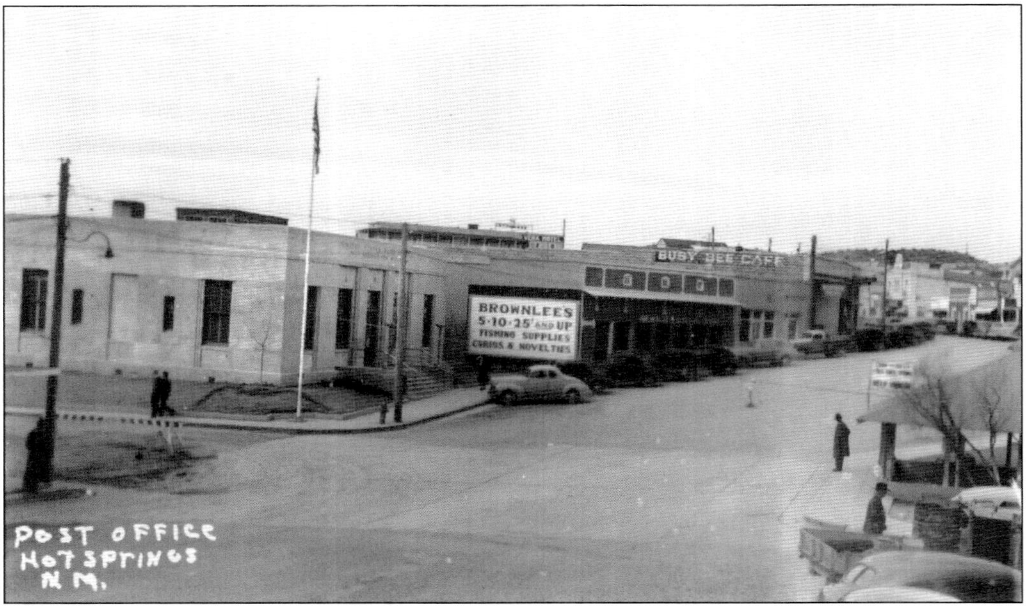

Charlie Gunter opened the Busy Bee Café, located just down from the post office. It was a popular eating place for both residents and visitors. There was also Brownlee's, where fishing supplies, curios, and novelties could be bought. The September 9, 1938, issue of the *Las Vegas Optic* noted that Hot Springs would receive $8,250 of WPA funds to create sidewalks and curbs.

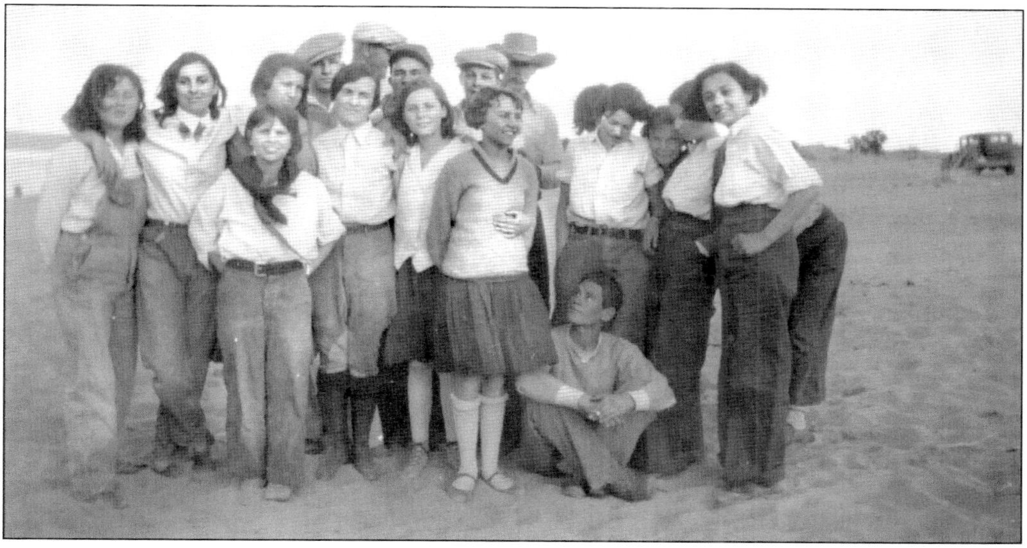

Members of the Hot Springs High School freshman class are shown on the beach at Elephant Butte Lake on April 6, 1931. In the 1930s, money was scarce, and unemployment was running as high as 25 percent. Though these were hard times due to the Depression, these young faces appear oblivious to the world's affairs.

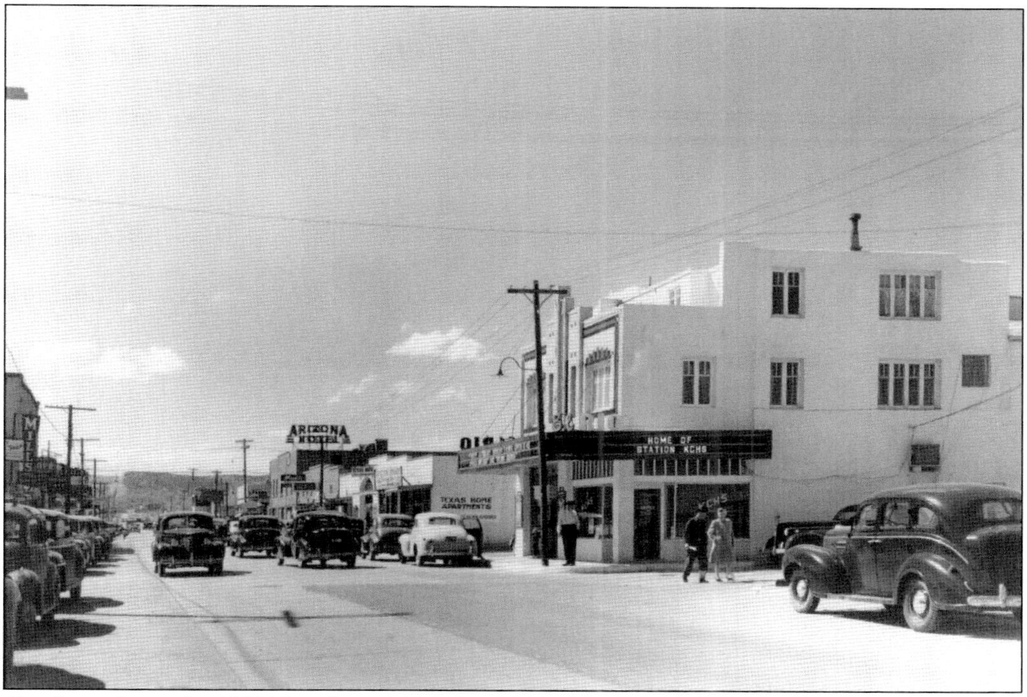

On the right is the KCHS radio station, the Texas Home Apartments, and then the Arizona Hotel. In 1964, Mr. and Mrs. Jim Landers purchased the radio station along with the Ward Apartments on Foch Street. Mrs. Landers's brother, Neil Baird, would run the station. The radio station still serves Truth or Consequences and surrounding areas. (Courtesy of Geronimo Springs Museum Archives.)

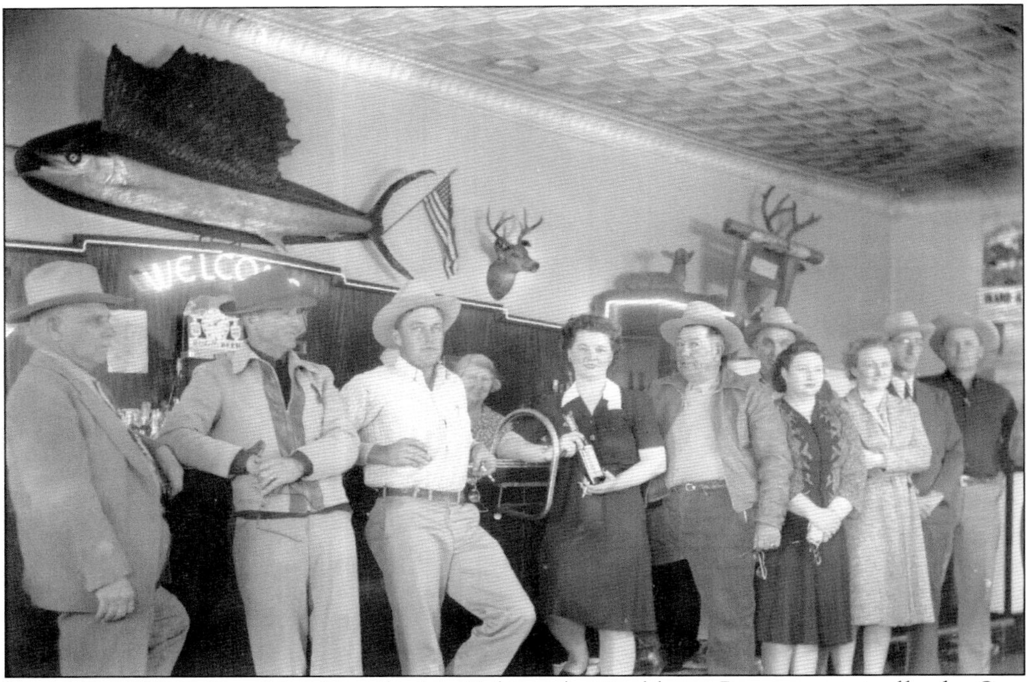

Located on Main Street and run by Joe Tafoya, the Buckhorn Bar was originally the Star Saloon. Joe's daughter, Cecilia Tafoya Cleveland, would later operate the bar. Cecilia Tafoya Cleveland would go on to serve as New Mexico secretary of state. (Courtesy of Geronimo Springs Museum Archives.)

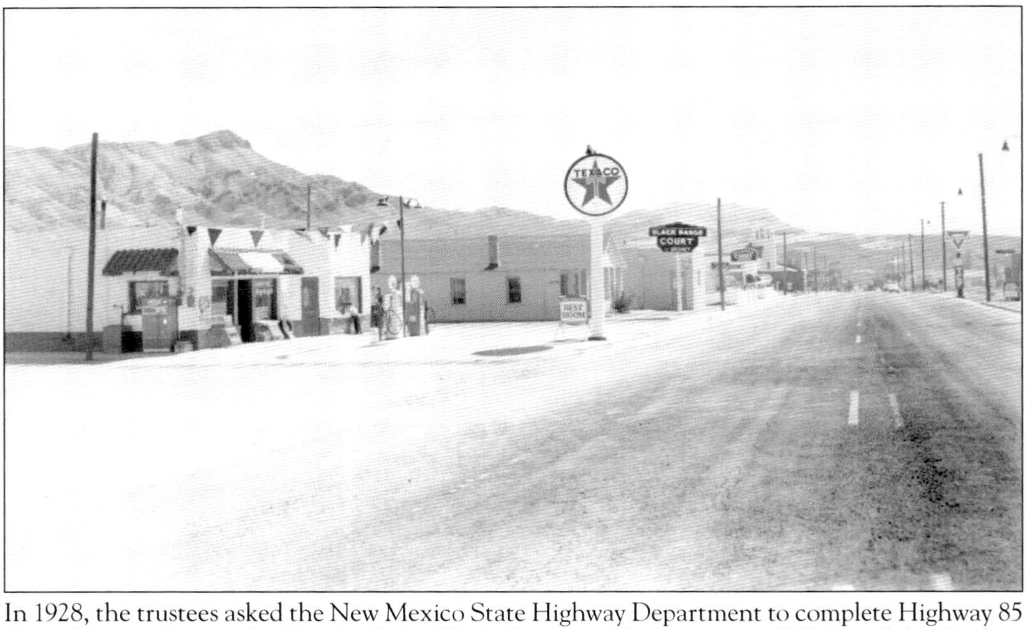

In 1928, the trustees asked the New Mexico State Highway Department to complete Highway 85 through town. During the New Deal, the Works Progress Administration (WPA) and the Civilian Conservation Corps (CCC) paved roads. Even today many of the sidewalks have the original WPA symbol and date on them. (Courtesy of Geronimo Springs Museum Archives.)

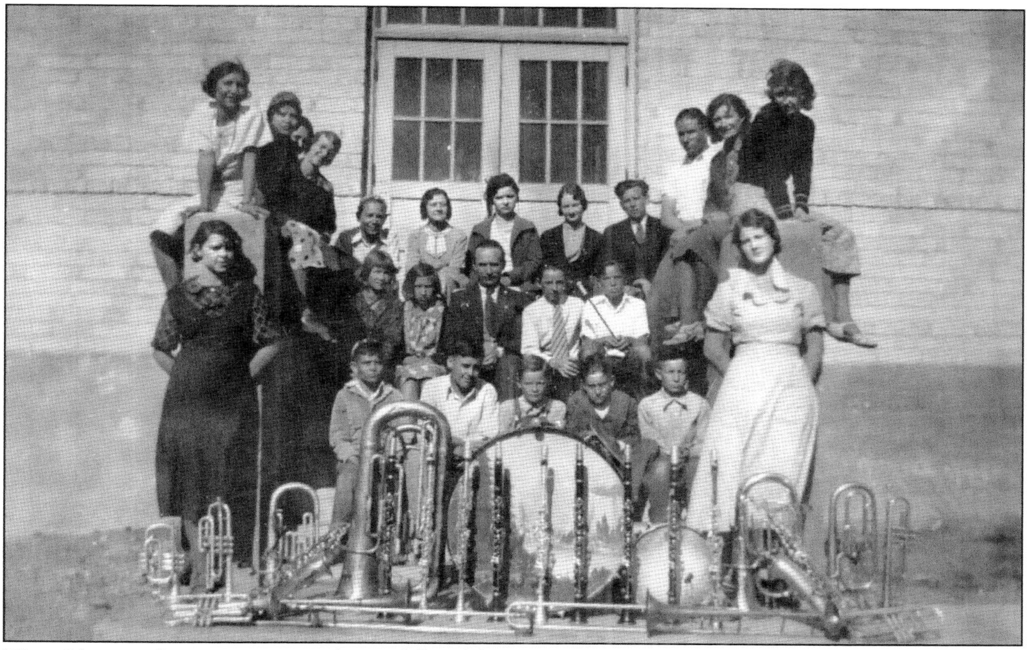

The older gentleman sitting in the middle of this group of Hot Springs High School band students was Sovereign Anderson, a member of the Woodmen of the World. The New Mexico-Mexico camp convention was held at Hot Springs, and these high school musicians were said to have played several difficult pieces in a very pleasing manner, receiving applause and praise from the delegates.

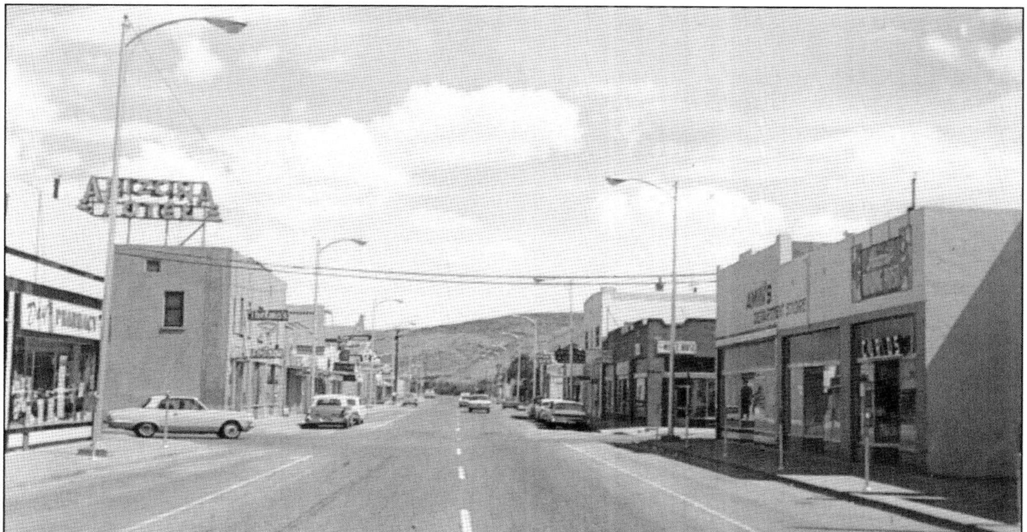

On the right is Amin's Department Store, and on the left is Day's Pharmacy. Just down from the pharmacy was the Arizona Hotel. Bars could be found on both sides of the street.

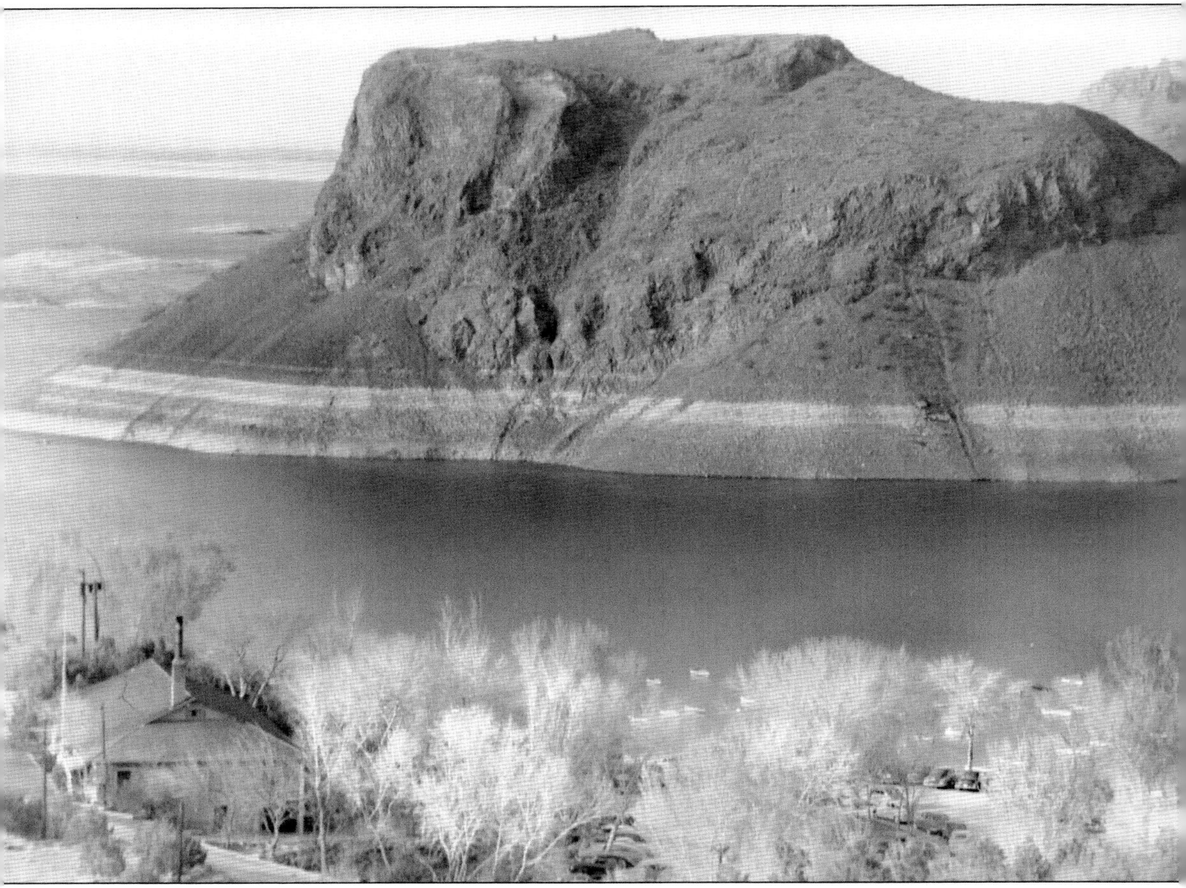

Looking at the left side of the land rising from the middle of Elephant Butte Lake, it is obvious why the butte got its name. Sitting on the water's edge is the U.S. Bureau of Reclamation office. In 1911, the structure served as the administration and engineering office for the construction of the Elephant Butte Dam. Today the building has been remodeled to not only add modern amenities but also to preserve the history of the original structure as a bed and breakfast and conference area. Visitors can stay in the rooms that have been decorated with antiques. (Courtesy of Dam Site Resort.)

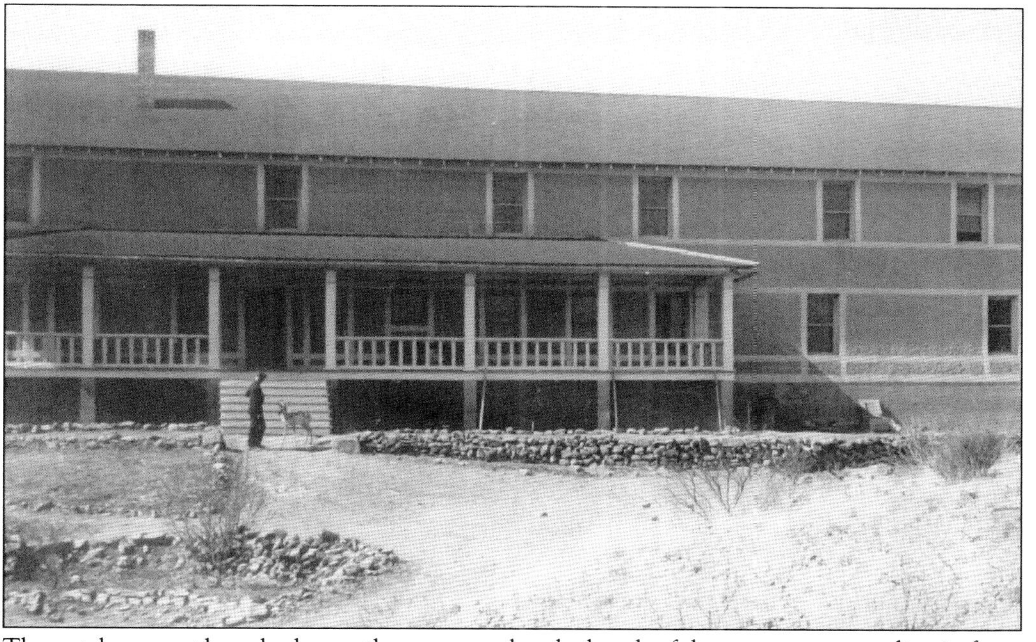

The antelope must have had more than one meal at the hands of the young man standing in front of the Hotel Elephant Butte. When the CCC worked at Elephant Butte during the New Deal, they put in roads, planted trees and shrubs, built boat docks, and constructed stone stairways and spiral walks. (Courtesy of Dam Site Resort.)

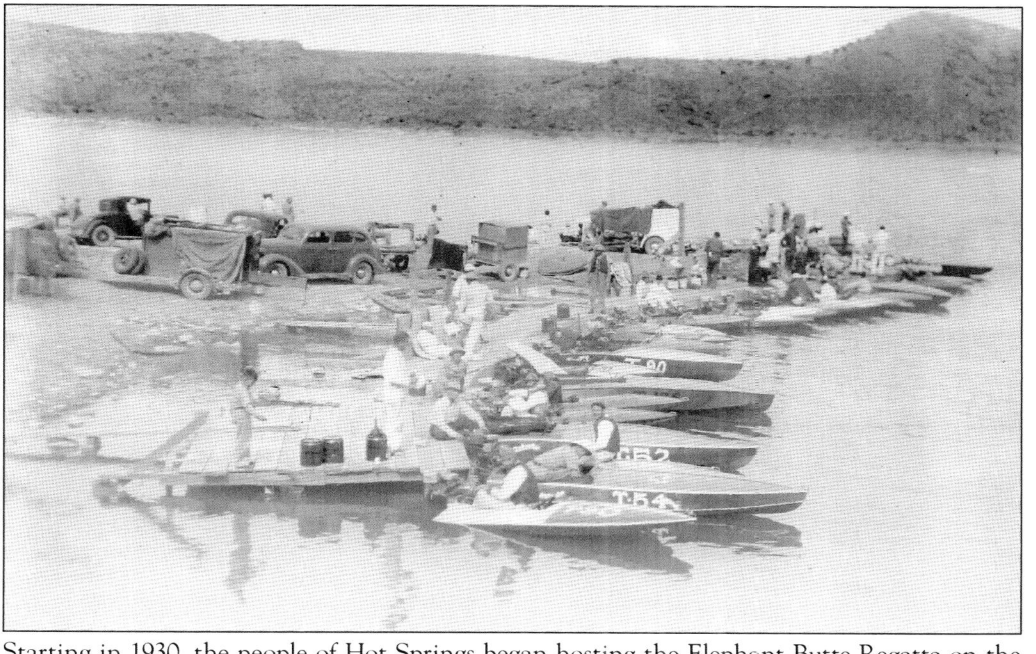

Starting in 1930, the people of Hot Springs began hosting the Elephant Butte Regatta on the first Saturday and Sunday of June. Boats and drivers from all over the nation came to compete in the speedboat races. Workers at the regatta were volunteers from Hot Springs; after expenses, all money made went straight to the winners of the races. (Courtesy of Dam Site Resort.)

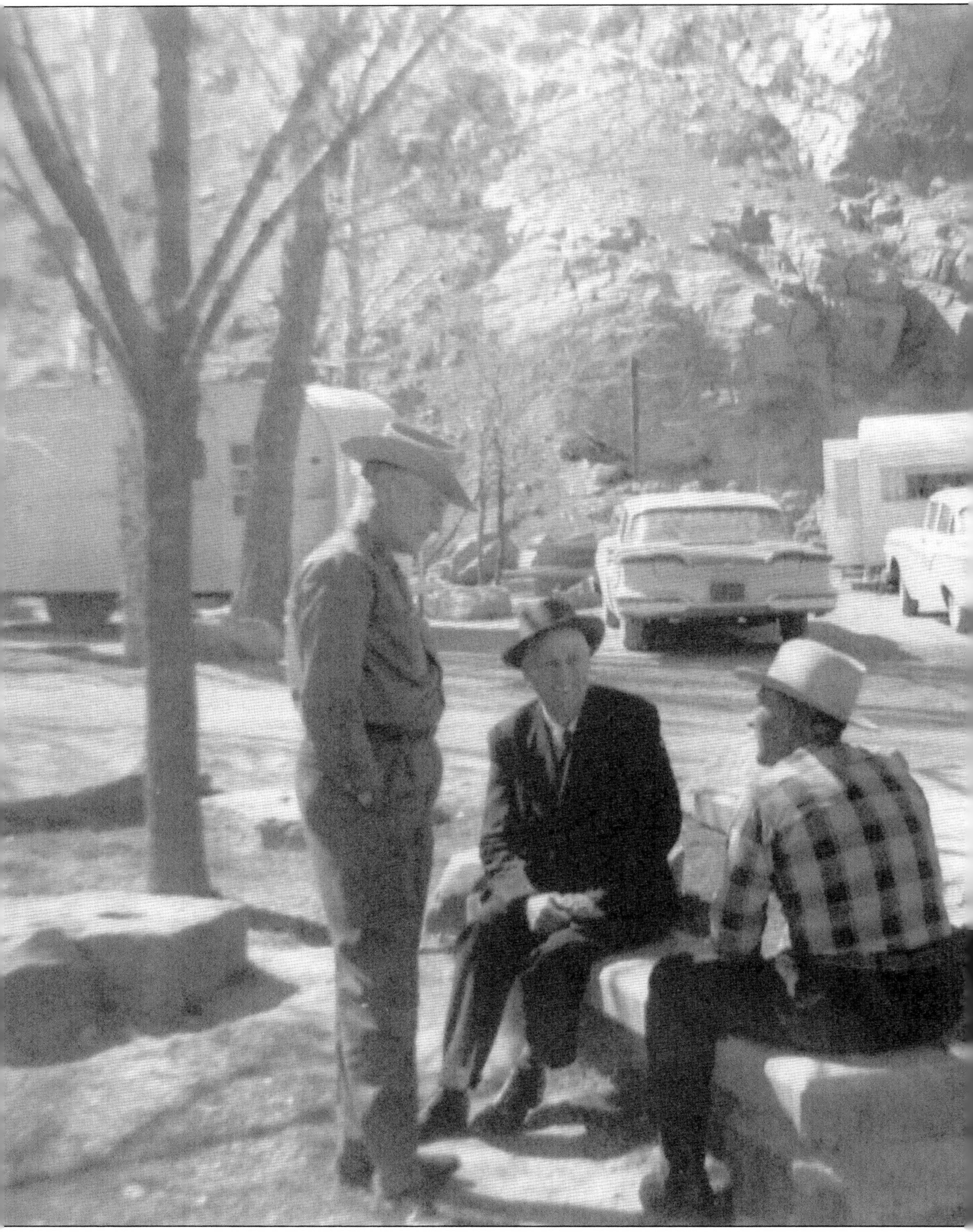

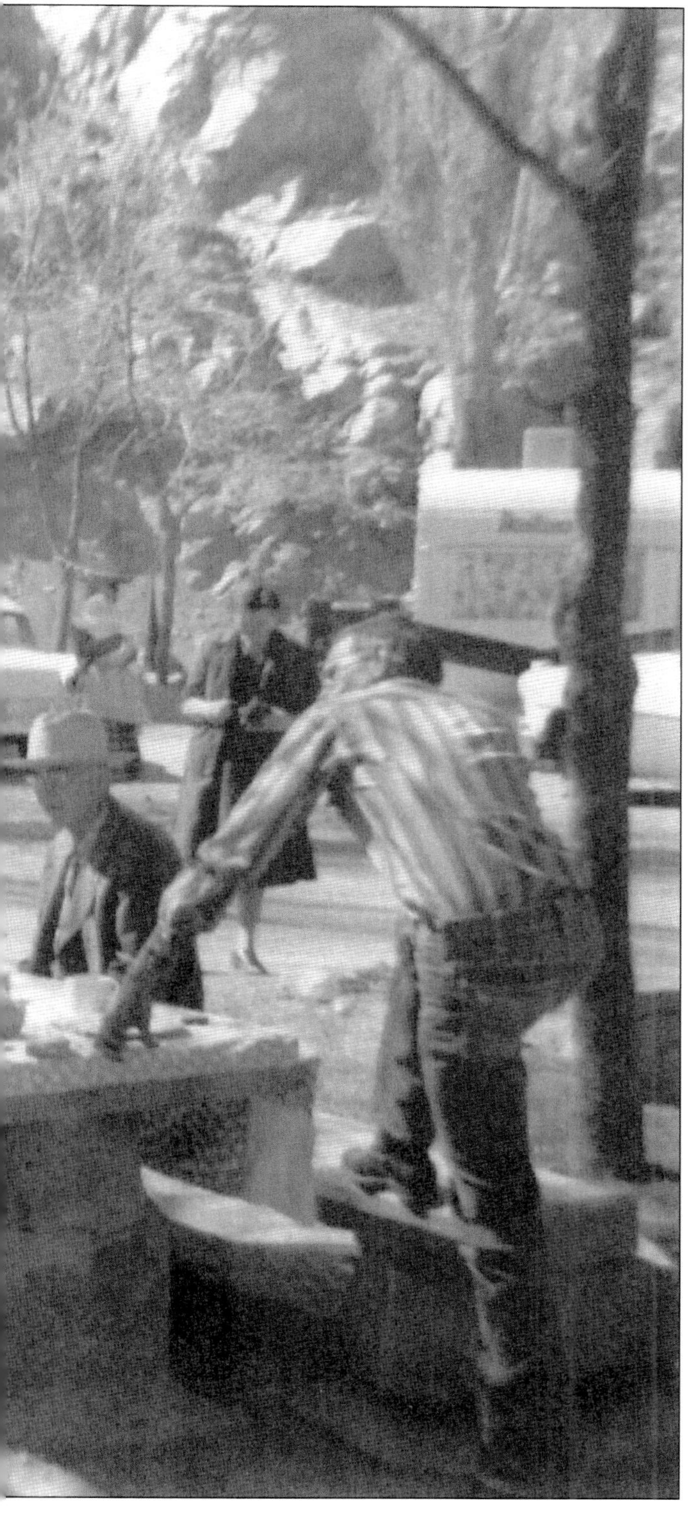

In his New Deal relief program, President Roosevelt promised to save "two of the nation's wasted resources, the young men and the land." In 1938, the CCC had completed the Elephant Butte Camp with space for 17 car-and-trailer units. Each campground was provided electricity, plumbing facilities, and cooking space. Two of the four piers had been completed, which would provide a swimming space marked by the docks and floating buoys. The adjacent park had been planted in shrubbery, and a sprinkling system had been installed by the CCC. Five of the fourteen holding ponds were also completed that year. A total of 140,000 bass were used to stock the Elephant Butte Reservoir. These campers seem to be planning their fishing strategies. (Courtesy of Dam Site Resort.)

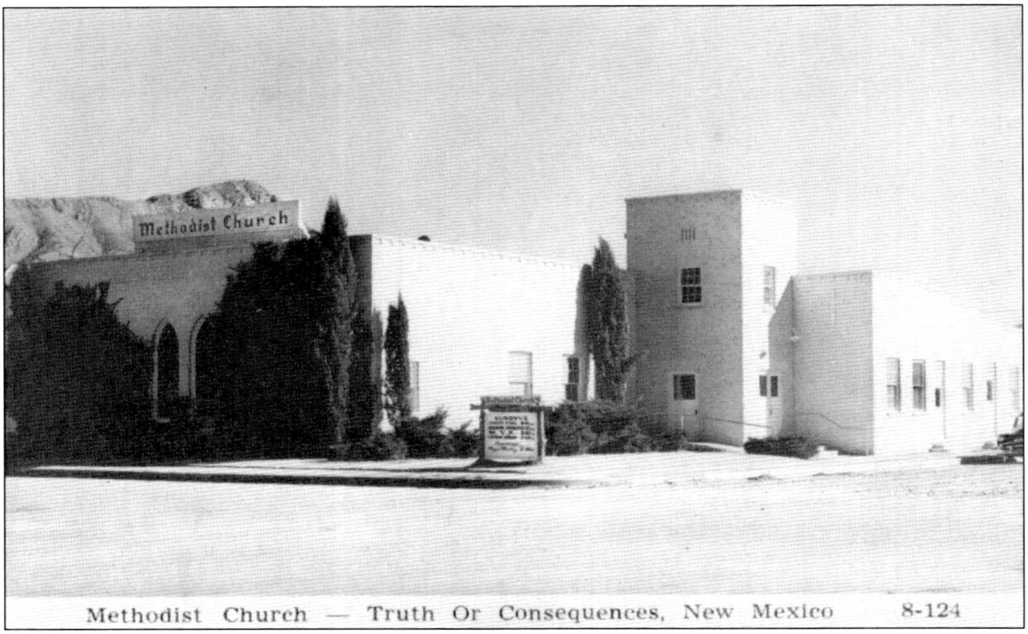

Before constructing the Methodist Church, local Methodists shared a building with the Community Church. In 1931, they began to meet in an old building with no electricity. Beneath a glow of burning kerosene lamps and lanterns, they worshiped and praised God. In 1929, floods destroyed the San Marcial Church, and the bell was brought to the First United Methodist Church, where it still rings for Sunday worship.

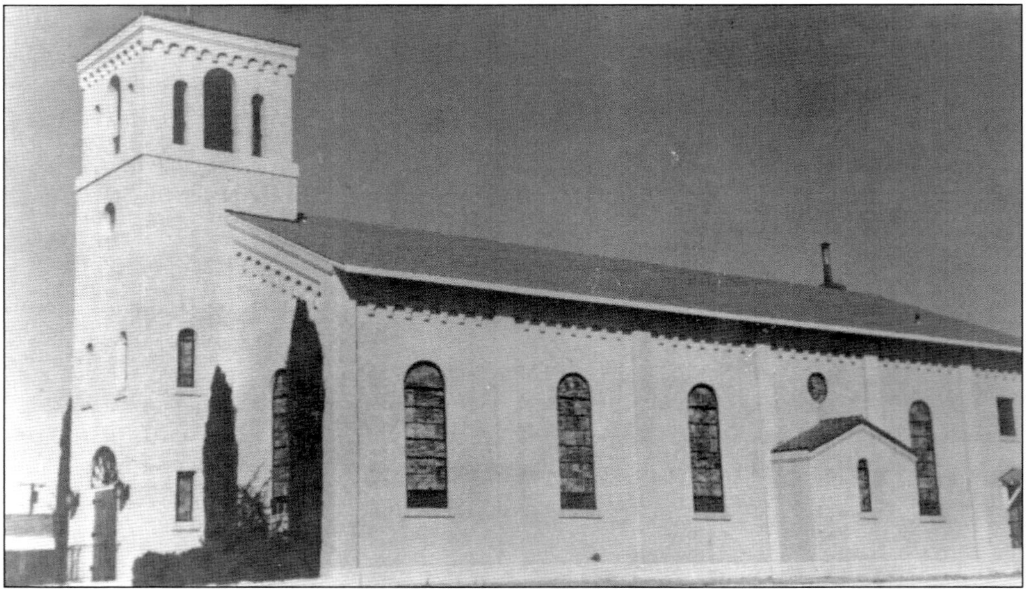

Our Lady of Perpetual Help Parish was dedicated on December 8, 1949, by Most Rev. Edwin V. Byrne, archbishop of Santa Fe. It still stands as a monument of worship on Date Street. At Christmastime, the bell tower is illuminated with the glow of Christmas lights, reminding passersby of the birth of the Lord Jesus Christ.

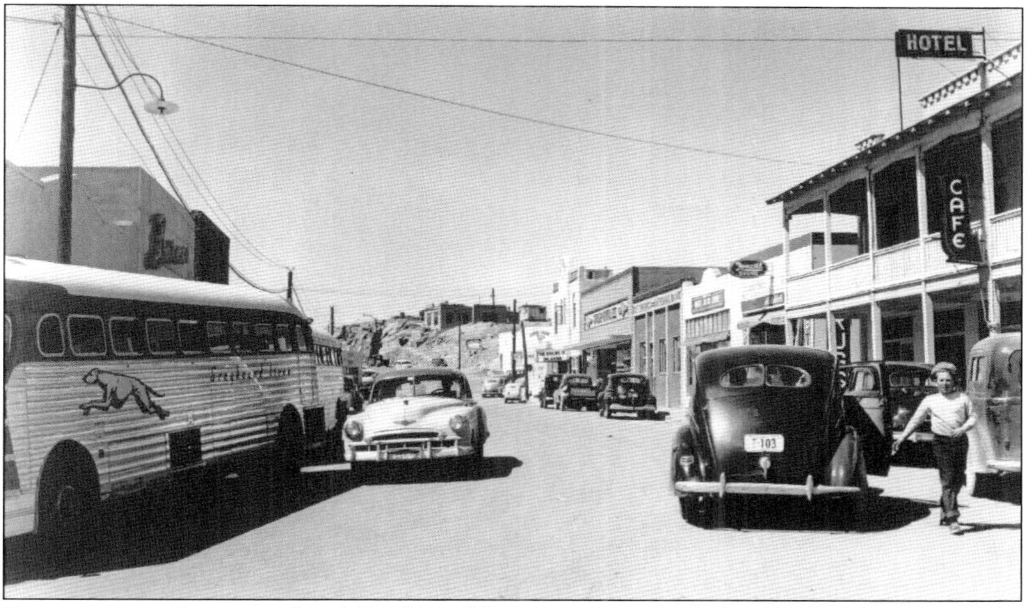

Bus companies Continental and Greyhound brought passengers in from both the north and the south to Hot Springs several times a day. At this time, the traffic flowed two ways where today this is a one-way street. It would be later on before the interstate system bypassed small towns such as Hot Springs, impacting the commerce that came in with the tourist.

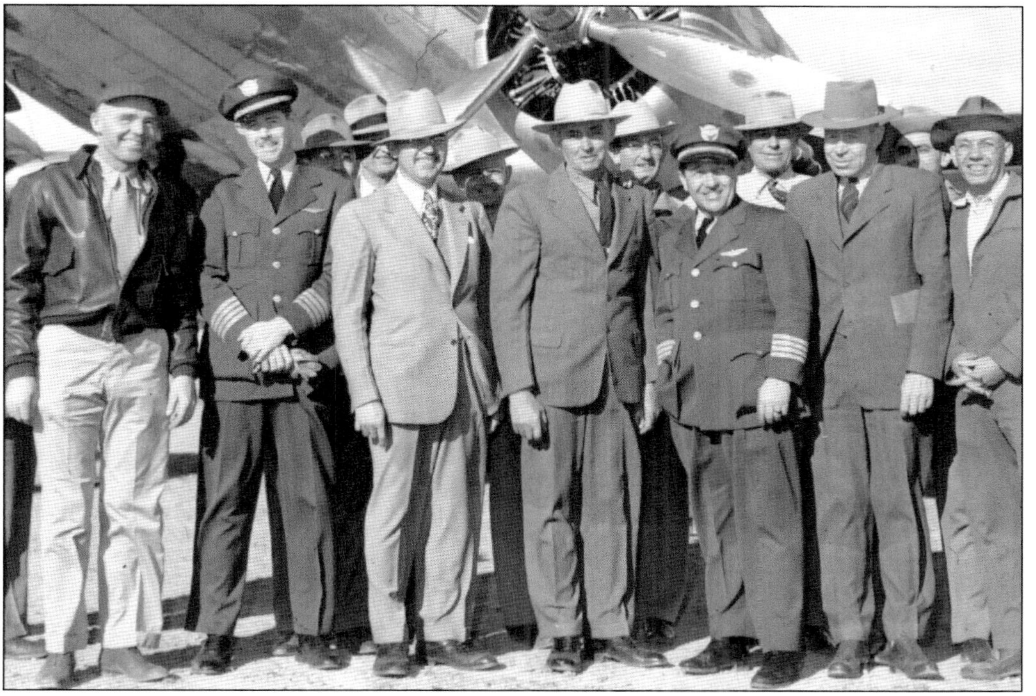

Airlines and airports brought travelers into Hot Springs. Fourth from the left is Jewell Glenn Mims, affectionately known as "Pop" Mims. Since his house was outside the city limits, he occupied room 15 at the Arizona Hotel so that he could run for mayor of Hot Springs.

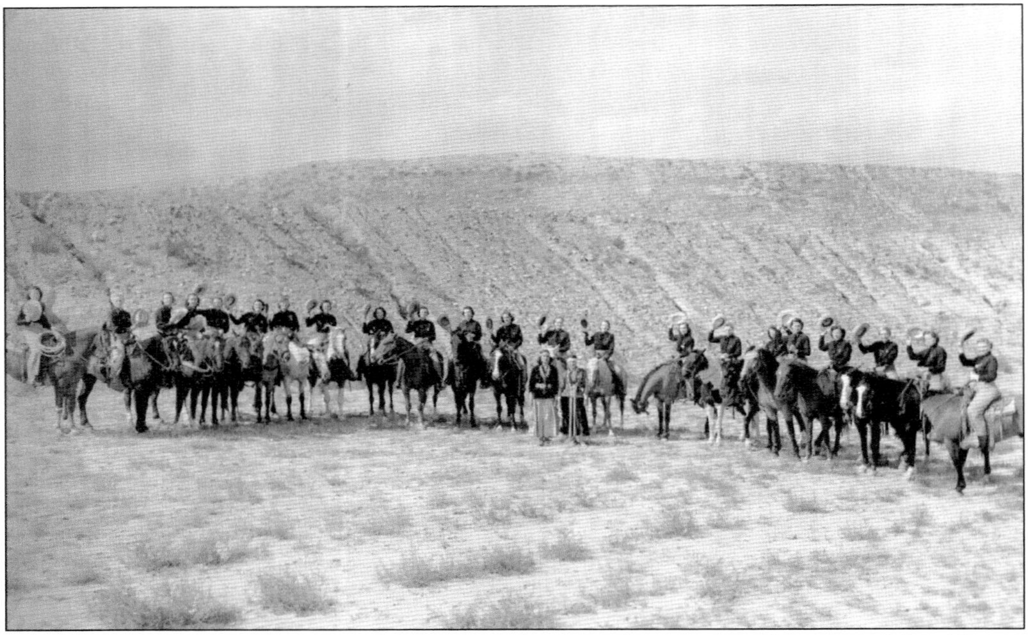

The Sierra County Sheriff's Posse was organized in 1939 by Roy Stovall, owner of the Aleman Ranch. The women of the posse were the Sierra County Sheriff's Posse Auxiliary. They focused on providing financial assistance to the posse's projects. In World War II, the FBI trained members of the sheriff's posse in case of custody of "aliens" during the war. (Both, courtesy of Geronimo Springs Museum Archives.)

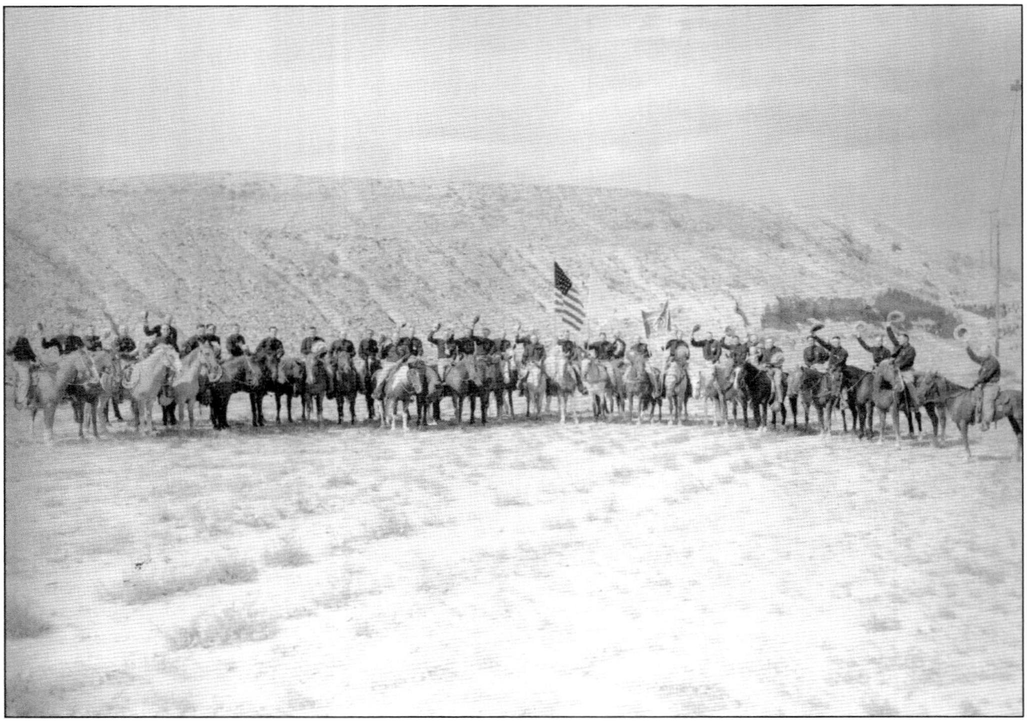

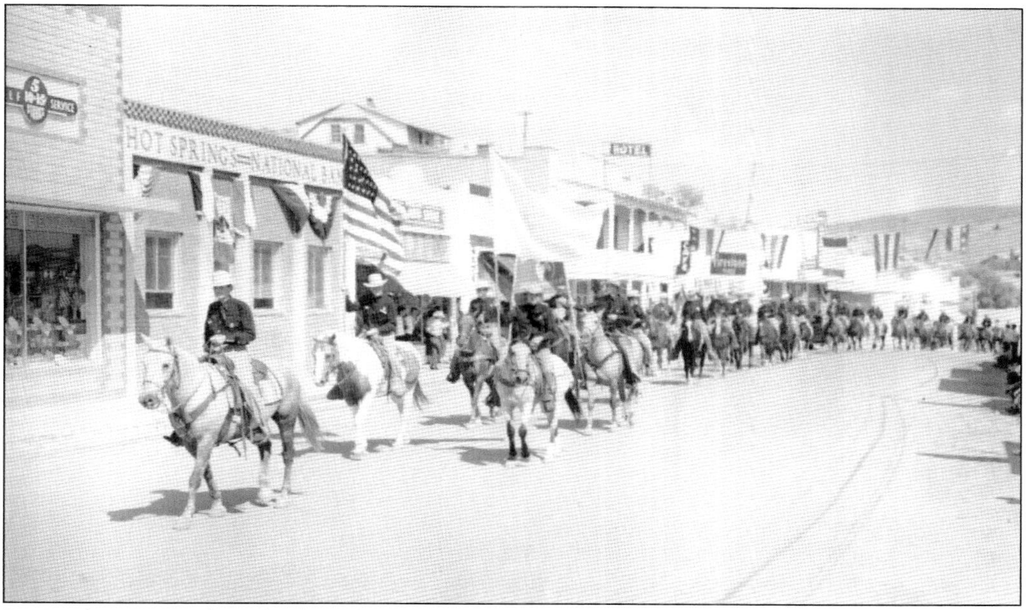

Joe Pankey is seen here leading the Sierra County Fair and Rodeo Parade. In 1920, Joe and his wife bought the Flying X Ranch in northern Sierra County from his family. Joe Pankey was one of many "managers" of the posse. Posse managers' duties, besides helping out the sheriff, were to promote the commercial, civic, agricultural, and recreational development of Sierra County. (Courtesy of Geronimo Springs Museum Archives.)

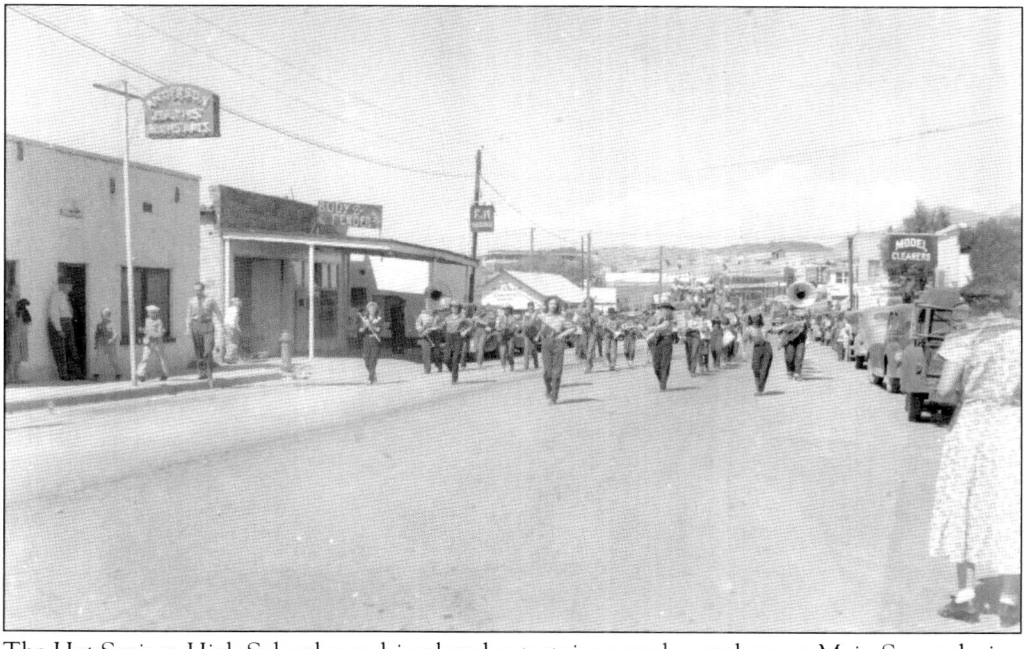

The Hot Springs High School marching band entertains parade watchers on Main Street during the 1948 Sierra County Fair and Rodeo. The businesses lining Main Street included Hannah Apartments, Anderson Baths, Model Cleaners, and Body and Fender. (Courtesy of Geronimo Springs Museum Archives.)

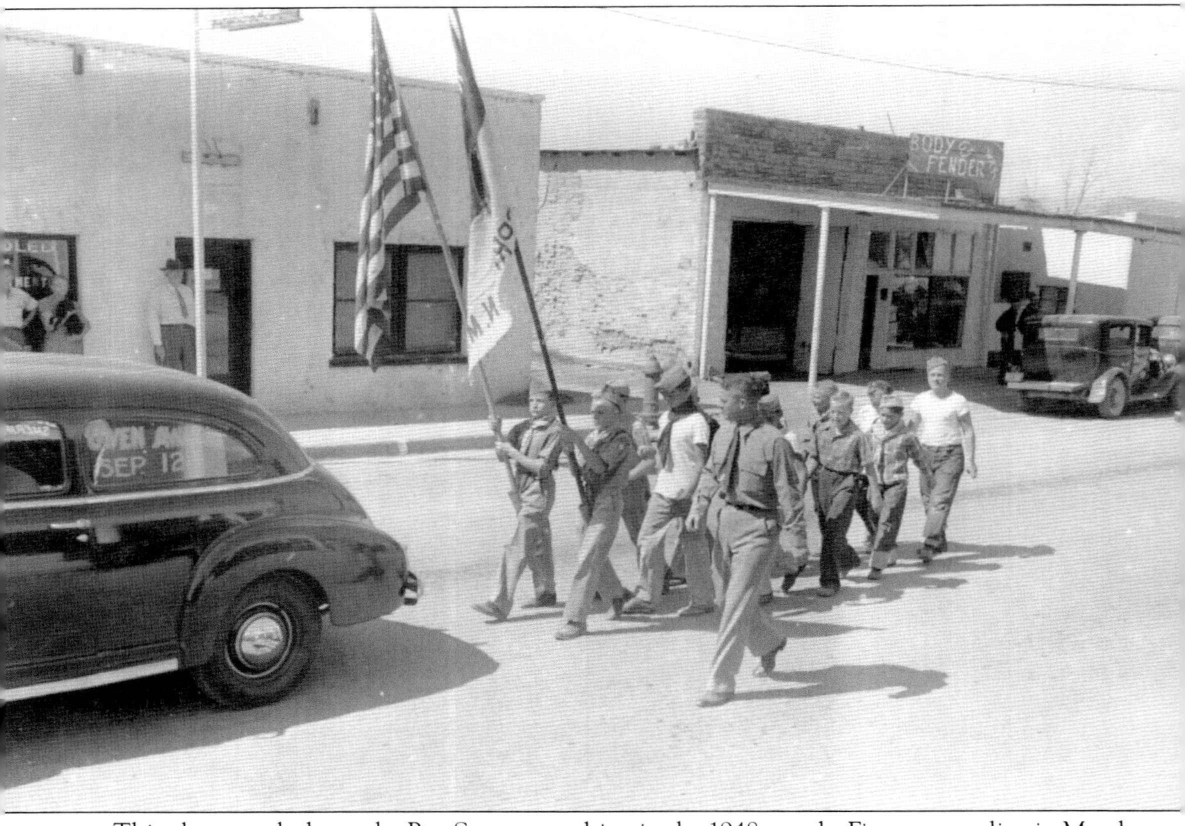

This photograph shows the Boy Scouts marching in the 1948 parade. Five years earlier, in March 1943, four Boy Scouts lost their lives in the waters of Elephant Butte Lake. The only body ever recovered was that of Robert Brock. Robert's body was recovered from the water by his brother Harley, Harley Thomason (their grandfather), and a family friend, Frank Ellis. This traumatic event would help precipitate boating safety laws throughout New Mexico. (Courtesy of Geronimo Springs Museum Archives.)

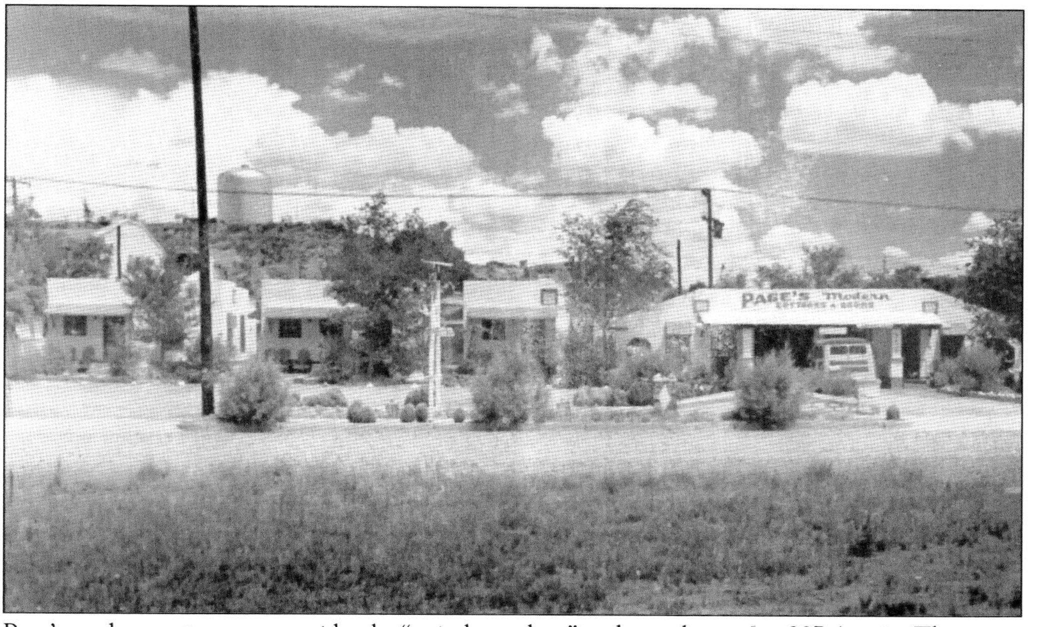

Page's modern cottages were said to be "strictly modern" and were located at 207 Austin. They were exactly one-half block from the bathhouses. Owner-operators Mr. and Mrs. M. Page advertised their units as "private bedroom cottages." The old territorial newspapers often printed the names of who was going to take the baths in Hot Springs.

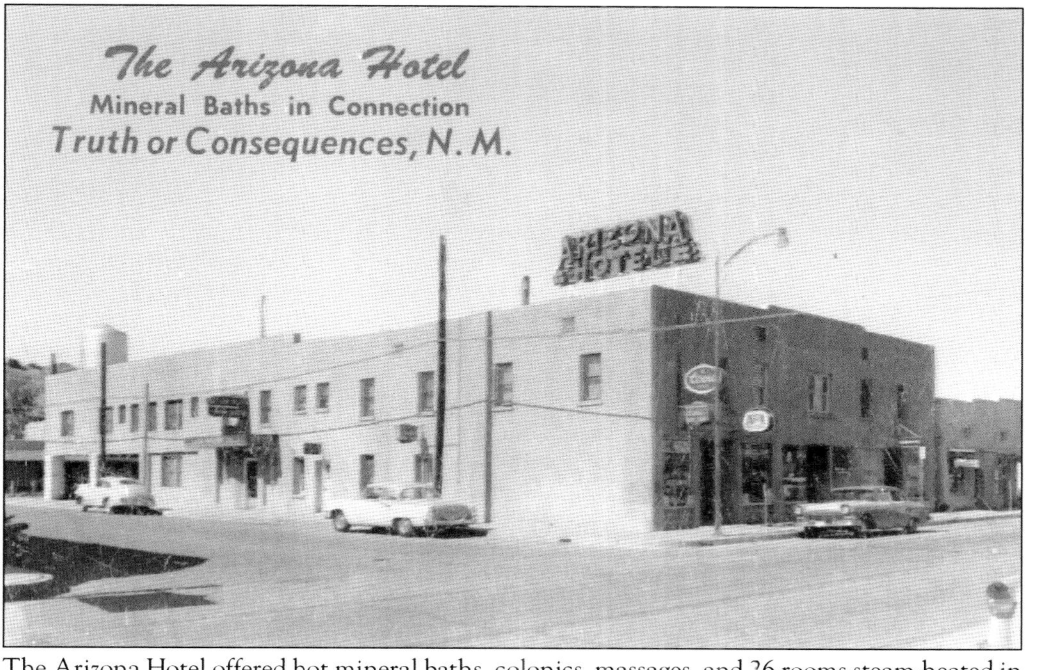

The Arizona Hotel offered hot mineral baths, colonics, massages, and 26 rooms steam-heated in the winter and air-conditioned in the summer. Their rates ran from $2 to $4 per day and $14 to $28 a week. In 1944, Ray Stanley had the license for the bar at the Arizona Hotel and controlled the gambling room.

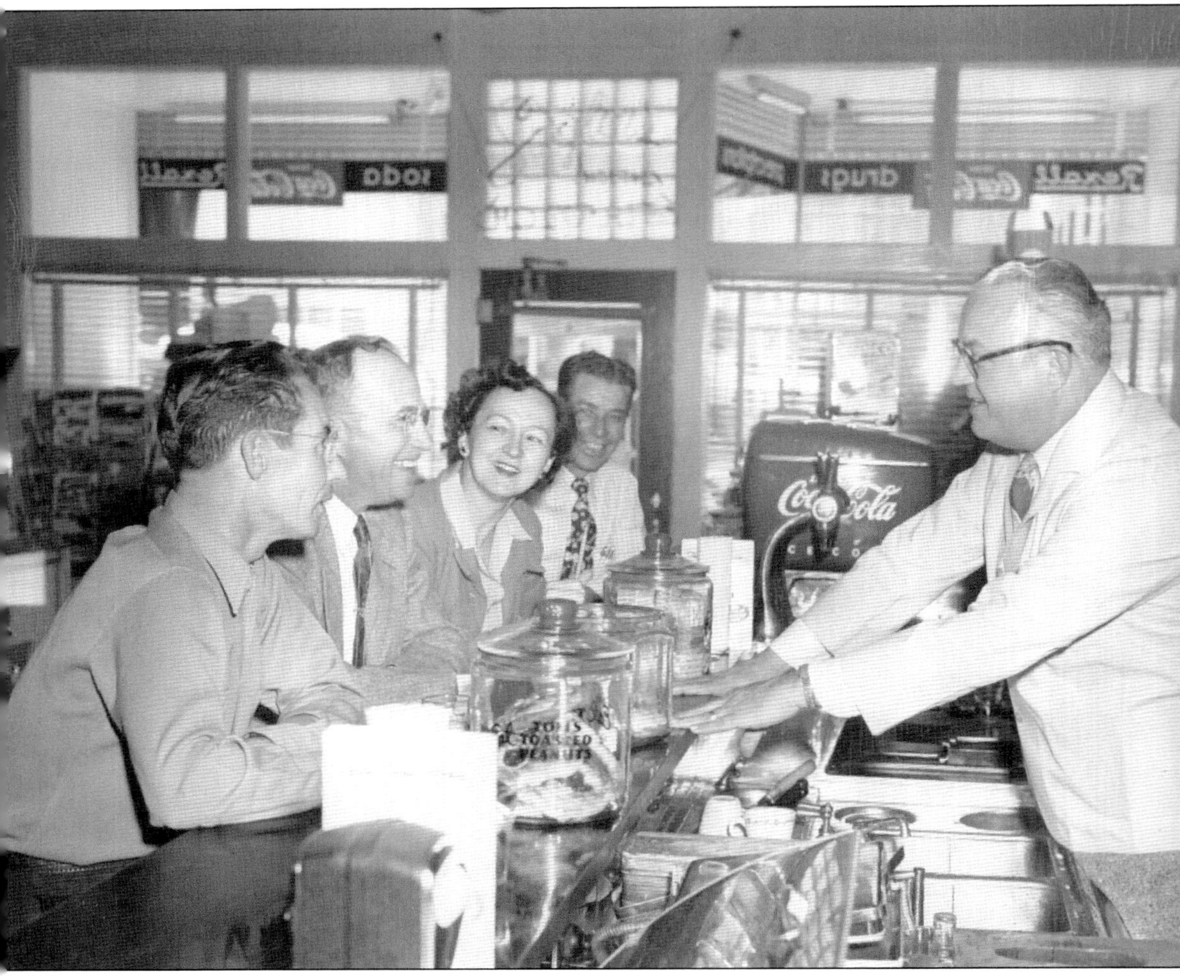

Seen here sitting from left to right in Riddle's Drug store in March 1950 are *Herald* newspaper editor Paul Tooley, Baptist minister O. L. Dennis, *Sierra County Advocate* editor Arletta Coleman, proscriptionist (one who prescribes prescriptions) Johnny Dobson, and drugstore owner George Riddle. All were said to favor the "notorious move," but they also expressed caution. The discussion centered on changing the name of Hot Springs to Truth or Consequences. Ed Bailey, the production manager of the radio show *Truth or Consequences*, had asked Burton Roach, the New Mexico state senator representing Sierra County and the manager of the Hot Springs Chamber of Commerce, to run the idea by the town's fathers. Not everybody was convinced it was a good idea, but it was already starting to bring in the publicity that the town needed to promote the area. Ralph Edwards, host of the radio show, guaranteed to promote the town to his coast-to-coast audience. The town was listening.

Five

A Man on a White Horse

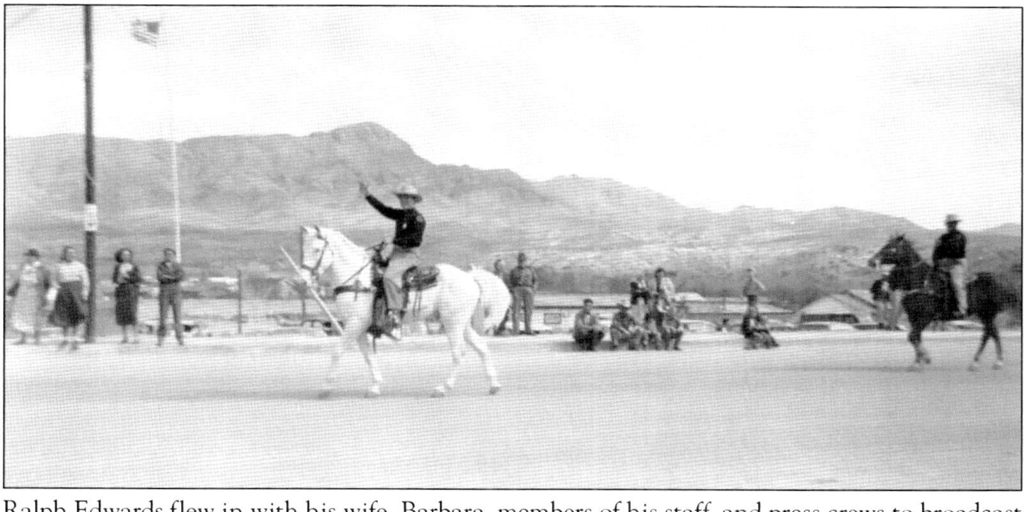

Ralph Edwards flew in with his wife, Barbara, members of his staff, and press crews to broadcast the 10th anniversary of his game show *Truth or Consequences* and the changing of the name of Hot Springs to Truth or Consequences. A special election on March 31, 1950, had decided in favor of the new name by a margin of 1,294 to 295. The next day, reporters and commentators responded to the news with sarcasm and even disbelief. It was April Fool's Day, after all.

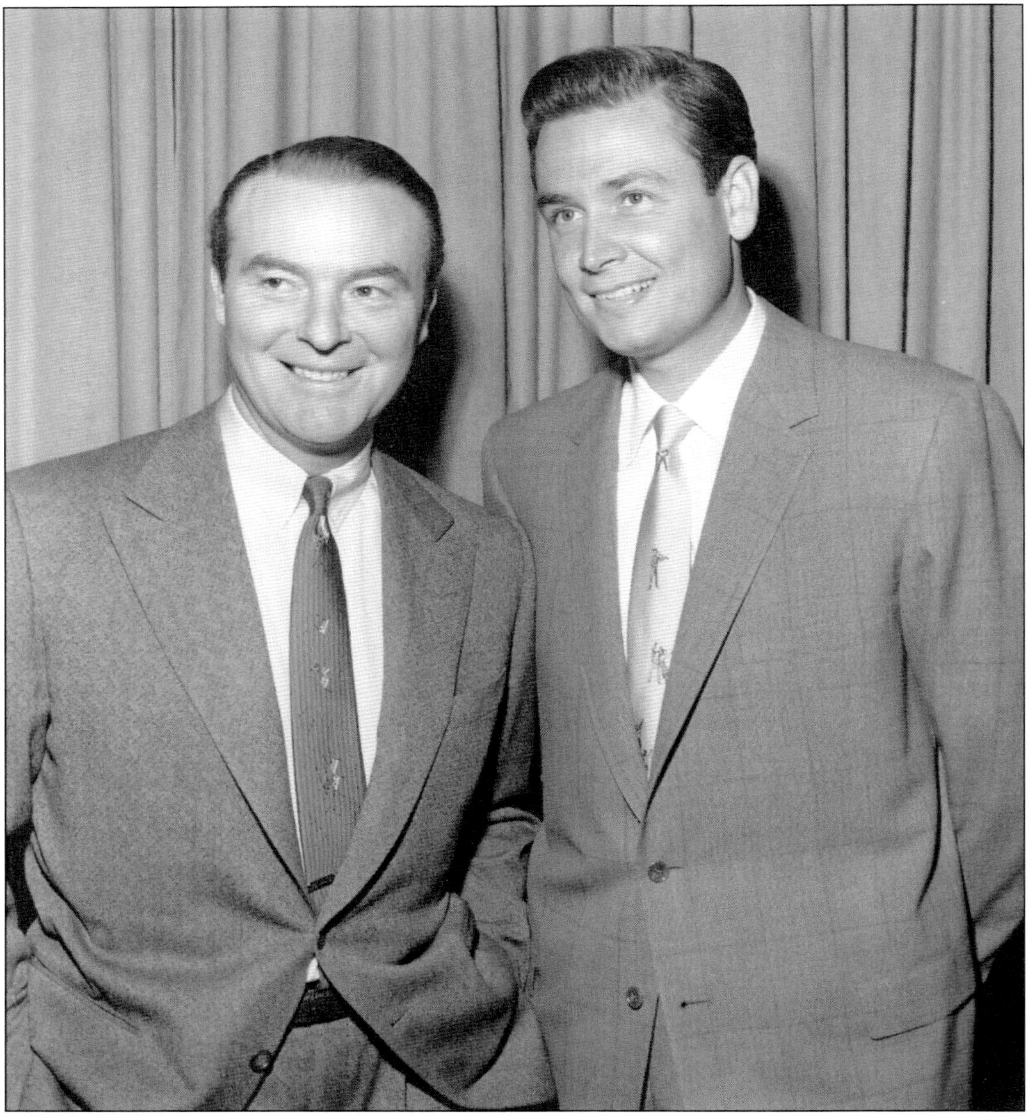

Ralph Edwards, shown here with fellow entertainer Bob Barker, plugged the city on the radio almost immediately after hearing the news that the city would change its name. He told all of his listeners, "We'll be down there in a few days ready to go fishing and take a motor boat ride on beautiful Elephant Butte Lake, the third-largest body of impounded water in the world, 44 miles long, behind the dam where large mouth bass really bite, they tell me. And since receiving this wonderful invitation, we've looked into the history of the city of Hot Springs, New Mexico, which will now be Truth or Consequences, New Mexico, 'City of Health' because of the mineral waters of the hot springs." He went on to mention the Carrie Tingley Hospital for Crippled Children and the humanitarian work of the residents in the area of arthritis. In the 1985 *Truth or Consequences Fiesta Souvenir Edition*, Edwards said, "The town had long administered to the needs of the sick, much like the radio program had done in its 10 years on the air."

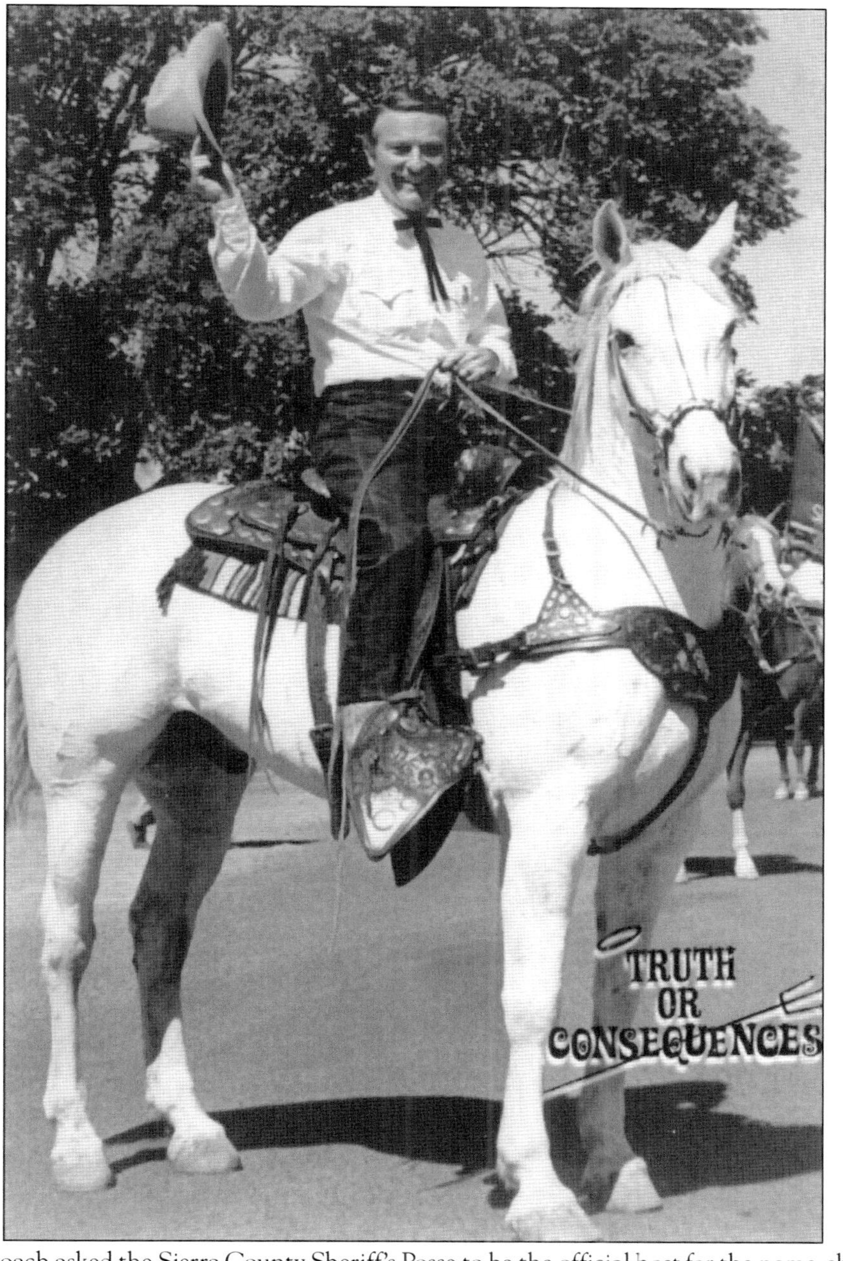

Burton Roach asked the Sierra County Sheriff's Posse to be the official host for the name-changing ceremony, and the group promptly made Edwards an honorary lifetime member. During the first fiesta, the Sierra County Sheriff's Posse initiated the radio host by undressing him on the street and having him put on the regulation posse uniform. Edwards then mounted Chris Trujillo's white stallion, U. J., and led the parade while his wife, Barbara, rode with the Sheriff Posse's Auxiliary. According to Mary Lou Trujillo-Smith, her father, Chris Trujillo, went on to keep U. J. until the horse died of old age in the pasture at the U. J. Ranch. Year after year, Edwards would return with his Hollywood friends to help celebrate the yearly fiesta. (Courtesy of Monty and April Brown of La Cocina Restaurant.)

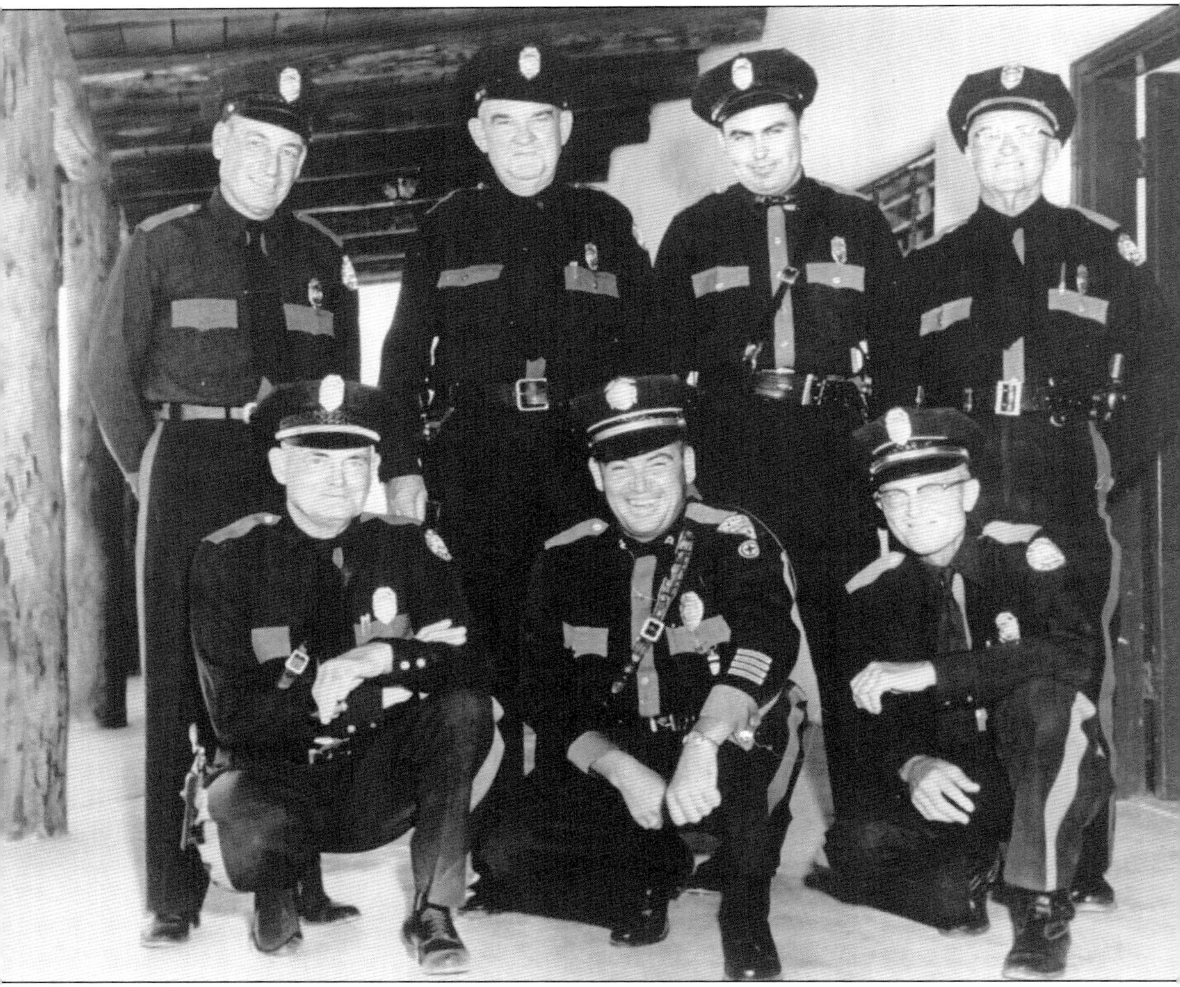

On April 1, 1950, the same day that Ralph Edwards was in town, the New Mexico State Police (though not specifically these officers) swept down on the bars and taverns in Truth or Consequences on a surprise raid. It was reported that the raid had come about due to complaints from citizens who had supposedly been approached by gamblers on the streets of the small town. The Buckhorn Bar, George's Bar, Jackson's Bar, Arizona Bar, Turf Bar, and the Tavern Bar were all simultaneously raided and had their gambling equipment confiscated. The bars saw their slot machines, dice tables, and roulette wheels taken to the town dump, soaked in gasoline, and burned. This amounted to $8,000 worth of equipment. The cash confiscated came to exactly $689.35 and was to be placed into the school fund. Judge Joe Osburn of Truth or Consequences fined 14 individuals a sum of $50 plus court costs for being found in the gambling establishments.

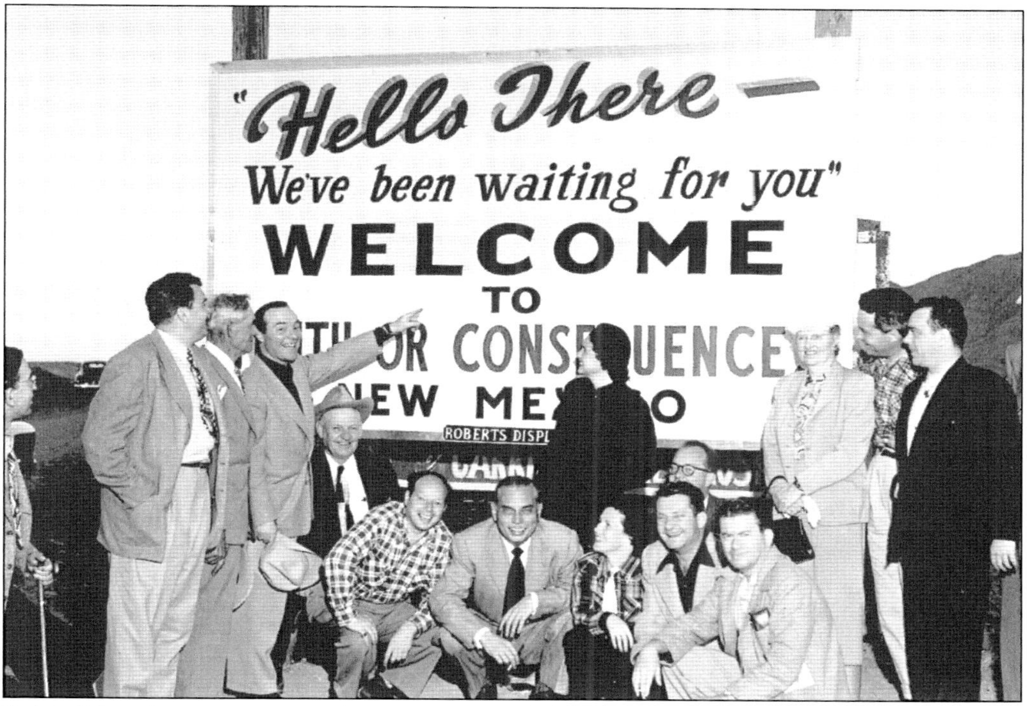

Ralph Edwards points to one of two signs provided to the new city of Truth or Consequences, New Mexico, with the words, "Hello there, we've been waiting for you." There could almost be two interpretations of those words. Had Ralph Edwards been waiting for Truth or Consequences? Or had the town been waiting for Ralph Edwards?

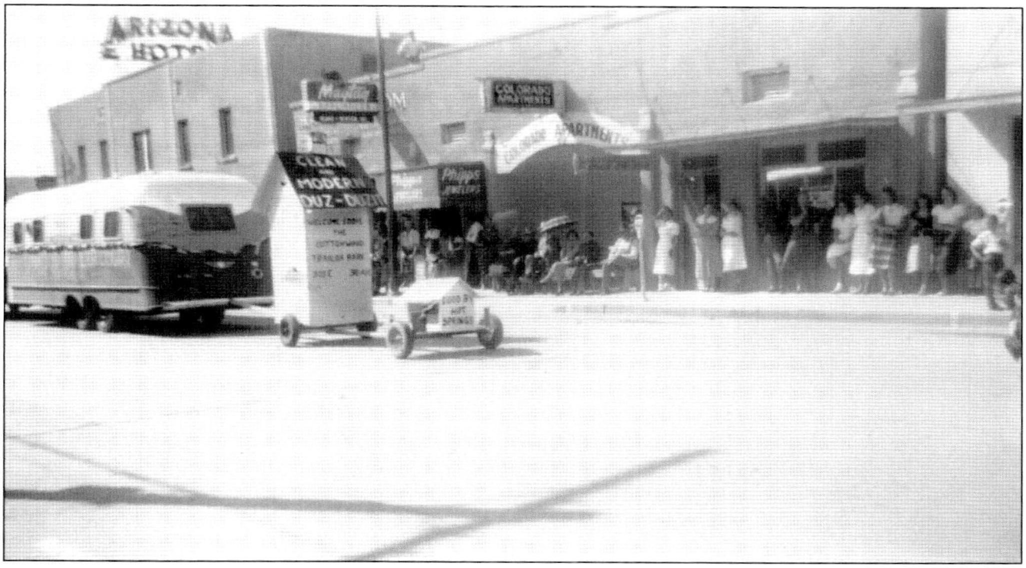

Proctor and Gamble, manufacturer of DUZ detergent and sponsor of the *Truth or Consequences* radio show, got their fair share of advertisement. Owen's Market Basket, a grocery store, filled its windows with boxes of the soap. The Colorado Apartments, shown here, were formerly the Texas Home Courts and are now the location of the Happy Belly Deli in Truth or Consequences.

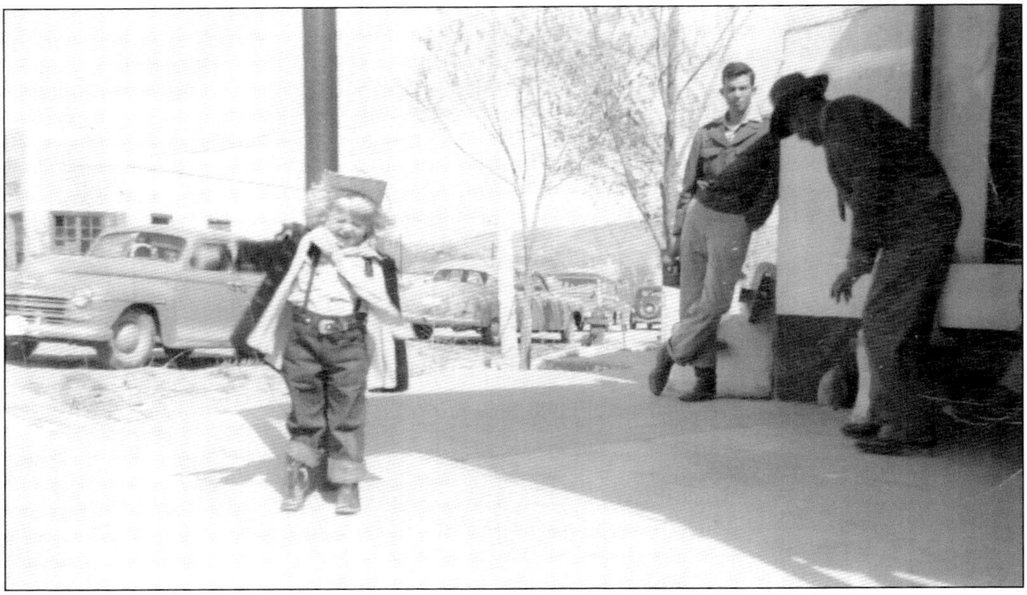

This young girl is waiting for the first Ralph Edwards' Fiesta and Rodeo. Unfortunately, not everybody was happy with the name change: an anonymous pine coffin was found near the cemetery filled with old bones and an envelope addressed to Hot Springs's next of kin. Inside was a joker from a deck of cards and the words "Hot Springs, born December 1916, died March 31, 1950." These parade watchers, however, seem unconcerned about the controversy surrounding the name change.

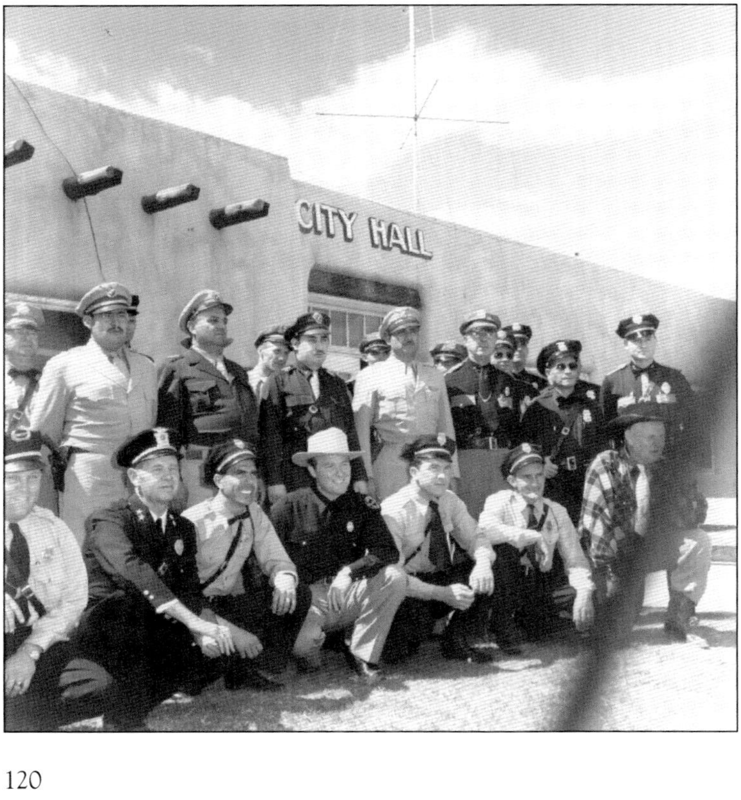

Kneeling fourth from the left is Ralph Edwards. Burton Roach, kneeling at far right, played a pivotal role in the name change. Besides managing the Ladder Ranch at one time, he was chairman of the Rural Electrification Administration and Sierra Electric Company, deputy game warden for Sierra County, member of the Albuquerque Game Protective Association, and deputy cattle inspector for the New Mexico Sanitary Board.

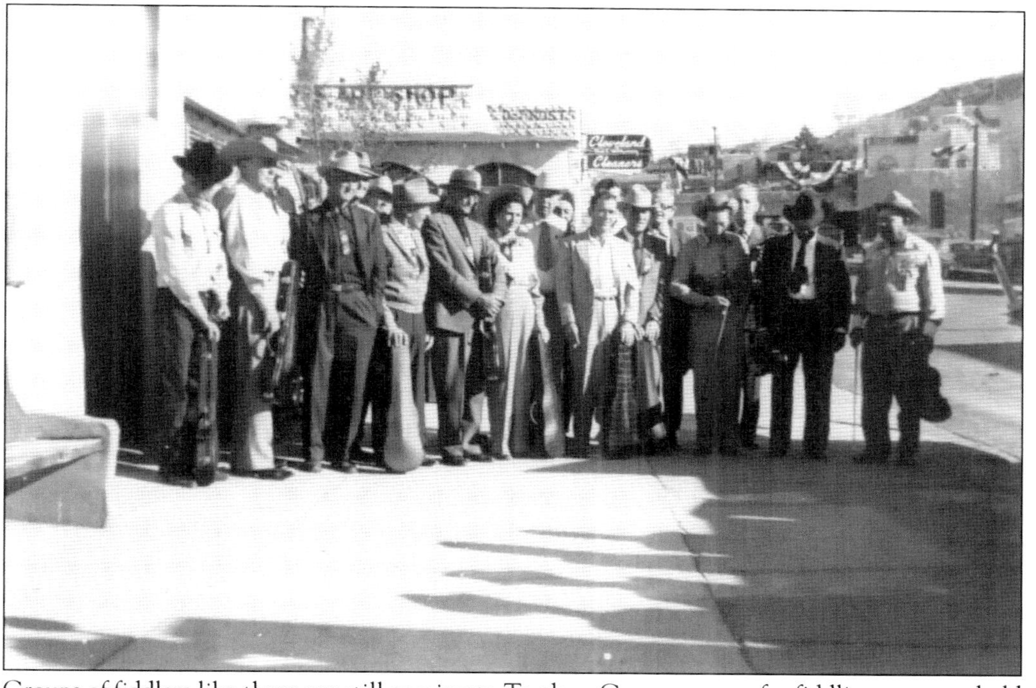

Groups of fiddlers like these are still coming to Truth or Consequences for fiddling contests held at the civic center. Since there was live entertainment in the bars and nightclubs of Hot Springs, fiddlers were known to frequent areas where appreciative listeners congregated. (Courtesy of Geronimo Springs Museum Archives.)

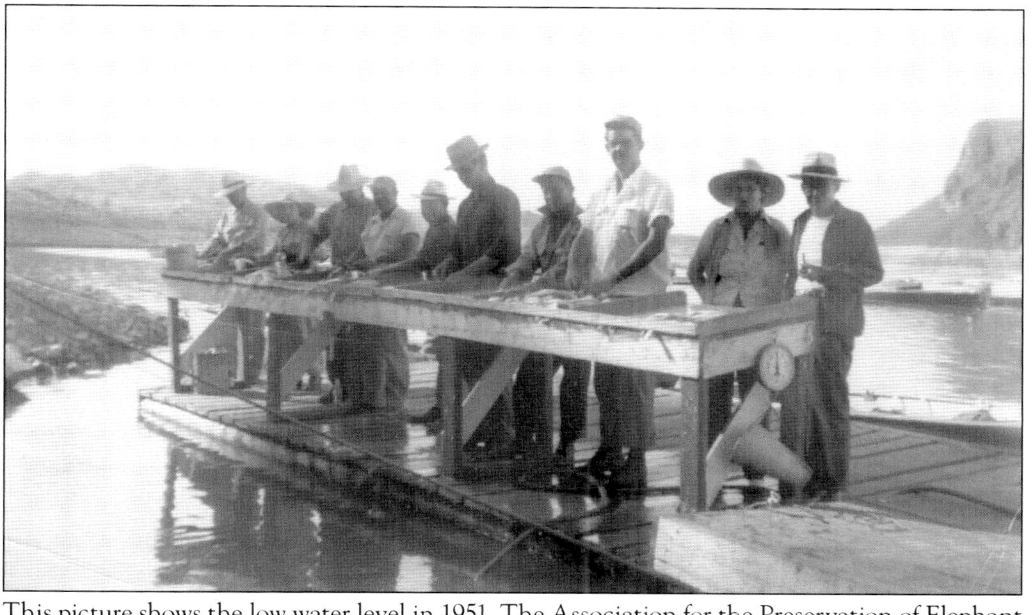

This picture shows the low water level in 1951. The Association for the Preservation of Elephant Butte Recreation expressed concern that the lake might be drained and said that this would result in no fishing for four or five years. They recommended leaving 15,000 acre-feet of water in the lake, claiming that this amount would not make a difference to the farmers losing crops.

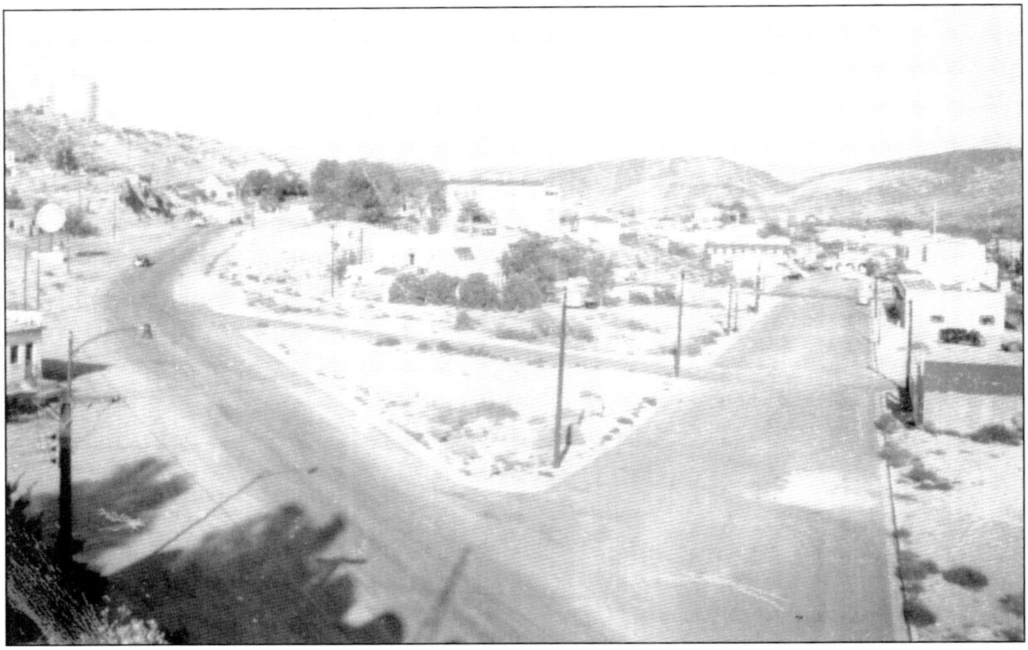

These two pictures signify the changes of the town's landscape from early Hot Springs to Truth or Consequences. Turtleback Mountain was identified in the newer photograph. The gas station located at Main Street and Broadway has since been torn down, and the area today is a parking lot for Bullocks Grocery, still located across the street. Locally owned, Bullocks continues to offer home delivery for the elderly and shut-ins. Down in the far left-hand corner is a Randy's Big A Burger, which had previously been a Dairy Queen.

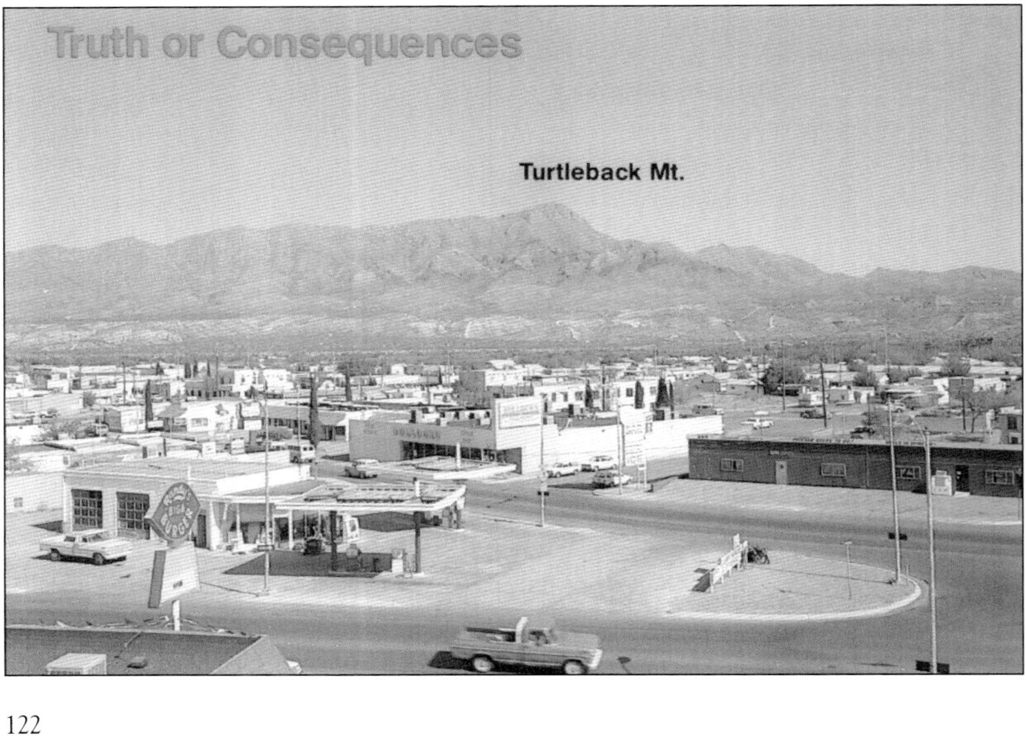

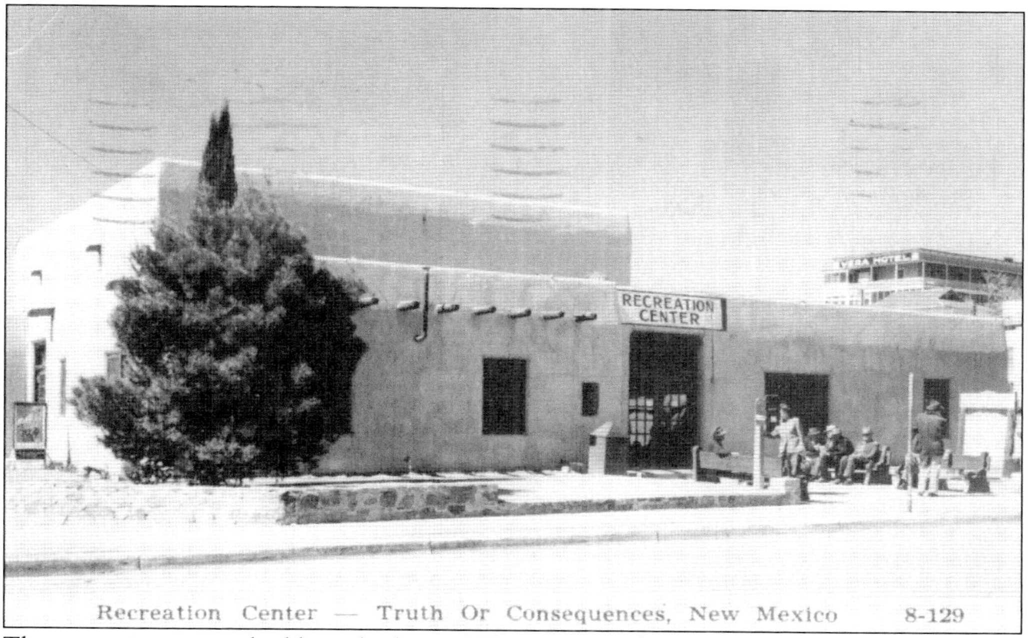

The recreation center had been built in 1935 at a cost of $19,036, paid for by Works Progress Administration funds. The architect was Willard C. Kruger, and the architectural style was Pueblo Revival. Visitors could play cards and shuffleboard, or dance at the center while waiting on appointments to see Magnolia Ellis, the local healer.

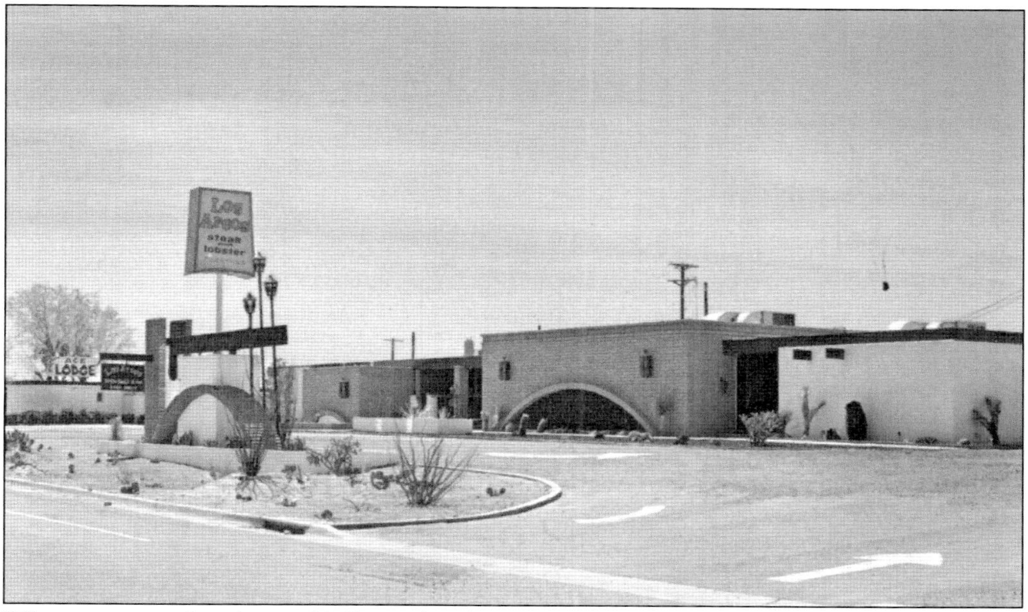

When it came to fine dining, Hollywood and Los Angeles had nothing on Truth or Consequences because Truth or Consequences had Los Arcos. The architectural style of Los Arcos was very similar to that of the other buildings that contractor John Guthrie built in T or C. He was responsible for building the structures currently housing Compass Bank, the telephone company, and Geronimo Springs Museum. The steak house continues to serve up fabulous food.

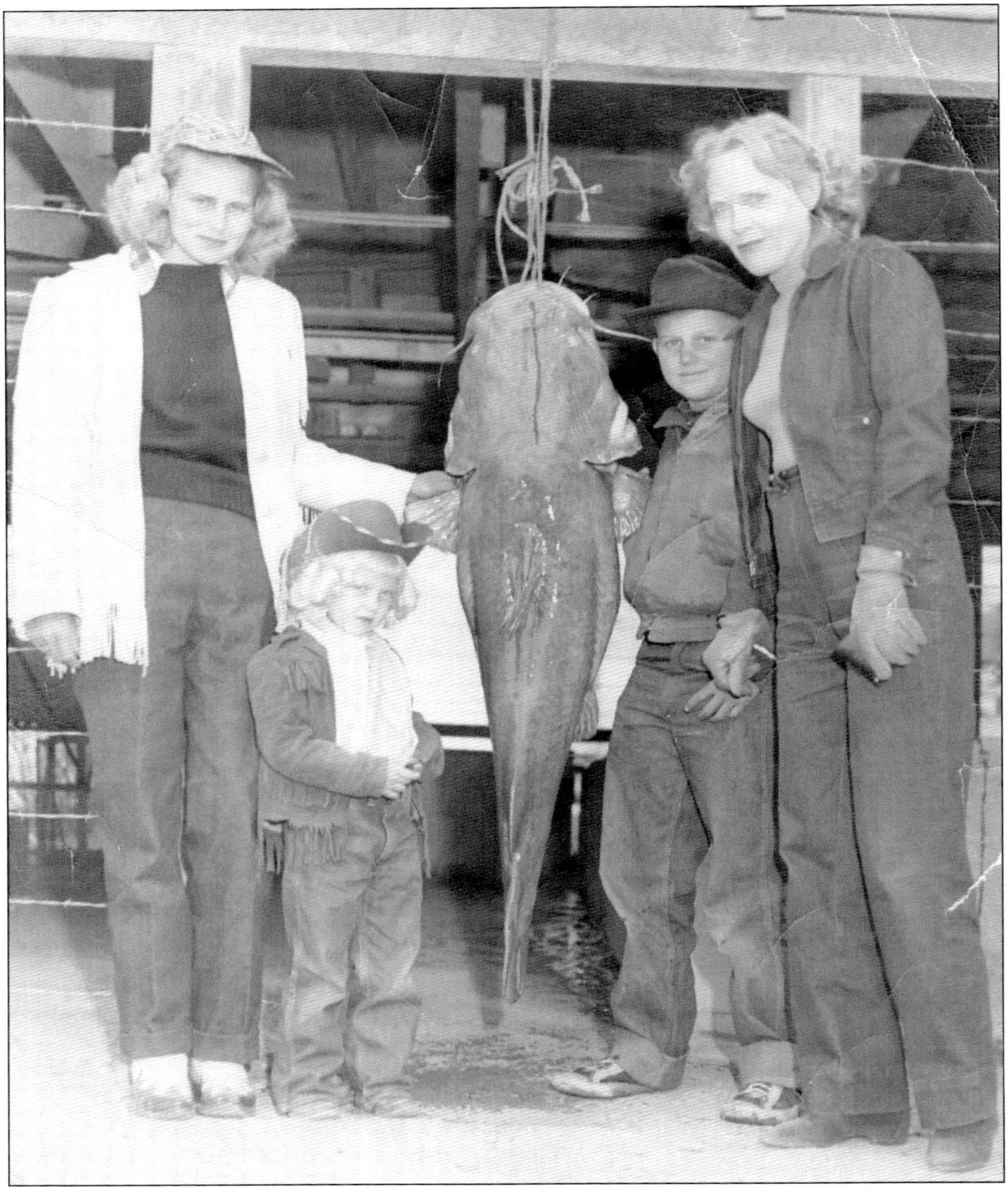

Shown here from left to right standing next to the state record catfish of the 1950s and 1960s are Maxine Fletcher, Sherry Fletcher, De Lane Fletcher, and an unidentified person. They are standing in front of the Mims Sporting Goods Store. On Friday, March 13, 1959, Maxine made the local paper when she saved two men whose boat had overturned on the lake (a third man unfortunately died). In that same paper, the headline asked, "A Space Station In Our Backyard?" The U.S. Naval Research Laboratory and the Bendix Radio Station had placed a station in the remote area near Engle to monitor satellites. In 2010, Truth or Consequences would again have a spaceport in its backyard, just 30 miles east of the town, when British entrepreneur Richard Branson chose to make the area the world headquarters of his Virgin Galactic space line and to use the Southwest Regional Spaceport as the company's primary operating base.

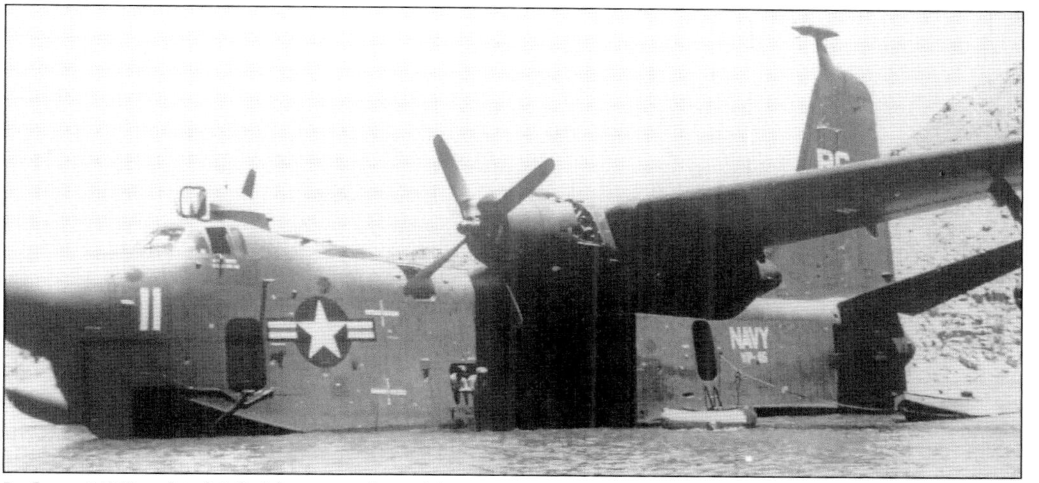

In June 1958, a big U.S. Navy seaplane blew a piston on one of its twin engines over Columbus, New Mexico. When the engine quit, commander Frank Meyer headed for Elephant Butte Lake with eight crewmen aboard. After the landing, Meyer reported that the men were having a ball fishing and swimming while they waited for the new engine part to be flown in from San Diego, California. (Courtesy of Dam Site Resort.)

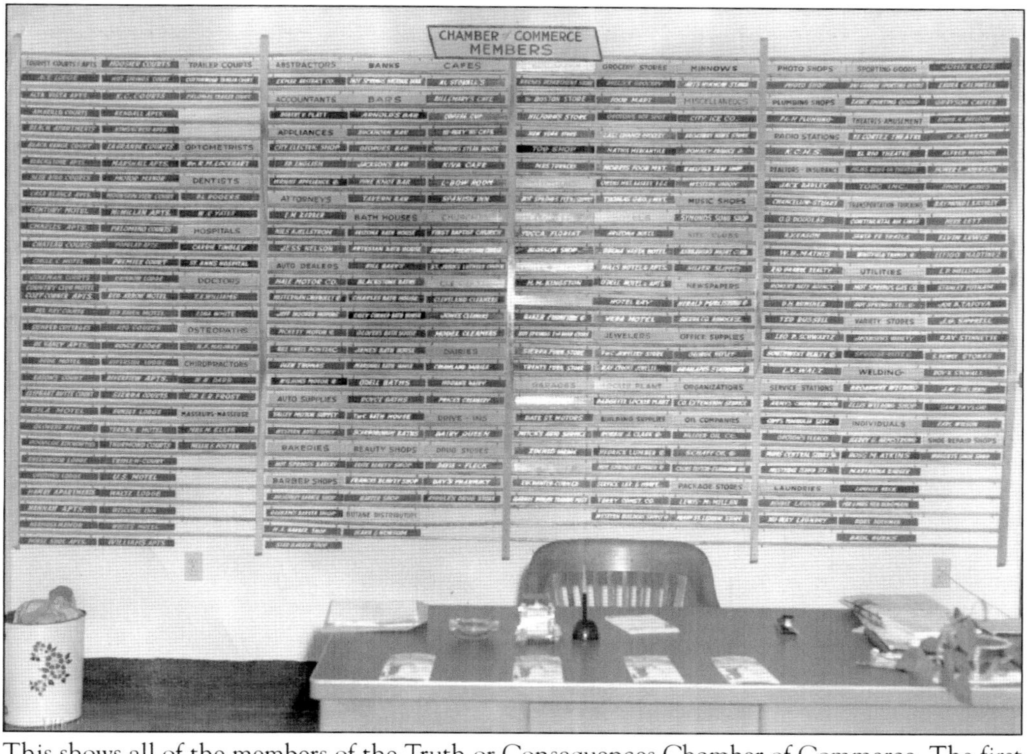

This shows all of the members of the Truth or Consequences Chamber of Commerce. The first chamber of commerce had been called the Commercial Club, and Otto Goetz was president. Their focus was the hot mineral springs that were touted for curing blood, stomach, and rheumatic diseases. The 1940s chamber directory listed 19 bathhouses. Today there are approximately 10 bathhouses listed. (Courtesy of Geronimo Springs Museum Archives.)

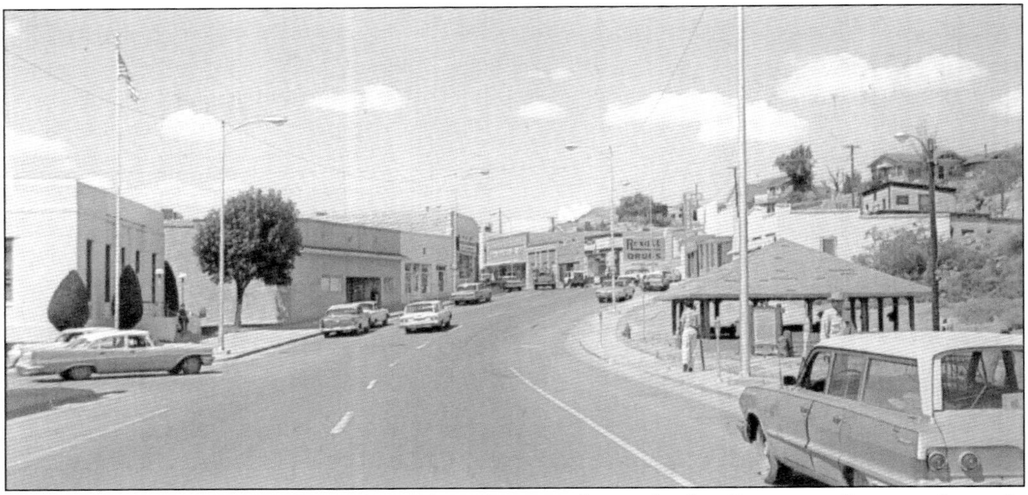

Just in front of the car to the right of this photograph stands the Geronimo Springs, formerly called Government Springs. It was in 1947 that a 20-year lease of Geronimo Springs from the U.S. government was executed by the city. Across from Geronimo Springs is the U.S. Post Office. Notice that the road is now one-way.

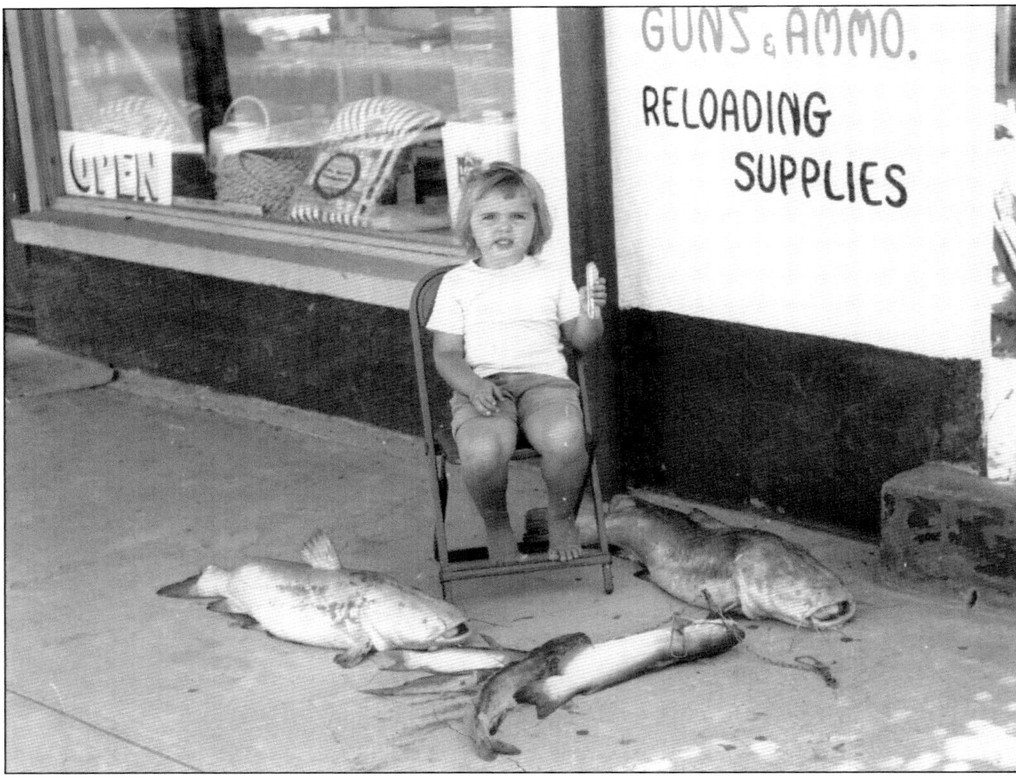

This young woman, Vicki Cecil-Sears, was quite a fisherman herself. She is sitting in front of her parents' sporting goods store. Notice that the store also sold guns, ammo, and reloading supplies. Hunting is part of the heritage of Truth or Consequences, so if residents get tired of fishing at the lake, they can hunt area quail.

This picture hangs today in La Cocina, a popular Mexican food restaurant owned by Monty and April Brown. Edwards also created and hosted the show *This Is Your Life,* where he surprised celebrities (and sometimes ordinary citizens) and would recount their personal and professional lives with viewers. (Courtesy of Monty and April Brown of La Cocina Restaurant.)

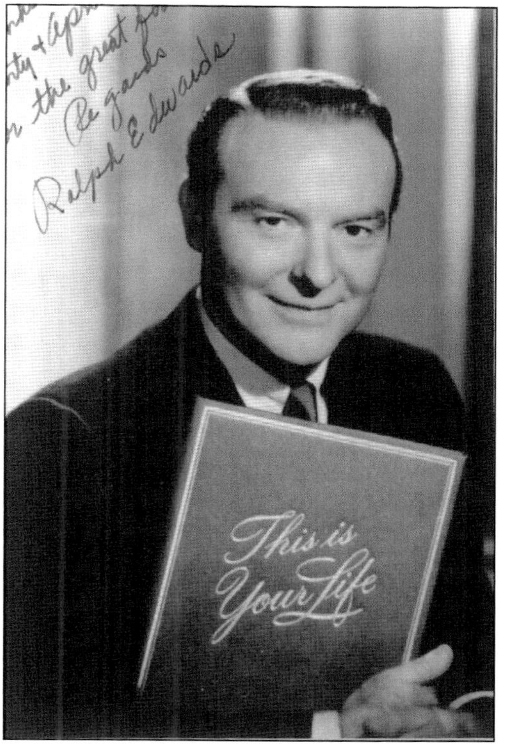

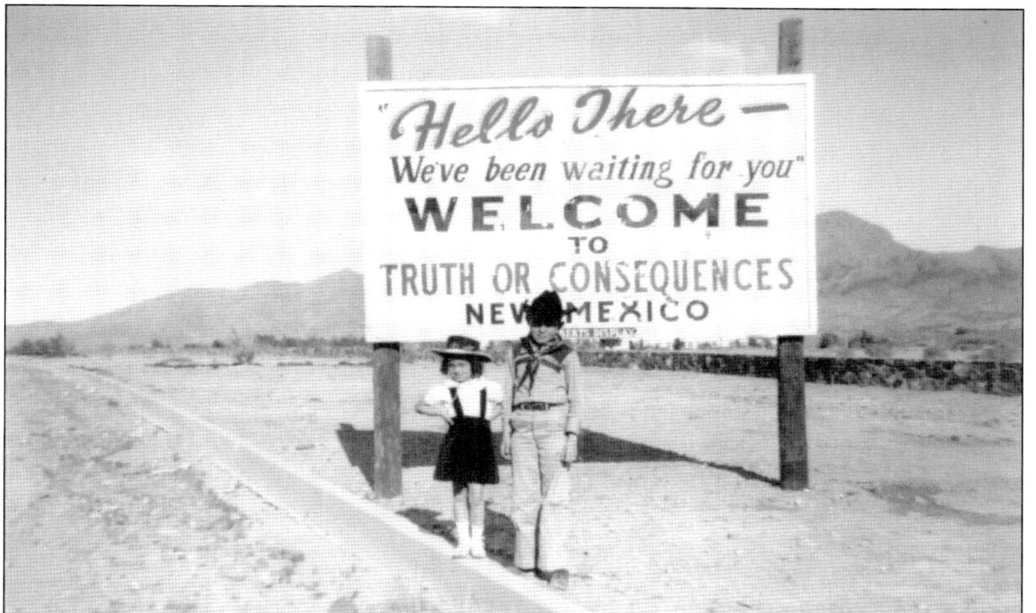

Ralph Edwards died on November 2005, but his legacy continues. The city of Truth or Consequences continues to wait for those who will come to this very proud little city that was named after a radio show. (Courtesy of Geronimo Springs Museum Archives.)